Miracle Healing: GOD'S CALL

TESTIMONIALS OF MIRACLES THROUGH SARA BUCKNER O'MEARA

BY
YVONNE LIME FEDDERSON

FORWARD BY
SARA BUCKNER O'MEARA

Miracle Healing: GOD'S CALL

Publishing

Paradise Valley, Arizona
ISBN 978-1463617882

First Printing - July 2011

**The Little Chapel Publishing®
is a registered trademark.**

*Designed by Rocky Berlier
Manufactured in the United States of America*

DISCLAIMER:

The publisher, authors, distributors and booksellers of this publication present the information contained herein for educational purposes only. This information is not intended to diagnose, replace or prescribe for medical, chiropractic or psychological conditions, nor is it to recommend specific information, products or services as treatment of a disease or to provide diagnosis, care, treatment or rehabilitation of individuals, or apply medical, mental health or human development principles.

Testimonials contained herein are anecdotal and the personal experiences of the individuals reporting these experiences. None of these testimonials or experiences should be interpreted or construed as implying, effecting or provoking similar experiences in yourself or others. Always consult a personal healthcare provider for all medical conditions and treatments of disease.

" Sara O'Meara is an angel upon earth who helps countless children and inspires others to be of service like her. "

– Doreen Virtue, author of more than 20 books including, HEALING WITH THE ANGELS and MESSAGES FROM YOUR ANGELS books/angel cards

" This extraordinary book is a manifestation of the power of God's love. I have witnessed the miracle of God healing people while Sara is praying for them. In fact, I myself was a recipient of such a healing. The true stories in this book provide absolute proof of God's gift to Sara and to the world. "

–Nick Bunick, subject of the New York Times Best Seller, THE MESSENGERS

" I've experienced God's healing love working through Sara in the Little Chapel numerous times and I have been the recipient of healings there myself. Open your heart and allow God to bless you as you read about these life-changing miracles. One of the greatest miracles is the friendship and working relationship of these two phenomenal women-Sara and Yvonne-for over five decades. "

–Efrem Zimbalist, Jr., GOLDEN GLOBE winner and legendary star of stage, screen and film

" Sara O'Meara is truly an angel on Earth. As an agent of God's healing power, Sara has spent her lifetime sharing her gift of love and hope to believers of all faiths. "

–Sharon Lechter, editor of OUTWITTING THE DEVIL and co-author of THINK AND GROW RICH – THREE FEET FROM GOLD and RICH DAD, POOR DAD

" Sara Buckner O'Meara, co-founder of Childhelp® with her colleague, Yvonne Lime Fedderson, have demonstrated unreserved spiritual love and service to healing the wounds of children and in the many areas of other human needs searching for Divine Healing. I honor Sara for her unlimited duty to her call from God to serve in the areas of her healing mission. "

–Father DiOrio, Renowned vessel of God's healing power and author of several books including the recently released, REFLECTIONAL THOUGHTS FOR MOTIVATIONAL LIVING.

Contents

Testimonials

Biographies

Dedication

To Sara

There is a Little Chapel where men and angels love to gather.
It is where you go for inner peace, and release all that does not matter.
Great truth from the Bible is read and taught to all who come.
Living the Ten Commandments is a must for everyone.
As you enter this Chapel you feel the power of love so strong.
It inspires you to forgive others, and ask forgiveness
for what you have done wrong.
Souls are touched, bodies are healed, and lives are made brand new.
It really does not matter if you are a Protestant, Catholic or Jew.
For God and His angels love and cherish every one of us, you see.
Because all of us are part of His creation
and a vital part of one big family.
Jesus, Abraham, Mohammed, our heavenly angels all continually pray
That our whole world will accept this truth, and live in peace one day.
Those who attend the Little Chapel are encouraged
to accept it in their hearts and know.
For God's angels are always present, lifting us up
to the light and heavenly glow.
The Chapel is fairly small, but no one denies it is mighty in power.
We know God will continue to bless it every day,
every moment of every hour.
For as long as the glory will be given to Him,
Great blessings and healings will never cease to begin.

*This photograph, taken on August 31, 1981
reflected a perfect cross focused on and around
the image of Sara O'Meara*

*This was the day that God's healing power manifested
itself through her… for the glory of God
…during a team ministry with Father Di Orio.*

Forward

What Sara Says About Her Healing Gift

"I have no special power, it all belongs to God. I am merely his obedient servant to be used as a conduit—a vessel—for Him. The credit in no way belongs to me and I am the first to know that."

I have often said that if I personally possessed the power to heal, I would travel across the country clearing out hospitals and ensuring that everyone I touched was rejuvenated in body and spirit. In sharing my personal story and the tale of others who have been made whole through The Little Chapel ministry, I seek to shine a spotlight on the greatest physician, psychologist, and wellness practitioner the world has ever known: The Holy Spirit.

Before the fabulous group *Doctors Without Borders* circled the globe saving lives, God was expressing his compassionate love and concern for us by healing our bodies and souls. There were never any borders dividing individuals through the artificial categories of race, creed, sex, class and religion.

Many ideologies seem to separate mankind into various camps and groups. I strongly believe that the Creator's intention was never to design isolating boxes. We need to amalgamate our religions, going beyond the divisions that separate us and seeking to meld our hearts and minds to a single vision of God. God made us all. In God's eyes, we are all his children.

Faith is the source of discipline, power and meaning in the lives of those who ascribe to any major belief system. It is a potent force. A shared faith binds people together in ways that cannot be duplicated by other means. The purpose of any church, temple, cathedral or place of prayers and meditation is to teach the love of God above all things. It is to appreciate and understand these teachings so much that you practice them and live them.

Mutual loving behavior brings and sustains peace within ourselves and this expands the potential of peace throughout the world. If we wish to honor our religions, it is our loving behavior that will demonstrate real affection for God.

Like a caring parent, God comes to comfort us when we are sick and afraid. Through His healing grace we will be touched spiritually and have new opportunities to refocus our lives to be truly centered in Him.

In the healing ministry, the one who is the channel for healing and those who are asking for His mercy are sensitized to the presence of God through the power of prayer. It is wonderful to have faith and positive thinking but healing is ultimately involved with the salvation of the whole person.

Divine healing includes one's relationship to God. When we are healthy and secure, sometimes we forget to honor God, but when we become sick, we rush to Him. It is important to instigate a dialogue with Him before we need His healing touch. It's God's call, but it's our dime. AT&T® used to have a popular slogan that said "reach out and touch someone." God is willing to heal but we must keep the lines of communication open, listen to his wisdom, and have faith in His counsel.

Faith does not demand miracles, but often accomplishes them. When God heals, He is leading the soul to a new life of service. In living a faith-driven life, we take advantaged of God's preventative medicine and save our souls from deterioration, inflammation and decay.

To remember God only when we are in dire pain and forget Him after being blessed is a sad response to His goodness. God's purpose for us when we receive healing is to draw our spirits closer to His will. God's intent through healing is to allow us the remarkable renewal of being touched spiritually. In accepting this gift, we are called upon to refocus our lives to be truly centered in Him.

Being healed can feel like receiving a new life. It is almost a rebirth. To extend the analogy of the parent by your bedside, God asks for little in return. Like the child who has been brought back to health, we should give all that we have.

Fortunately, God wants little more than for us to believe in Him, act in love and fulfill the destiny He has devised for our lives. Each one of us has a purpose and mission. God wants us to find, pursue and complete that divine goal. By our awareness, we can recognize these heavenly aims and by attempting to fulfill His purposes for us, we will reap rewards greater than our fondest dreams.

In breathing our souls into our bodies, God gave each of us an assignment; a mission to further His kingdom on earth. These individual purposes, however humble and modest our own may seem, are supremely important because no one else can accomplish each component like we can.

Each one of us has a particular talent to share with the world. When we recognize our individual skills and work towards God's greater good, we are truly united. It is then unlimited what God can do for us and through us.

Hold firm to God's purpose for you and He will faithfully take you step-by-step through all necessary preparations. Your greatest role is to give Him yourself and let Him be the guide. The Bible tells us that the Lord is glorified in a people whose heart is set at any cost, by any road, upon the goal which is God, Himself. Any road, even a difficult path beset by enemies, can be traveled if the passionate desire for good holds you steadfast in God's guidance. God will sustain you through adversity and direct you through challenges if you let Him.

Begin to open yourself completely and give your life to God. It is never too late to place Him first and ask for His divine guidance. Open up your heart and ask God to reveal His plan. He will reveal it to you. The ultimate purpose of following your destiny to a place of divine healing is to manifest the works of God and give glory to Him.

The intent of healing has one focus: becoming closer to God. The physical and mental healings are marvelous, miraculous demonstrations of God's love and compassion in action, but the primary purpose remains spiritual growth: finding God as your very own miracle worker.

I always think of God's plan like a tapestry. Each personal history is a thread that God is weaving. Each stitch is important in His pattern for our lives. Without our loved ones and those who are so unique and different from us, we would not have such a beautifully designed piece. When we fight God's will, fraying His handiwork, we unravel His masterpiece to rags. When we return to Him in forgiveness and faith, when we ask to be healed in spirit as we are in body, He will patch up our tapestry with golden threads and mend our souls for eternity.

God bless you on your journey,

Sara O'Meara

Introduction

The Little Chapel

Health is a state of complete physical, mental and social well-being, and not merely the absence of disease or infirmity. ~ World Health Organization, 1948

T he Little Chapel is a welcoming house of fellowship and healing in Paradise Valley, Arizona where believers of all faiths congregate to celebrate the journey towards a healthier, happier, more spirit-driven life through God.

Focused prayer, inspirational services and the thousands of remarkable documented healings that have taken place in this sacred space have attracted dedicated theological scholars, medical doctors, scientists, practitioners of alternative medicine and those seeking solace in a deeper truth.

God did not create us to suffer. He created us to be expressions of His love and light here on earth. Problems are great opportunities to grow if we look for the lessons they impart. When we are brought to our knees because of the challenges we face, God can guide us through these obstacles with the powerful force of His healing love. We may ask God for what we want but those desires may not be the best for us. We must learn to accept that it's "God's call."

Surrendering our will to His is an everyday and moment-to-moment process. When we allow God to be the center of our lives, miracles do happen. The more we open our hearts, the more God's wisdom and understanding helps us make better decisions. Wise choices and a positive attitude pave the way for God to work miracles in our lives.

Forgiveness is an action we all must take for ourselves and our loved ones. Forgive and let go of the past. The more we hang on to unpleasant situations, the more it affects our future. The emotions we feed keep growing. If we continue to nurture negativity it will destroy our physical bodies. Negative thoughts and actions are toxic to our health and interfere with balance and harmonious functions. It is vital we learn to forgive, forget, move on, bless life, find faith and be free.

Even the faith of a tiny mustard seed can bring about great miracles. Jesus said over and over again in the New Testament, "Your faith has healed you." When we feed our minds with positive, loving thoughts, the direction and quality of our lives (including our physical bodies) changes. We can truly see the results of love in action.

God transforms the troubles that come our way and turns them into stepping stones that take us to a higher place. Making that first step is the hardest, but once we take that leap, watch what happens. No matter where we are in life, God has much more in store for us. As we open our hearts to His love, He will help us to grow and reach our full potential.

Founded on the principles of positivity, forgiveness, openness and above all, love, The Little Chapel has become a destination for weary hearts worldwide that come seeking a higher good and profound understanding of God's plan for their lives.

Love is a most powerful force and it is able to manifest what we call miracles. There is not one thing that enough love and light cannot change for the better. Love is positive and nurturing and does not work to bring negative or hurtful outcomes to anyone. Through love, miracles happen.

Most who have entered the Little Chapel describe a feeling of immediate love, peace and warmth that envelops them. Some are overcome with emotion while others feel their hearts opening to a new experience. While a few people fear they are not worthy, it is one of life's great lessons that each person is worth God's love. In passing through the doorway of this hidden Paradise Valley haven, all people are equal and all needs are important.

The pews of the chapel are a microcosm of America: a senator sits by a man who has recently lost his job, a religious leader sits by a sick child, a doctor sits by a challenged teen. In the world their paths may never cross; at the chapel, they are all one. The Little Chapel belongs to everyone for we are all God's children.

This book is a compilation of just a few testimonials by those who were touched by God's healing power at The Little Chapel. About 80% of those who take part in this ministry are blessed with a profound healing miracle. Each individual in this book had a life-changing experience because when one is healed physically, it also touches the soul.

May these stories of faith and healing help you to grow spiritually and open your heart to receive a deeper understanding of how great God's love is for each one of us. Every day is a gift from God. What we do with our gift makes all the difference in our lives. It's God's call, are you ready to listen?

In Appreciation...

The Little Chapel Workers: John & Celeste Hopkins, Taryn & Karl Gosch, John & Jennifer Costello, Ron & Katie Walker, Greg Oswalt, Orlando Alvarado, Robbie Britt, Carol & Jim Hebets, our Prayer Warriors led by Joseph Don Vito and the congregation that collects in love, faith and healing.

Special Thanks to...

Daphne Young, Michelle Robinson, Gloria Javier, Randi Rodarte, Rocky Berlier, Wendy Young, Victoria Bowmann and every helping hand that brought this book to life.

For more about Sara O'Meara and The Little Chapel...

Please follow **@OurLittleChapel** *on Twitter at:*
> **http://twitter.com/#!/OurLittleChapel**

Enjoy Sara O'Meara's blog and chapel updates on her website:
> **http://ourlittlechapel.blogspot.com/**

Email:
> **solittlechapel@gmail.com**

Address:
> **The Little Chapel**
> **6135 E. Palo Verde**
> **Paradise Valley, AZ 85253**

This Miracle Changed the Course of My Life Forever

Sara O'Meara

" Almost forty years ago, I was a young woman with a family, rewarding mission advocating for children, and all the responsibilities of a busy mother and nonprofit founder. The philanthropic spirit instilled by my faith and upbringing had led me from country to country and I was filled with energy and a passion to change the world. Much like today, my schedule was hectic and my calendar had no room for a day off with the flu, much less something more serious. It was during this time that I was diagnosed with an incurable cancer and given three months to live.

I felt all of the emotions that come with such frightening news. My mind instantly focused on my children (my own and those I sought to save through my work) and the effect my illness would have on other loved ones in my life. There was so much to do, so many people to take care of and I was struck by the natural sense of being somehow cheated by life.

Hopeless in my hospital bed, I waited for more tests and began the arduous process of attempting to face my fears of death. A deep, dramatic, mesmerizing voice boomed from the television. A thin woman in a flowing dress pointed her long index finger straight at the camera and said, "If you need a miracle, come to the Shrine Auditorium this Sunday!"

Being brought up Presbyterian, and spending years as a Presbyterian Sunday School teacher, I had never been to a healing service. I though of them as "holy roller" affairs replete with snake handing and speaking in tongues. They seemed overly theatrical and slightly silly. Still, her voice chilled me and I was moved by her words.

There is something powerful about having nothing left to lose. Our vanity, defenses, and prejudices fall by the wayside and we open our hearts to options we may have never considered. The evangelist was named Kathryn Kuhlman. She hosted a regular program called I Believe in Miracles and conducted "healing crusades" throughout the country. Healthy happy Sara might have flipped the channel, but this new version of myself, still in pain from the surgery that had not been successful at cutting out my cancer, knew that I had to be at her upcoming service.

I was not supposed to get out of the hospital for days, but I talked the doctor into releasing me. I falsely assured him I would stay in bed and not move. I had an incision which was about 36" long and clamped together to heal. That was before there were fading stitches and the wound was vulnerable to the elements.

The doctor said, "You could bleed to death if you move, so I really hesitate to let you go home." Nevertheless, I successfully talked him into letting me go home, knowing I was planning to attend the healing service on Sunday.

I called the Shrine Auditorium and asked if there was a section where very ill people could sit. I had seen the winding lines on television with crowds trying to get in and standing for long periods of time. I could barely walk and knew I would not manage in the middle of the masses. My name was put on a list and I was told to enter through a special door for terminally ill patients.

A friend drove me and dropped me off at the curb so I would not have far to walk. I was instructed when to be there and arrived on time. Nevertheless, when I ambled up to the door I was told, "Everything is filled and if you had wanted a seat in this section, or anywhere, you should have been here an hour ago."

I was dejected. My hope vanished and I felt foolish for believing that God had sent me some special message on the television. Probably everyone straining to pack into this place had the same feeling I did. We were all desperate to save our lives and grabbing at straws for salvation. I turned around to leave.

My friend, Ruth Martin, had been in the auditorium and recognized me on the street. She had gone outside to her car to get a sweater because it was cool inside. She said, "What in the world are you doing here, Sara?"

I said, "I don't feel well and I'd hoped to get in but every seat is taken. My friend and I are going home."

She said, "I will give you my seat and my husband can give your friend his seat." Usually, I would have been polite enough to say, "Oh, no, no, no," but I jumped at the chance. I was poised for miracles and this was the first one of the day.

The seat was located way up in the balcony. As I climbed the steep stairs I saw that I was stepping in my own blood. I was bleeding from the long incision that began underneath my neck and trailed to my left side. I was so weak by the time I reached the top that I almost fell into my seat, which was fortunately at the end of the row.

I tried to right myself and was struck by a strange sense of lightness. I felt that my body was lifted up and I hovered above myself looking down. In my peripheral vision, a pink cloud the consistency of cotton candy was floating on the left side of the auditorium. It was slightly transparent but a seemingly solid mass. While still above looking down, I watched it float around my body. My rational mind concluded three possibilities: I was about to faint, I was hallucinating from the pain or I was slowly drifting towards death.

I don't know the length of time that passed. The sermon was quiet in the distance and the crowd has dissipated around me. I was so intrigued by the vision and wanted to turn to the friend next to me and ask her if she saw what was happening but I couldn't. I was frozen. My body was just there.

Kathryn Kuhlman stopped her service and her booming voice cut through my consciousness; "There is a healing of a girl with cancer riddled throughout her body."

Kathryn continued her service and then stopped again, "This girl in the balcony is being healed. She is having a phenomenal experience! She feels a thousand needles going through her at this moment."

I came out of the cloud and back into my body. It felt as if needles were coursing through my skin. It must be like the sensation of being shocked through an electric current. The entire row where I was sitting fell over like dominos in the seated position—feeling the overflow of Holy Spirit going through me. Kathryn emphatically called out, "This girl is sitting in the last row of the first balcony in a red dress. God has saved you for a very special purpose. You are annointed!"

I was wearing a red dress. There was a great commotion around me because everyone had been knocked over by the power. The ushers had seen this and came over to me and said, "Aren't you the one that's being healed?"

I said, "I think so." I must have sounded pretty confounded because light laughter rustled through the auditorium.

An usher instructed me to stand up and give my testimony. I was hesitant. Even with the profound nature of the events unfolding, my self-consciousness and sense of doubt crept in. I was concerned to look foolish in front of the crowd. Because of my extensive charity work for orphans and former life as an actress, I was well known and active in the Los Angeles community. What if someone I knew was there?

As I hesitated, I heard a very clear voice speak to me, "You mean that I would do this for you and you would deny me?"

I jumped out of my seat, and as I did a tremendous energy flowed from the top of my head to the bottom of my feet. I was filled with a sense of knowing that I was a new person. There was no pain. I felt energized. The bleeding had stopped and as I walked downstairs from the balcony, I found I was literally gliding the long distance to the stage. I knew that this touch of God's grace had given me a second chance.

As I walked down the aisle towards the stage to give my testimony, there were other people who had been healed that were anxious to get on stage to relate what had happened to them. I could not push through the throng of people but I spoke privately to God, "Oh God, I'm here. You see I'm here. I'm not going to make it up there, but I want you to know that I'm here to testify."

Kathryn Kuhlman came to the edge of the stage and pointed at me, "The girl in the red dress in the back, would you make way for her to come forward? The glory of God is all over her!"

There are rare moments in life when all education and rationalization give way to pure feeling. It is the rush of emotion we experience when falling in love or dreaming or experiencing childbirth. It comes in dramatic waves and when it's over, it is virtually forgotten. When we attempt to give it words we render ourselves speechless. I went up on stage and gave my testimony. I spoke from the heart and recounted exactly what happened.

When I had finished, the usher said, "Miss Kuhlman would like your phone number. She wants to know how to reach you, would you mind?" I gave it to him. Driving home with my friend, I was still in a daze and my mind was swirling as I praised God over and over again.

When I undressed that night, I realized my skin had mended over the clamps. The deep gaping wound had closed around each clamp. I felt repaired and at peace. The following morning, at my doctor's appointment, the doctor was amazed when he examined me. He left the examining room and approached Yvonne Fedderson, my dear friend anxiously sitting in the waiting room. Discarding professional medical terminology, he exclaimed, "You have the kookiest friend I've ever seen! I am in a state of disbelief. The skin has healed up over the clamps." The newest x-rays showed I was completely cured of my cancer with the doctor declaring he had no explanation for it.

The next day, I received a call from Kathryn Kuhlman and she asked if I had a copy of my x-rays before and after the healing. I told her I did and she asked if I could bring them with me to film a segment on her national television show. I was initially concerned about just giving a testimony on stage and now I was slated to appear on national TV. Still, the actress in me was able to step forward and share my story even though the young woman who had been healed felt slightly terrified.

After the appearance, Kathryn asked if I would oversee the VIP section at all of her services in Los Angeles. This section was set aside for recognizable celebrities. Before six months was up, she had placed me in the most difficult section which was where the wheelchair bound seekers and terminally ill patients sat in the hopes of healing. It was there that I realized I saw light around the person that God would touch and heal during the service.

As is my nature, I wanted to ensure I was not imagining this bright glow around those who had been chosen, so I tested myself for months. Soon I developed the courage to tell illuminated individuals that the Holy Spirit and God's touch was upon them prior to Kathryn calling out a healing in the wheelchair and terminally ill section. I became adept at identifying the exact one on whom the Holy Spirit fell.

Because I told them they would be healed prior to Kathryn's acknowledgement many were bolstered to receive their healing. Sometimes it seemed like faith needed a nudge to flourish but when it did, miracles happened.

When I finally spoke to Kathryn about my gift, she threw her head back, laughed and said, "It's just the beginning for you, Sara. It's just the beginning. God has a great plan." I thought she was speaking about my work healing abused children. I didn't know that she was talking about the beginning of our work together and a treasured friendship as well as what my future held for me.

I traveled to the Holy Land with Kathryn Kuhlman and it was there that she strongly reiterated that God had saved me for the special purpose of healing. My purpose was not only for the organization that my friend Yvonne and I founded for abused children, but also a gift of healing to be used for His glory.

While Kathryn, my dear friend Yvonne and I were having lunch at a little restaurant overlooking the Red Sea, Kathryn said to me, "I hope you recognize what God has done for you. He has given you the gift of healing." I knew that I had developed a knack for sensing what ailed others and I had experienced a healing of my own that was nothing short of miraculous, but her words were weighted with such responsibility. I wasn't sure I was ready to accept such a profound purpose, nor was I sure the mantel had truly fallen on me.

Reflecting back on that day, I wondered if Kathryn knew about her own health or felt the need to pass a torch so that her ministries could continue. Shortly after our trip, she passed away on the same date as my healing. I was heartbroken because of our close friendship. I felt there was so much more to learn from her and countless people who needed her guidance.

I suppose when our senses are awakened by God's love, we open our eyes to new signs and symbols He makes available to inspire our consciousness. My oldest son, John, was born on February 20th, I was healed on February 20th and Kathryn Kuhlman died on February 20th. This meaningful date in my life was one sign that I was on the correct course to continue as a conduit for God's graceful healing.

A year after her death, a famous healing priest named Father Ralph DiOrio from Massachusetts, was doing research on Kathryn Kuhlman. He read a chapter she had included about me in her book and he began to search for me. People told him if he wanted to know more about Kathryn he should contact Sara O'Meara. He didn't know how to find me because my phone was unlisted. However, while he was a guest in Danny Thomas' home in California, he asked if Danny and his wife, Rosemary, happened to know me. As fate would have it, they had been active in my children's charity. They replied, "Yes, we're friends."

The Thomas' invited me to dinner to meet Father DiOrio. I was unsure why he would want to speak with me but I went. I told him my story and he listened with rapt attention. He confirmed that God had granted me with the gift of healing and I must use it. He offered to mentor me and ended up playing a major role in my life. We began conducting some services together to bring God's mercy to those who needed it most. I spoke and helped with preparations but I had not been officially introduced as a healer.

Months later, at a service that Father DiOrio and I were performing together in New York, he surprisingly announced that Sara O'Meara would be praying on one side of the podium and he on the other for people who had not received a healing during the service. I was overwhelmed because I thought, "This audience doesn't know me at all." There were 3,000 people in attendance and I recoiled fearing that nobody would know me and they would all go to Father DiOrio's line. I was right. Not a soul stood in my line.

At the end of the long snaking line for Father DiOrio, I saw an extremely tall man speaking to two or three people gathered around him. They appeared to be members of his family. He looked towards me several times and I inferred he was discussing whether or not to try me for fear he might not make it to Father DiOrio.

The tall man made his way towards me and I nervously thought, "Oh no, he thinks I can do something for him." There were mixed emotions. On one hand, I was embarrassed no one was in my line but I was also apprehensive that the tall man was on his way to see me and there was nothing I could do to help him.

The tall man said, "Would you pray for me?"

I asked, "Well, what is wrong with you sir?"

He said, "I have an inoperable cancerous tumor on my face," as he pointed to a prominent lump on his right cheek.

My heart went out to him. The baseball-sized tumor distorted his features and clearly made him self-conscious. His eyes were filled with such expectation and I was afraid God would not heal him through me. I prayed all the time but felt paralyzed. I couldn't think of a single prayer. I reached into my heart for the first words I could find, "Dear God, heal this man."

As soon as I spoke, there were screams from his family. They gasped and created quite a commotion. The swollen tumor had begun to deflate. It was disappearing before all of our eyes. I was even more shocked than he and his family.

All of a sudden a rush of people came to me. A second healing occurred with a woman suffering from a skin disease that no one was able to cure. The visible gauze that had been sticking to her body began peeling upward to reveal her newly repaired skin.

An 82 year old gentleman who was totally deaf in one ear and had 80 percent hearing loss in the other, explained that for 50 years he could not hear but suddenly my voice rang clearly through the cathedral. The day was filled with miracles as I continued to pray for people and practically everyone I prayed for was healed. It was then and only then that I consciously accepted that God wanted to use me in this way.

I returned to my California home to find the answering service filled with messages from people requesting prayer. Word quickly spread throughout the country that there was a lady on the west coast who had a healing gift. I began prayer services. Numerous miracles from God touched those at my gatherings. The crowds grew and grew and I realized a larger meeting place was required.

I decided to build a small chapel that would seat over 100 people so I could conduct healing services. In 1987, donations from friends, many of whom had personally experienced healings, made it possible to break ground on the Little Chapel in Tarzana, CA. A marble statue of Jesus was commissioned in Italy by the Fedderson family. It took ten months to complete and another two months for shipping. Whatever one's religion, the statue is an open-armed welcoming symbol of love and acceptance.

Yvonne and I moved to Paradise Valley, Arizona with our families. It is where we live now and where the charity we founded is headquartered. I knew that I still needed to continue my healing mission and began establishing a new and final version of the Little Chapel designed exactly to the specifications of a divine plan revealed to me. It seats over 200 people who come to experience the healing work of God.

I have spent almost 40 years allowing God to work through me. If people look to me to create miracles, they are looking in the wrong place. I have no power. That has to be made clear. If I could, I would save every sick child, dying loved one and injured person I could reach. The work I do is strictly God's call and it is between God and the individual that needs the healing. He simply uses me as a conduit. I don't like to be known as a "healer," but rather as God's servant.

The Little Chapel services occur only once a month because of my philanthropic travel schedule. The night before a service, I remain cloistered in prayer. My "Prayer Warriors," a group that sends blessings for all who need God's intervention in their lives, pray in the chapel separately the night before a service. When offering services in other cities, I always tell my healing story to ensure that the audience does not spend time wondering "How did she get this gift?" Throughout my years of performing healing services, I have witnessed the incredible miracles that God has given, and continues to give, His people.

I have seen God perform miraculous transformations for the health and hearts of those who are suffering. The most amazing part of the healings is the change of spirit for those who have been blessed. What happens to individuals when they realize how much God loves them can change their lives in an instant. The joy is not just what the healing does to the body, even though this is wonderful, it's what it does to the soul.

Illness can sometimes be the manifestation of an ailing spirit. We have to be careful in our commitment and agreement to God on the day of our healing so that we accept His grace and never stray from His glory. The root of the problem can cause it to reoccur if we don't acknowledge God's magnificent healing power and become closer to Him. We must completely lean on God and put Him first.

The day I was healed changed my life forever. The most important realization comes from knowing, in the depth of my soul, that God loves me enough to give me a miracle and He loves each of us enough to heal our bodies, minds and spirits through his merciful grace.

"Seek Ye First in All Things His Kingdom."

Accept Your Miracle!

Becoming a Partner with God

Missy Anderson

Missy Anderson was born and raised in Scottsdale, Arizona with her sister, Jinger. The two outstanding women have always been extremely close. Missy has been happily married to the very handsome and successful Lyle Anderson for over five years. Lyle is president of the Lyle Anderson Companies. Her lovely daughter, Ashley, by a previous marriage, lives with them in Paradise Valley, Arizona.

Missy is an avid tennis player and over the years has twisted her knees many times during a game. Her accident in May 2002 altered her life forever.

When tragedy hits us, God is always there to help us. Many times a painful circumstance turns into being our greatest blessing. We always have opportunities to grow. We must stay alert and keep our eyes and ears open to take advantage of each golden moment. Missy allowed her misery and pain to become a beautiful, joyous blessing. It changed her life and she, in turn, has helped others to come to the light and change their lives.

Missy has been blessed with outward beauty, a gifted mind, a sweet soul, and fortunately uses her position in life for good.

" In May, 2002, I was playing tennis, which I do quite frequently, and I twisted my knee terribly. Having had a history of knee problems, I knew it was bad the moment it happened. I had already had five knee surgeries, three on one knee, and two on the other. Nine years ago, I had my ACL reconstructed and it had four pins and was an ordeal because it required major surgery.

The minute I twisted my knee I had that familiar feeling. I thought, "Here it goes again." I was so frustrated as I came off the court in excruciating pain. For the next couple of days, I did the traditional thing of icing it, and then putting on the heating pad. Ice, heat, ice heat, ice, heat—for several days I kept up the routine and hoped the pain would lessen. By the end of a week I was in such pain I could not function. I could not walk, and because it was my right knee, I could hardly drive. People had to drive me everywhere.

I dreaded going to see my surgeon, but I did and he ran all the tests and took X-rays. He said I had definitely torn my inner meniscus. He hesitated for a moment and then went on to say that it looked like I had ruptured my ACL. He hated to tell me, but the surgery for fixing an already reconstructed ACL is much worse than the first time around.

Tears rolled down my face as I said, "You've got to be kidding." The first surgery caused me to be non-functioning for nine months. I had to wear a brace and spend a lot of time in rehab. I went on and on to the doctor about our summer plans. He replied that I must schedule the operation for the next week if I was going to go anywhere during the next few months. I could be in a brace or using crutches. It would depend on how well the operation went and how I healed.

I left his office on Friday sobbing and the first phone call I made was to my husband, Lyle. I kept saying, "I can't believe it." Saturday, I believed it. I was in such pain I had to spend the whole day in bed using the ice packs and then the heating pad. That night I took three Vicodin. My dear husband was up and down all night with me, and had to leave on a business trip Sunday morning.

Bright and early on Sunday, my mother, Marilyn, phoned and said she wanted me to go to the Little Chapel for a healing instead of going through another operation. That sounded wonderful to me, but I felt awful, and I wasn't sure I could even get out of bed.

My mother has lupus and was told to go to the Little Chapel by our dear friends, Carol and Jim Hebets, who had another friend healed of lupus through Sara's ministry. She kept saying, "I needed the healing more than she did, and she was picking me up in two hours, so get ready!" You don't argue with my mother. Mothers always know best.

As we walked through the doors of the Chapel, I was greeted by friends, and I knew I would be surrounded by loving prayers. The service was wonderful, but I could hardly sit through it, because I was used to having my leg propped up with ice on it. My leg had to be straight down. I was the worst wiggle worm trying to get through the 1½ hour sermon waiting for the healing part of the service.

When the healings began, Sara went to several people around me. She had the most incredible message for my mother, and then she had a beautiful message for the lady who sat on the other side of me. Then Sara went to the lady behind me and to many others all around us, but nothing for me. My heart sank, but I told God I understood it just wasn't my time.

As we walked out of the Chapel, tears were streaming down my cheeks, and Carol Hebets thought they were for my mother because the Holy Spirit had given her, through Sara, a fabulous message. My mother explained that we really were here for me, and told her about my upcoming operation.

Carol took me back in the Chapel and asked Sara to pray for me privately for about thirty minutes. I felt the most incredible heat come through her hands as she placed them on my knee while she prayed. God gave Sara a message for me, and then told me to get up and walk. It still hurt a lot, so Sara said another beautiful prayer. At the end of the ½ hour, she gave me a message that God needed me to hear, and it was much more about my spiritual healing than my knee.

It was about me holding on to things that were of this world, and being so concerned about perfectionism. A lot of us want to please everybody, and do what people think we should do. We get caught up in what the world thinks of us, instead of what God thinks of us. I was always thinking about what society thought of me, and forgot to think about what God thought of me, and what He wanted me to do with my life.

I am blessed to be in a position of influence, and God asked me how I was using my influence to help others. This had been mentioned to me before through other spiritual individuals, but this time it hit me hard. Was I only thinking of pleasing me, my family, and my circle of friends? There are so many others that I could influence in a positive way if I wanted to let God use me. We limit ourselves so much.

The third time Sara laid her hands on me, I knew I had been healed. I stood up, walked around the Chapel, and the pain was gone. We were all crying and thanking God. At this time it was 85% healed. Sara explained that this was like having knee surgery, and that I needed to take it easy for a while. She told me to be good to my knee and be tender — not to play tennis the next day or walk on high heels.

I was told to continue praying for a 100% healing. A lot of times, God heals us in stages. That is for our spiritual growth along with our physical healing.

Pain makes us stop and think. It is really a great blessing if we learn the spiritual lesson behind the pain. It is a great teacher, if, we, as students, will just listen, learn and grow through the pain.

Monday morning, my surgeon phoned. He had put together a team for the surgery and wanted to set a time. I told him I was feeling better and wanted to wait for the surgery. He said he had given me some severe pain medication, and that the drugs were making me feel that way. I was afraid to tell him about the Little Chapel service but I did tell him I hadn't taken the prescribed drugs for 24 hours. He said that my body must be in shock, and he was concerned that I was going to be going down a stair and the ACL would completely give way. He didn't want to take that risk as my doctor and I said I was willing to take that risk. I released him of any responsibility. I never had that operation.

Many of us who attend the Little Chapel services ask for a physical healing. I think it is important to ask for a spiritual healing also. There is a spiritual lesson to learn through every physical healing.

I have a weakness in my knees and it is my responsibility to work out and keep my knees strong. We have a responsibility of keeping our bodies strong and healthy through proper diet and exercise. We cannot continue to abuse ourselves and say to God, "Heal me." It doesn't work that way. God heals us and then expects us to do our part to keep the healing. We must become a partner with God, and together we can have healthy bodies and happy, productive lives that make the world a better place in which to live.

Another important part of healing is to surround yourself with people who will support you, and who are on the same positive path of higher thinking and living. I want to be an example for God. I ask God daily to use me to reach others. As I tell people about my experience, I pray that I will be able to touch their souls and help them to stay on the path of light and love.

God's Love and Light Does Heal You

Lynn Andrews

*L*ynn was born in Seattle, Washington, and is delighted to be living now in Cave Creek, Arizona. She has been blessed with a wonderful gift her entire life of seeing the light and truth around people. Lynn works with the mind and heart of individuals to help them accept a higher consciousness—a higher way of thinking and living.

Lynn is able to see around people their state of disease, and works to help heal them in a spiritual way. She is an internationally acclaimed best selling author of over 18 books, including *Medicine Woman*, now in its 39th printing.

Lynn had heard about Childhelp, the organization Sara and I began in 1959, but had no knowledge of the Little Chapel and Sara's healing work. One day, while speaking to a mutual friend, Nick Bunick, he mentioned the Little Chapel. As tears rolled down his cheeks, he told her of his healing, and shared with her numerous other magnificent healings he had witnessed which touched her heart deeply.

She asked Nick the date and time of the next service, because he was so insistent she meet Sara. Here is Lynn Andrews' story.

❝ I was mesmerized by what Nick had told me about the Little Chapel, and looked forward to attending the next service. The time came, and I almost forgot about it. I got up early Sunday morning and was busy cleaning stalls in my barn, when I suddenly realized this was Chapel day. I flew in the house and hurriedly changed my clothes. All the way while I was driving fast to not be so late for the service, I was praying to be calm when I arrived so I could enjoy the morning and be open to the many blessings.

Years ago, my mother suddenly passed away, and it put me into a tailspin. Ever since that day, I had suffered terrible neck problems. My life was always about helping others, and I never took the time to think about my sore neck and why I was always in pain.

The minute I walked through the doors of the Little Chapel, I felt great peace come over me. I found a seat quickly as I wanted to be still and enjoy every moment in this spirit-filled place.

I looked around the room and prayed for all those souls who were there for a miracle. Throughout the service I continued to pray and send positive energy out to all those in need. I could see the beautiful light around Sara as she spoke, and knew she allowed the Holy Spirit to work through her for great miracles to occur. That day changed my life. I never connected my neck pain with the death of my mother until that Sunday morning.

The healings began after the service, and Sara walked up to me, not knowing who I was and said, "You don't have to carry that pain any more in your neck. Your neck hurts, doesn't it?" She looked very directly into my eyes—it was as if Sara had moved somewhere else and the Holy Spirit was speaking through her. It was just so powerful. Nothing happened to me. She didn't touch me, and I didn't feel a particular energy coming through me, but all of a sudden, she asked me to move my head to the right and left. I hadn't been able to do that in years. I did so and the pain was gone, and it has remained gone.

Sara didn't realize she put a little bit of the sacred puzzle together for me. What I realized sitting there, that little piece of the puzzle, was that you don't have to be educated to get there. Faith is something that is unto itself, and if you open yourself up to the light, as she was talking about that day, that light does come through and it heals you. I think it's a process of coming to the Chapel asking for the healing and not just *hoping that it will* happen, but having faith and *knowing* that it absolutely will happen. Mine did.

I am relieved to be free of the pain in my neck, and so grateful to God for all the other miracles that happened in the Little Chapel that unforgettable Sunday morning. Even though I have my own school for sacred arts and training, and have been in this work all of my life, this experience gave me a renewed sense of miracles.

Sara is truly a light in this world and a blessing to us all. If you want power, you have to make a place inside you for power to live.

Unconditional Love Opens Your Heart to the Healings from Jesus

Alexis Angeles
by Renée Angeles

Renée was born and raised in Scottsdale, Arizona and graduated from Arizona State University. She has been married to Jesus for ten years and they have two young daughters. Bianca Marie Angeles, age 8 and Alexis Katherine Angeles, age 3, are blessed to have such loving and devoted parents.

Renée was first invited to go to The Little Chapel approximately seven years ago by a co-worker named Maria Petrick. Her mother, Katie, never likes to miss a service and is part of the prayer group who meets and prays the night before. She is a real prayer warrior for God.

Katie has witnessed so many healings at the services in The Little Chapel, and knows deep in her heart that God can do anything.

Katie is so happy that Renée, Jesus and their girls are all spreading the word about how great the love of Jesus Christ is for each of us.

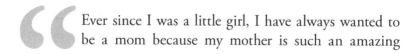 Ever since I was a little girl, I have always wanted to be a mom because my mother is such an amazing

woman. She is a great role model who loves life, is always willing to help others and has unconditional love for her friends and family. Today, I have been blessed with two beautiful girls who have helped me understand what unconditional love means. It is a very powerful thing.

On August 24, 2008, my youngest daughter, Alexis, was outside playing with all the neighborhood kids. She ran, jumped and played like any normal two-year-old would. The next day she woke up complaining of pain in her ankle. It was swollen to about five times its original size, red, hot to the touch and she could not put any pressure on it. I immediately took her to see the pediatrician, who thought she may have sprained her ankle. The doctor suggested we take her to an orthopedic surgeon to take a look. We did just that and the orthopedic surgeon's diagnosis was a hairline fracture. He told us to keep her off it and keep icing it down. After doing exactly what we were supposed to do, we saw no improvement.

For three months my baby could not walk. She cried whenever pressure was put on her little ankle. She would cry and whimper throughout the night. We saw eight different orthopedic surgeons, one of whom put Alexis in a cast for six weeks. When the cast was removed, there was no change – she was still in pain. Finally, one orthopedic surgeon suggested I take her to a rheumatologist to rule out JRA – juvenile rheumatoid arthritis. There was no question in my mind - I would take her wherever I need to in order to rule out everything and find out what was wrong with my baby.

On November 26, 2008, the day before Thanksgiving, I was hit with devastating news. The rheumatologist we consulted diagnosed Alexis with Poly-JRA, not only in the ankle that was symptomatic, but also in the other ankle, both knees, both hips, her right shoulder and the fingers on her left hand. They told me the course of treatment was chemotherapy and steroids. I was told my baby girl would loose her hair, get sick after every meal and suffer from horrible mouth sores. But, the doctor said, "After all this she will feel better!" My only thought was, "You've got to be kidding me!" I was in total denial. I cancelled all our Thanksgiving plans and stayed home all weekend, crying, praying and questioning my faith. I held and carried my little angel all weekend. I didn't want to put her down.

By the following Monday, I still could not accept that I would have to give my baby chemo and put her through what I knew would be the most horrific pain a two-year-old could experience. That morning, the doctor's office called to see why I had not filled the prescription. Nurse Laura, who I believe was an angel in disguise, told me that if I didn't start Alexis on the medicine within three months there would be so much damage to her joints that she would be committed to a wheelchair for the rest of her life. She said that if I wanted to see what that looked like, to come see at the office any day. She also told me that Alexis' blood work came back positive for the diagnosis. I was heartbroken and became physically sick at work. Later that day, we decided to start Alexis on the drug regimen the doctor recommended. Still, I knew in my heart that there was another way, a better way, to help my daughter.

So, I prayed harder and more diligently for God's guidance because I truly believe that God only gives us what we can handle. I kept asking Him to help me understand why this was happening to our family and to give me strength. And then it came to me, what would my mother do? The answer came loud and clear, and I kept hearing the words in my head – Call Sara! Call Sara! Ask her to pray for a healing for Alexis.

On December 3, 2008, I left an emotional message for Sara. I explained Alexis' diagnosis as best I could. To this day, I'm amazed Sara could even understand my message! Later that day, Sara returned my call. Her voice was like an angel speaking to me, very sweet, very calm and very confident that something good was going to happen. Sara did tell me that sometimes it takes more than one healing to heal children and she really wanted to make sure I was ready to accept what God had waiting for me. I was ready!

All the healings were done over the phone. During the first healing, I held Alexis who was restless and fussy at first. As soon as Sara started to pray, Alexis became amazingly calm. Sara confirmed with me that the Holy Spirit was at work and told me to let Alexis go to sleep. Sara said that when Alexis woke up she would be healed and feeling better.

Well she was. After her nap, Alexis got out of bed and was walking like a normal little girl. Unfortunately, that was short lived and soon she was back in pain and didn't want to walk. I called Sara again and left a message saying that we needed to continue praying over Alexis. Sara called me back immediately and prayed over Alexis. Again, I held my baby. This time, she was very calm but as the praying went on her body got very hot. Sara assured me again that the Holy Spirit was at work. Suddenly, Alexis opened her eyes looked at me and said, "Mama I want to walk." Not knowing what to do, I asked Sara, "What should I do?" "Let her walk," she replied. "The Holy Spirit will do the rest."

We prayed over Alexis two more times. Sara told Alexis and me to thank God every day for the healing and praise Him for His work. Not a day goes by that we don't take a few minutes to give thanks.

On January 8, 2009, we had a follow-up visit with the doctor. He had told us previously that he would be increasing her medication and starting her on daily Epi-shots. When we arrived, however, the doctor examined her, looked at her again, and then asked me, "What did you do?" I explained that I don't have any medical experience, but I do have a Jesus and I left it up to Him. The doctor was amazed, but still wanted to run more blood tests and asked us to return in six weeks. I told him I was certain Alexis was healed, but would be happy for him to run whatever test he needed.

Six weeks later, the test results confirmed that Alexis had no signs of JRA in her blood and that she was a normal little girl. Again, the doctor asked me what I had done. I reiterated that I turned to Jesus to guide me and answer our prayers. The doctor was speechless.

He explained that sometimes doctors can't explain why patients heal—they just do. He had tears in his eyes and, needless to say, so did I. He said to keep doing what I was doing, since it was obviously working. I fell to my knees when he left the office and gave thanks to Jesus, the Holy Spirit and Sara for healing my baby.

On a follow-up visit, one year to the day after Alexis was diagnosed with JRA, the doctor declared her fully healed and said we didn't need to come back for six months. With tears in his eyes, he told me I was a great mom and to keep doing what I was doing. I owe that credit to my mother who taught me to love unconditionally. He looked at Alexis and said, "Kiddo, you're all better!" Alexis replied, "Thank you doctor and Jesus for healing me. Mama, can I get my ears pierced?"

Every single day we thank Jesus for his blessings and praise Him for His work. I thank Sara for her strong spiritual connections, her healings and her love for people. I would also like to thank Yvonne for the opportunity to share my story with all of you. I challenge each and every one of you to open your hearts and minds to accept the healings of Jesus.

Learning to Never Limit His Blessings

Betty Appleby

etty lives in Detroit, Michigan and attends the *Renaissance Unity Church* there. Marianne Williamson told the congregation Sara O'Meara was going to give a healing service the following Saturday at the church, and that announcement somehow touched her heart. She prayed about attending the service, and the Holy Spirit let her know she should definitely plan to be there.

Betty had several people around her whose thinking was narrower than her own. She was a great deal more open and didn't doubt the possibility that God could and does heal through certain individuals.

She has been blessed with a son who is married and has made her a proud grandmother. Living with Betty is a very ill niece and her blind young son. She works closely with him daily and feels he is very spiritual. Betty is known as a warm and giving soul and is most grateful to God for blessing her mind, body and spirit at Sara's service in Michigan.

I have had the privilege of working for two Governors in Michigan and I've been a civil rights representative for years. I volunteer my time now in helping Marianne Williamson to establish a U.S. Department of Peace.

I have suffered with health problems over the years, so when I heard about the healing service I knew in my heart I wanted to attend. The spiritual side of my life is very important to me, and I'm always willing to learn more about God. I enjoy doing Reiki and Therapeutic Touch.

As Sara began to speak at the service my heart completely opened up like a flower in bloom. I felt such inner peace, and the Holy Spirit was filling my entire body with God's love and healing energy. In fact, the power was so strong my entire body began to vibrate. I felt heat and a prickly feeling and then the tears began to flow. I cried throughout the entire service. They were happy tears-such a release like I had never experienced before.

I had to laugh through my tears when I thought of those whom I love whose thinking is so small, it could fit into a tiny "box"; and this service would definitely upset and confuse them. I prayed hard to stay strong in my faith and that I would never go back into that little "box" thinking again which is so limiting.

After the service I felt I had definitely received a healing of that mind set and self sabotaging. I was also healed of arthritis in my left hip. I am so grateful to be released of that chronic pain. Since that glorious day when Sara spoke and allowed the Holy Spirit to heal me through her, I have had no pain or discomfort.

I feel now I can move forward with my vision to return to Africa one day to help uplift the people there. In the meantime I am doing what I can to help others, especially children in Michigan.

I promised God that day of my healing I would serve all His children. My heart desires to help the abused and neglected children and I'm sure God will honor that.

God is so good and it is important we never limit His blessings. I'm so glad I did not limit Him. I am free!

Replacing Pain with His Love

Bill And Jill Babb

*B*ill and Jill Babb live across the street from our home in Flagstaff, AZ. When we go up to Flagstaff we like to rest and be with our family, so we haven't met a lot of our neighbors.

One day Jill came over with a plate of her delicious fudge and introduced herself. She invited us to attend a prayer group the following week in her home. We were only staying for the weekend in Flagstaff and had to decline her nice invitation.

Our dearest Friends, Carol and Jim Hebets, joined us for a couple of days and, after they had arrived, we told them about our nice neighbor who had just brought us all homemade fudge. Jim and Carol knew Bill Babb and went across the street to say hello. Now we are all enjoying spending time together as often as we can. Bill and Jill are beautiful souls and we are thankful God brought us all together.

Carol and Jim recently purchased a home in Flagstaff a few blocks away from us. Jill is decorating their home and in her spare time she began a Childhelp Chapter there. She has bought and given away many copies of our book Silence Broken, which is the story of Childhelp, along with copies of our Lifetime movie, For the Love of a Child, to most all her friends. The Childhelp Flagstaff Chapter is doing well – thanks to Jill and Bill and their loving and generous hearts that touch and heal many little lives. Jill also serves on the Childhelp National Board.

Bill and Jill are so grateful that God healed each of them, and they want to give back. They not only help the little children of Childhelp®, but they are spreading the word all over Flagstaff about The Little Chapel and the great work that God is doing there. They have brought many people with them to The Little Chapel and they too have been healed and touched in a profound way.

One small loving act, like bringing us fudge, can have quite a beautiful ripple effect. We could truly change the world if each of us would do small things with great love everyday.

"" My story (Bill) actually started in 2003 when I was diagnosed with hydrocephalus. Hydrocephalus is fluid or water in the brain. One day I knew something was wrong when I went out to the parking lot where I work and couldn't find my car. We have a small parking lot, so I thought I'd better check things out with my doctor.

Once the doctor determined I had hydrocephalus, he recommended surgery within 30 days. They had to put a tube down my spine and put a shunt in my stomach. They drained the water from my brain down the tube into my stomach. That helped immensely, but I wasn't getting a whole lot better. I had to have another surgery in September 2003, which helped, but I still wasn't happy with the results.

Carol and Jim Hebets were having lunch with us one day and I told them it looked like I was going to have another surgery at Barrows Neurological Institute. Jim spoke up and said, "Here's another option for you. This may seem a little strange, but let me tell you about the Little Chapel in Paradise Valley."

When he finished talking about Sara and The Little Chapel, I looked at Jill and said, "What do I have to lose?" I had much more to gain than to lose, so I was anxious for the next service.

It was in February 2004 when Jill and I walked through the doors of The Little Chapel. It was a powerful moment and one we will always remember. The feeling of love was everywhere and everyone was so friendly.

I noticed brass plaques with names on them on the pews and I first thought they must have assigned seating. We were told anyone could buy a plaque, but that didn't save you a seat.

It was already crowded so I ended up sitting behind a pillar. I could only see half of Sara when I leaned around the pillar, so I started thinking to myself maybe I'm only going to be half healed. Oh well, half a brain is better than none!

Jill and I prayed all through the service and all of a sudden near the end of Sara's sermon I got this very sharp pain in the side of my head. I looked at Jill and said I thought I was having a stroke. She was trying to find a cell phone to call 911, and I thought how awful this was to happen in the middle of this healing service. I thought this was going to be bad P.R. for Sara when an ambulance pulls up and carries me out of the Chapel.

The feeling of a knife in my head turned out to be the beginning of my fantastic healing. The arteries in my head opened up and all of a sudden I could see everything. Sara was still talking and hadn't even started the healing portion of the service. I was so happy I wanted to shout out loud what had just happened.

The healings began and Sara asked people to raise their hand when they received one so she could confirm it. I'm thinking I don't have to raise my hand. I know I'm healed. I never had to have that surgery!

I lost my first wife nine years ago to brain cancer. The pain in my head was exactly in the same place where the scar was on my wife's head after the removal of her tumor. The doctor said that there have been cases where an individual feels so deeply about a loved one's suffering that they absorb the pain and take the illness on themselves.

That was a beautiful day for me and my lovely wife Jill. We had faith that God could heal, but our faith has increased so much since attending the services in The Little Chapel. I'm grateful to the Holy Spirit for my magnificent healing through Sara. I'm thankful for Carol and Jim for telling us about The Little Chapel, and my wife for being a good neighbor and delivering her fudge with a smile on her face and a glow in her heart. God works in mysterious ways His wonders to perform. **"**

"My (Jill) dear husband, Bill, received his wonderful healing in February 2004 and on Sunday, May 23, 2004 I received mine.

I had suffered with lower back pain for almost 20 years. I had tried almost everything possible just short of surgery to stop the pain. Ice and heat had been my only form of relief. I had learned to tolerate the pain and accepted it as a way of life.

Sara and Yvonne were in Flagstaff for a few days, and so were Carol and Jim. We had a wonderful dinner together Friday evening and I mentioned to the ladies an idea I had for Childhelp. Sunday afternoon I thought I would walk over and show them my idea. My back was hurting more than usual, and I realize now God was trying to impress me to ask Sara to pray for a healing of my back.

After arriving at the house and talking with Yvonne and Carol, they mentioned how they had stayed up late the night before praying. It was amazing to me that they would spend even their off time thinking about others. I must say it didn't surprise me.

As I was getting ready to leave I asked if they would pray for my back that evening during prayer time. Yvonne said, "Okay, but better yet, let me get Sara now to lead us in a special prayer for you before you leave." I really didn't want to interrupt their Sunday morning, but Yvonne insisted.

Soon we were in one of the bedrooms with Sara kneeling on the floor next to me with her hands on my stomach and back. She began to ask God for His tender touch to heal my back. Sara is always sure to point out that all things are possible through God's grace and love and our faith.

My back began to feel very warm, but not uncomfortable. After her prayers, Sara asked me to stand up and see if the pain was all gone. I was so nervous to stand up. What if God didn't hear her? After all it was early in the morning, Sara was in her robe and we were not in The Little Chapel. Where was my faith?

I realized that none of those things really mattered and that God is everywhere and always hears our prayers. I stood up, then I sat down, then I stood up and walked around. Yes! Yes! God did hear our prayers and I was completely healed. I didn't even have a slight ache.

We thanked God over and over for my beautiful healing that changed my life. I, too, thanked Sara for being the instrument that God used to heal me. Since that glorious summer day in May, I have not had one pain in my back. Every morning I thank God I am pain free. God replaced my pain with His love and that is my miracle.

Bill and I cherish our miracles and thank God daily for our many blessings.

A Toast to "Two" Miracles

Joanne Bateman

*J*oanne Bateman is a mother of four, grandmother of eight, and great-grandmother of four, and has lots of energy for all of them. She loves children and has volunteered many hours at our Childhelp Village, a residential treatment center in Beaumont, California, where 80 abused children live.

" In the fall of 1998, I had the flu and couldn't seem to get rid of it. I had no energy at all, and only wanted to stay in bed. It just went on and on and on. I had chest X-rays and was taking antibiotics, but nothing worked. The doctor told me he thought my immune system was not working. He said maybe I had gotten stuck with a needle because of my occupation as a surgical assistant. He insisted I take more tests.

A few days later, my husband, Ben, and I were getting ready to celebrate our anniversary. Love filled the air as we were reminiscing about our beautiful years together, and how happy they were. I was on my way to get the bottle of champagne that was chilling on ice when the phone rang. It was my doctor, phoning to tell me the report of the tests I had just completed. He said I had multiple myeloma (cancer of the bone marrow). He proceeded to tell me that it is fatal and there was nothing to be done, and it was just a matter of a few months.

I hung up the phone and turned to Ben with tears rolling down my cheeks. I struggled to tell him the devastating news. The champagne on ice was put on hold, and there was no anniversary celebration.

We began calling the family and when we reached our dear friend, Vita Cortese, she said, "Oh, yes, there is something you can do. You can ask God for a miracle." Vita phoned Sara and the prayers began. Sara told Vita I was #1 on her prayer list until I redid the test to confirm the healing.

I then went to an oncologist in Palm Springs who told me it looked like I had multiple myeloma, but I couldn't have treatments for it. He wanted me to run more tests. Sara kept praying, and I went from denial, to anger, denial, to anger, and tried to have faith, but it was hard—real hard. She kept telling me to trust God—that He was healing her.

The doctor finally phoned and asked me to come to his office immediately. I was nervous but anxious to hear the news. When I saw the look on the doctor's face, I knew I had received a miracle. He told me to "Take this piece of paper home and frame it—you no longer have multiple myeloma!"

After phoning all my family and sharing the fantastic news, I phoned Sara. She was so grateful to hear that God had given me more time to be with my loved ones—a miracle indeed. Ben and I opened the bottle of champagne and belatedly celebrated our anniversary.

A few days later, I got another call from the doctor telling me that they discovered I had ovarian cancer. He said I had a large growth and numerous clusters on the left ovary. It was necessary to go through several more tests. I was then sent to a gynecologist. He showed Ben and me the spots on the ovary through an ultrasound. One was especially large.

Some more direct calls were made to Sara! Ben and I had planned a motor vacation, and I asked the doctor if he thought that would be OK. He said to go, but he wanted to see me right away for more tests when we got back home. When we returned, there was a message on our answering service from the doctor, telling me to go to the hospital immediately. Ben drove me to the hospital and patiently waited while I took another ultrasound test.

All of a sudden, a broad smile came across the doctor's face as he turned to me and Ben and said, "I want you to look at this screen—there is nothing."

"Where did they all go?" I asked.

"It's a miracle!" the doctor said.

I burst into tears and quietly uttered, "Somebody said prayers for me, and they were answered." That somebody was Sara.

It was six weeks of living misery, but a miracle ended it all beautifully—not once, but twice. I was so relieved after my healing that I just kept walking around thanking God. My prayers continue to increase daily. When I see an accident or an ambulance drive by, I say a silent prayer for those involved. I don't take things for granted anymore.

Yes, miracles do change your life, and I had two so I had to change twice as much!

My Grateful Heart Wants to Love More, Give More and Inspire Others by My Actions

Jane Bell

Jane and Ted Bell first learned about the Little Chapel through their son, Jim. All three of them regularly attend the service. Jane and Ted generously serve ice cream for everyone to enjoy after the service while Little Chapel attendees share their experiences and blessings of the day.

Jane was born in Chicago, Illinois. She moved to Seattle, Washington 48 years ago where she met Ted. They married a year later and have one son Jim.

Ted's work took them to many interesting places to live including Singapore, Iran, China and Saudi Arabia before they moved to Arizona in 1966 where they reside now.

Jane taught physically challenged and blind children to swim wherever they lived. She has such a beautiful heart for children, which now includes helping the abused and neglected children through Childhelp. We are so fortunate to have her as a part of our Childhelp family.

"Our son, Jim, told us about the Little Chapel and insisted we attend a service to hear Sara speak. He went on and on about how her sermon touched his heart and he also mentioned that Sara and Yvonne began the organization, Childhelp. He felt we should meet the ladies and get involved in helping the children as well as attend a chapel service.

We agreed to go to the Little Chapel, which turned out to be the special Christmas service. I made a prayer request for our son, Jim, to be given help to get his new business started. God answered my prayer quickly. Ted and I regularly attend Chapel now and while setting up the ice cream buffet Ted started to suffer from shortness of breath, and could hardly stand up. Sara was entering the Little Chapel and saw Ted gasping for breath. She stopped and said a prayer for him, and then proceeded into the Little Chapel. By the end of the service, Ted was breathing properly. He was completely healed. He feels every breath he takes is a gift from God.

In January 2009, Jim's business took off and has been doing very well ever since. Ted and I always arrive early to set up to serve ice cream after the service.

In August, I had abdominal surgery and while I was in the hospital they discovered my appendix had ruptured and I had developed mucinous epithelial neoplasm, which is a tumor that looks like Jell-O®. It was not cancerous, but had to be removed. If one cell is left it will start growing again, so the doctors had to keep checking me.

Four months later, the doctor continuously monitored me after I was released. They took a scan of the area and said a detected tumor growing again and asked me to come back for more tests, I put in my prayer request to Sara.

I felt the presence of the Holy Spirit so strongly at the service. I prayed, Ted prayed, Jim prayed. We all believe that positive, loving thoughts open our lives to great possibilities and miracles. I needed and wanted a miracle so I released it all to God. During the service

I felt such peace and warmth throughout my body and knew God had touched me.

When I went back to the doctor for another scan he was shocked because he couldn't find anything. He said he didn't know what I had been doing, but whatever it was I should keep it up and continue to do through my belief in God.

The three of us love the Little Chapel with all our hearts for it has helped us in so many ways. It has lifted us up to a new dimension and opened our hearts and our eyes to look at life in a different and more positive way.

We have learned that garbage mental habits can trash our lives. Our personal spiritual growth takes a lot of inner work every day that we found unequivocally to be worth it.

We have had another bonus added to our lives by attending the Little Chapel. We have been given the opportunity to joyously give our time and energy to help the abused children through Childhelp. The more we give from our hearts, the more God continues to bless us. We are so grateful.

My Best Friend, Jesus, is Back with Me

Jenny Bertolini

*J*enny Bertolini was born in California and moved to Colorado with a girlfriend when she was 18 years old. She loves to ride horses in the wide-open spaces in Colorado when she has free time. However, she is married, has a son and works full time as a hairdresser in Aspen, so her days are rather busy.

Jenny was raised a Catholic, and never heard about healing services. One day, while talking to one of her clients, Joyce Bulifant, she learned about Sara O'Meara and her wonderful healing gift. Joyce got her attention, and she promised to attend the service in Snowmass the next time Sara came into town. It wasn't long after that, Sara came to Colorado, and Jenny kept her promise to Joyce. Her life has never been the same.

I was so curious; I just had to attend the service. What kind of people would go to one of these services, I wondered. I adore Joyce, so I trusted that nothing bad would happen to me if I went. In fact, she said something good might happen and besides, she said there would be some good music, and I love music.

My friend and I went to the service. Sara called out a healing that was meant for my friend, but she didn't take it. She wasn't ready for it yet. I sat through the service in awe. Everything Sara said seemed to go right to my soul—it touched me so deeply and I felt such total peace within. My body felt elevated and so filled with God's love. I had never experienced anything like that before.

Sara asked someone if they felt the heat from the Holy Spirit. I sure did, as my body began to vibrate. I was a Christian before, but truly received a spiritual healing that day.

My entire life changed as a result of that service. God opened my eyes, and they became the windows of my soul. It's a whole new world for me and my family.

Jesus was my best friend when I was growing up, but somewhere along the way I forgot about him. I let that friendship slip away. At Sara's service, I found him again, and I was so grateful I cried all the way home. I've had a hunger for more spiritual qualities for my life ever since.

At another service that Sara had in Aspen a few months later, I received a healing of the heart. Sara said that I was going to climb far up the spiritual ladder. I just needed to let go of the last rung on the ladder. Every day I'm working on letting go and letting God help me with things so my life will become easier and more serene.

A few months later, my husband, Rick, and I, drove to Arizona for a Chapel service where I gave my testimony. Rick had injured his knee some time ago, and had never gone to see a doctor. It hurt him to walk, but we didn't have the money for him to have surgery, so he just lived with the pain. He was thrilled beyond words when he felt the magnificent healing power on his knee. There was no longer any pain. Another miracle! I also received a healing of my shoulder. I had torn my rotator cuff while water skiing and it is now perfect.

My mother, Robin Fuller, had gone to a couple of the healing services in Aspen and loved them. When she learned she had cancer, we phoned Sara in Arizona right away. The next day, mother was operated on, and they removed her appendix, her ovaries and her uterus. She refused to take chemo and said she was trusting God for a complete bill of health. She is doing great! At another service in Aspen, I brought a friend with prostate cancer. He is now cancer-free.

God just keeps blessing me. The last service my ear, neck and back all received healings, along with a great emotional healing. A friend had been very depressed and I allowed her negativity to get to me. Sara saw the sadness around me and said God was lifting up the situation around me and everything was going to be all right. She told me I must learn to protect myself from the darkness, and keep in the light so I can be of more service to God. At that moment I felt this dark cloud lift out of my heart. The depression is completely gone now, and I pray for love and light to protect me every day.

I never want to miss a service, because they always make me feel so much better in every way. Every single day I ask God to use me to help others with their problems. I try to let God work through me to help them.

There is a beautiful statue of Jesus in the Arizona Chapel. While I sat in the audience during the last service I attended, I looked up at the statue and He spoke to me. He said, "Do you feel that?" I said, "Yes," and Jesus said, "That's me." My life has been completely turned around since I met Sara and attended the services. I'm grateful for all the many blessings, but having my best friend Jesus back with me is by far the best gift of all.

Following the Path of Light & Love

Rebecca Bloom

Rebecca was born in Michigan and raised in Coco Beach, Florida. Now she is a certified hypnotherapist in her home state of Michigan. She has a son, Christen, and a daughter, Nina, who has one little boy.

Rebecca was a heroin addict for 15 long years. She tried to stop her addiction many times, but was unsuccessful. She was taught about God as a child, but she never thought about spiritual things as she grew older.

One day she felt she was at rock bottom and couldn't go on anymore. She fell to her knees and asked God to help her stop this terrible habit. God saw her heart truly wanted to stop, and He answered her prayers. It has been over ten years now since she has been free of drugs.

This was the beginning of her new life. She is so happy that God lifted her up to a new way of thinking and living.

> I have lived through hell, and now I feel I am enjoying a little piece of heaven on earth. I have God in my life, and I am free of drugs. Sometimes when we don't go through

great suffering, we don't appreciate how good God is and all the things he has blessed us with to enjoy.

I was diagnosed with Crohns disease, which ties up your bowels and intestines in knots, and causes severe pain. The doctor could only recommend prednisone as a remedy, but there is no cure. I refused that treatment.

In the fall of 2003, Marianne Williamson announced that Sara O'Meara was coming to our *Renaissance Unity Church* to do a healing service. My friend and her husband told me about the service and I was anxious to attend. I was tired of the pain, but did not want to take prednisone. I wanted a spiritual healing with all my heart. God helped me with my drug habit and I knew He would help me again.

The sermon was great, but I couldn't wait for the healing part of the service to begin. After the healings began to happen throughout the audience, Sara announced that someone was being healed of intestinal problems. I quietly raised my arm, and at that moment I felt a lightening bolt of electricity go through my entire body, followed by intense heat. I immediately claimed my healing in the name of God.

Sara came by where I was sitting and verified my healing. I was one grateful lady. Since that wonderful day in October 2003 I have had absolutely no pain. I tell everyone who will listen about my healing.

I have promised God to use my gifts for His glory. I love to read spiritual books and to meditate. My heart goes out to stray animals and I feel a great need to take care of them.

God has been so good to me, and I want to be His hands and feet to help others in every way I can. I know what it is like to not be on God's path, and my only desire is to follow the path of love and light.

Love is the Golden Key that Opens Up Heaven for Us

Kathy Bowen

*K*athy Bowen has lived most of her life in Arizona and was raised with three brothers whom she adores. She now has two grown daughters, Lani and Traci, and a wonderful son-in-law, Larry. Lani and Larry have a beautiful baby daughter Sofia. Family is everything to Kathy and she loves to have all the family and friends over for one of her gourmet meals. This is only one of her many talents.

She always greets you with a big smile, and her heart is always open to help anyone she can. She is a wonderful example of love in action.

Kathy tells the following story, praying it will help you to believe in a deeper, more meaningful way.

In the spring of 2000, I went to the doctor and was told I had a melanoma spot on my face and must have surgery right away.

Carol Hebets, my sister-in-law who is just like a sister, said "I'm taking you to a special healing service next Sunday. You won't need surgery, I promise."

A group of us women came together to The Little Chapel, and we were all so happy and full of joy during the entire service. The healings began happening all around us, which were unbelievable to watch. The heat began rushing through me, and Sara looked my way. I thought she was going to speak to me, but the lady in front of me stood up. I was crushed and said to myself, "No, no it's me—it's not you!"

Then I started telling myself, "Okay, I'm next," but Sara went all around me, and went to just about every woman who came with us that day. She never came back to me.

I knew I had received a healing-I felt it. I was on fire inside, and I just knew it. I left saddened, however, because it hadn't been told to me directly; for Sara points out almost all of the healings which happen. She sees a light around the person from the Holy Spirit.

I got in my car and looked in the mirror, and the melanoma spot was gone. I looked at my face and the texture was changed and the depth was changed. I thought "Oh my gosh! Wednesday I'm scheduled for a doctor to be cutting up my face, and he doesn't need to do it."

On Monday I called the doctor and told him that I thought he might want to look at me before I went in to surgery. He asked me to come in right away so he could look at it. When he saw it, he agreed that it had changed. I said, "Well, I promised my two daughters that I would have another biopsy done just to be certain but I know it's gone. He did another biopsy and it came back negative. Yes, I had received a healing!

I developed a close friendship with Sara and Yvonne. After a few weeks I had a bad fall. I dislocated my shoulder, cracked three ribs, dislocated my thumb, and on and on. I was sore all over and physically a mess, but I didn't want to give in to the fact that I was hurt; and I needed to take some time off just for me. I wanted to keep on working and ignore the pain in my body.

My sister-in-law, Carol, kept asking me to say something to Sara when I saw her, but I said I didn't want to bother her. Carol said I was silly not to ask because she knew I would get another healing. Why stay in pain when God wants us to be free of pain? Just ask!

The next time Sara and I were together she asked if she could pray over me. I was secretly happy she brought it up, and I didn't have to do the asking.

Sara sat me in a chair and put her hands over me as she prayed. Once again, I felt that rush of heat going through my body and I knew I was being healed. All of a sudden it felt like someone had turned on the lights and I thought someone had come in the room. I opened my eyes and the entire room was filled with light. I knew the Holy Spirit was there and working through Sara to heal my body. I felt my angels giving me such love that it was overwhelming. That moment proved to me that love is the "golden key" that opens up heaven for us. It brings in the light and eliminates the darkness.

Sara told me to treat the areas on my body as if I had surgery. They needed to be treated gently, so she advised me to take a couple of days off from work to relax. God had given her those words to tell me, and I said okay—and then went right back out and started working. I didn't listen.

When I saw Sara the next week she looked at me and said, "You didn't listen." I admitted the pain was gone, but the weakness was still there. She prayed over me and this time I listened. I have learned to listen because God only tells us what is best for us. I didn't want to ask for a healing, but I know now that we must ask to receive. Help is always available, but never forced.

I'm glad I learned to ask because several months later I needed another miracle. My brother Jim and Carol were taking a group of us on a trip to Europe, including Sara and Yvonne and their children. A couple of weeks before we were to leave, I awakened at four in the morning without my front tooth. The tooth was inside the cap, so I had nothing but a hole right in front.

The next morning the dentist took an x-ray and said how strange it was that the tooth just separated and fell out. He was not able to book surgery for me for six weeks, but he was able to fix it temporarily for the trip.

Two weeks later we were on the plane to Europe. Every time I ate something I'd have to look for my tooth in a piece the food. The tooth became abscessed, and I was just a mess. One morning after we arrived in Italy, we decided to take a tour of the Vatican. While sitting on the bus I reached across the aisle and told Sara I was in great pain, and asked if she would please say a prayer for me. She did and immediately the pain began to leave, and soon the infection disappeared. She prayed again for me that evening, and I remember the entire room was filled with white light. That pain never returned.

It was phenomenal! For twenty-seven years I used nose spray and lived on Sudafed®. After those beautiful prayers that day, I have no more sinus problems. God did it again! Thank you God, and thank you Sara. I have learned to always trust in the flow of divine love. Our God is a loving God and only wants to bless and heal our aching bodies and mend our broken hearts.

Love is the Energy that Heals Even the Deepest Pain

Victoria Bowmann

*V*icki was born in El Paso, Texas. She moved to Arizona in 1968 to attend ASU and graduated in 1972. After graduating, she continued her studies and went on to receive her PhD in Homeopathy and Natural Medicine in 1999 and a doctorate in Homeopathic Medicine in 1995.

She has one adult son who is married and has blessed her with four grandsons. She also has three horses and one cat that she adores.

It was Dr. Doris Rapp who first introduced her to The Little Chapel in 1998. Vicki was in a car accident in December 1999. She tried many things to help alleviate her pain over the next 12 years. When she attended a service in The Little Chapel she would always ask for a healing. She could feel the Holy Spirit surrounding her with love and blessings, but in those 12 years she never received a complete and lasting healing. She never gave up and kept a positive attitude. She knew that God would heal her one day. She had the faith that sincere prayers with a lot of love have power to produce miracles. She witnessed at every service what God's unconditional love can do and she had peace in her soul that one day she would be completely healed.

" " In December of 1999, I was driving home from the west side of town on the freeway and a whole group of cars suddenly stopped as did I. Someone a few cars back didn't stop and six of us were hit. The impact of that collision put the driver's seat in the car all the way to the back, the ashtray was in the back window, and yet I was able to drive my car home—just barely. That impact caused a lot of damage to the left side of my body mostly in the hip joint and lower back. The hearing in my left ear was affected and one tooth also died and had to be treated by my dentist.

I'm a natural practitioner, and I don't usually like going the traditional medical route. Instead, I was in a chiropractor's office that afternoon, and I got a lot of care and treatments in the next few weeks. I've done many natural things but the impact was so horrific that my left hip and particularly the socket were severely damaged. I felt incredible pain. I could no longer sleep on that side of my body, and when I got up in the morning, I was limping badly. I have to move around for a few minutes to warm up so I could walk normally.

As for my genetic background, my mom has both osteo and rheumatoid arthritis. If you saw her hands you would cry, and I know the difficulties that she goes through and the pain that she has endured for most of her life. One of my commitments in taking care of my body is because I don't want that to happen to me. But in this instance, I could only think about the amount of arthritis I might have and the amount of damage from the collision that was aggravating my body.

For the next 11 years, I had treatments in osteopathic manipulation with an incredible physician. I also had different types of massage therapy treatments, prolo-therapy and prolozone therapy. These are all natural treatments and I am so grateful for each person who worked with me. Many of these practices have helped my condition and yet still there's a deep pain and constant ache in the hip socket.

At work, whenever I'm working on someone that has had a hip replacement, I ask a lot of questions because I have been worried that I might have to look at doing that surgery someday and it frightens me.

A few years ago, I was sitting in The Little Chapel and Sara called out a healing for a lower back and I could feel the Holy Spirit. I raised my hand and for three or four days it was magnificent but it didn't hold. Sara talks about progressive healings and I feel like I've been a progressive regression!

Then there was a time that Sara did a private prayer for me and again I could feel the Holy Spirit and that didn't hold either. Christmas of 2010, I was enjoying the service but my hip and my back were hurting so badly that I acted like a five year old wiggling in the chair. Sara called out a healing for a low back and I remember Jim Hebets saying out loud, "The age that we are, we *all* have low back pain!" and Sara said, "Well, I better do a blanket healing."

As she slowly passed her hand across the crowd and it reached me, the pain stopped. I thanked God but again, the healing didn't last.

Now, I must admit that as a child, I was rambunctious, and even today I sometimes refuse to grow up. I still want to do the active things I love to do. I don't want to be limited by a pain filled body. I'm determined about what I do and my mother would probably tell you that I'm stubborn. I bring this to my testimony because this stubbornness might be something that God wants me to examine more closely.

In each of these healing instances, I questioned why God would touch me one moment and then take it away. I realize now that God had some things He wanted me to learn through this. He gave me time to think about my life, to look deep inside myself and correct some of my weaknesses. It was actually a gift from God in order for me to grow more spiritual before the physical healing would occur permanently.

One healing I witnessed really strengthened my own faith. A gentleman, Ron Jones, gave a testimony at The Little Chapel of how he had been healed of kidney failure and he was taken off dialysis completely and stayed off! I know it was truly God as there is no medical answer. Once you're on dialysis, you stay on dialysis unless you're fortunate enough to be in line for a matching kidney transplant... and even that isn't always successful. The story of Ron Jones *(page 217)* and his magnificent healing is included in this book. It pays to read it and digest it for it will lift up anyone's faith. It certainly did mine.

Then in January 2011 I had something very unsettling happen at work and it worried me deeply. I was speaking to Sara about it and she said she would pray for me during the next chapel service. When the healing service began she said she would look at me and I would know that the Holy Spirit was working on the situation. I was sincerely praying for God to help me with this disturbing situation.

When the healings began to happen after Sara's sermon, she looked at me and pointed like she promised and said, "Yes." I nodded because that was our earlier agreement. I could feel the Holy Spirit so strongly in my body and I listened to each and every healing as I continued to affirm that God was touching my work challenge with his Love. When we stood up to sing the closing song I realized my hip was free of pain and I was healed. I was so happy for finally receiving the healing of my hip, but was still concerned about my work situation. I told God that I would be willing to live with the pain in my hip if He would please help me with the problem at work. A little voice inside me said, "When your hip doesn't hurt, remember God can do all things."

My hip was completely healed and I began to thank and praise God. At one point I felt a little tingle of pain and quickly said, "Get thee behind me Satan, God has healed my hip and you can't take it away from me." The pain left immediately and has never returned.

In time, He answered my prayers at work also. God is so good.

One of the physical things I enjoy is riding my horses. As I was returning from a wonderful afternoon ride my horse started to limp. I felt it was better that she didn't have to carry my weight, so I climbed out of the saddle and began walking beside her. The was an area along this path that had grass growing and it was wet. I didn't realize that it had grown over a hole in the ground. Well, I slipped and my horse slipped. I landed on my hip and she, fortunately, didn't land or step on me. I struggled to get up and I thought maybe I had damaged God's healing. Something inside me said, "Vicki, you can't hurt what God heals." It wasn't something I did intentionally and God protected me as I tried to protect my horse.

I do believe that it is our responsibility to take good care of our bodies; which are His temples.

I'm so grateful to say I'm still pain free. That pain and deep ache is gone. I can sleep in whatever position I want and I wake up rested. Each time I see Sara I wiggle from side to side, "Look, look at me now." Before any movement was always with pain and now I can dance, wiggling everything!

Every morning and every evening I acknowledge God's healing and thank Him for using Sara as an instrument of His great love for each of us. I will always continue to seek Him first and ask for the knowledge and wisdom I need each day.

And a Little Child Shall Lead Them

Cindy and Ashley Brines

*G*od loves the little ones who have just arrived here from heaven. So often they come to teach and help the family they were born into. All members of a family are brought together for spiritual growth. Ashley came with a mission and God helped her accomplish it right after she was born.

My name is Cindy Brines, the mother of Ashley. In 1993, I was happily married to Mike and we were expecting our first child. My friend, Amy Katz, and I were in law school together. Of course, I was always talking to Amy about my baby, and how excited we were to have our first child.

Ashley surprised us and came 5 weeks early in August of 1993. Because she was premature, she was very, *very* sick. She was put into the neonatal intensive care unit at Cedars Sinai in Los Angeles. Many times we thought we were going to lose her. We tried to keep positive, but it was hard when we looked at this baby trying to breathe and fighting for her life.

I poured my heart out to Amy every day. She was such a good friend to listen and comfort me, and kept assuring me everything was going to be all right. She didn't tell me at that time that she had a vision about me taking our baby to see Sara O'Meara.

I did know Amy had put together a prayer chain for Ashley, so she wouldn't die. Sixteen days later, our daughter came home from the hospital, and we all thought she was perfect. She made a miraculous recovery—one that most people thought she was not going to make. We thanked Amy for her prayers, and for all the others in the prayer chain who joined her. We were thrilled beyond words to have our baby daughter home with us.

As a result of all the things Ashley went through in her intensive care stay and all the medications she had taken, a couple of months later they needed to test her eyes and her ears. There were no problems with her pretty eyes, but the ears they were concerned about. During the first tests she took, they had a problem getting any response, but they also had problems with their machines. So I hoped that it was a problem with the machines, not my daughter's ears.

We decided to take Ashley to the Children's Hospital to check her hearing. They performed a whole series of tests. Unfortunately, the results were the same as before. They said Ashley couldn't hear, and that there was no chance there would be any recovery. We thought maybe because she was premature, there was still development to continue on, but they informed us that was not the case. They proceeded to get us in touch with all sorts of organizations for deaf children. It was pretty severe—she had very little hearing in one ear, and none in the other, and a lot of complications.

This was all pretty devastating to us. When I shared the sad news with Amy she smiled and said, "It is time for both you and Ashley to go see Sara and attend a Chapel service."

Amy knew I was Jewish and not even very religious, but she also knew I did have strong beliefs and faith and was open to learn. My husband Mike was raised a Lutheran, but at this time he had very little belief and faith in anything.

Both of us are on the rigid side, so trying something new wasn't necessarily normal or easy for either one of us. But God knew what he was doing when he sent us little Ashley. She had captured our hearts and we would do anything for her. We looked at each other and then at Amy and said, "Yes, of course we'll be there!"

We were most anxious for Sunday to come around. God was already preparing us because something made us feel so good about going to the Little Chapel and meeting Sara. The Little Chapel was in California at the time, attached to Sara's home. Because we had the baby with us, we sat in the solarium, which was considered the extended chapel. When the Chapel was filled to capacity, people would watch the service on closed-circuit television in the solarium, and we felt such peace as we entered the area. The view of the garden outside made us feel so serene and calm. It was the perfect place for us to be during the service. There was something about it that was magical, even though it was a cloudy day and not much sun.

Before the service started, Sara came out to meet us and talk to us briefly. She laid her hands on our daughter's head and said a prayer. Then the service began, and it was all about having strong faith. That was exactly what we needed to hear. After the beautiful service, the healings began. Then Sara said to the congregation that there were parents there who were praying for their daughter's hearing and she asked us to place our hands on our baby and pray for her. As the prayers began for Ashley, the clouds opened up and a ray of sunlight came down just on our daughter's head— nowhere else in the room. She began to squirm and cry because at that moment in time she received a healing and could hear the background music and the loving prayers from all the wonderful people around her.

Before that precious Sunday morning, October 17th, we had played loud music, beeped horns, talked, yelled and did everything to get her to respond. We knew there was a definite difference, and that God had touched her.

After the service, the famous actor, Efrem Zimbalist, Jr. and Emma Borders, Sara's housekeeper, came running up to us to share what they had seen. They confirmed how the light from the sky came right on our baby Ashley at the time she was healed. Efrem was so overjoyed and said it was absolutely miraculous to see the light that came through that window, right on our child. It was kind of like God had shown those who were seated in the solarium that indeed, He was blessing our baby.

On October 19th, my father went with me to take Ashley to the House Institute. They said they would be happy to retest her hearing, and told us about many new kinds of surgeries they could try on her.

My gut feeling was she was healed and would not need any surgery at all. I hung onto that with all the faith I could muster. We felt this was the best place for her to be tested, and I was so happy my father was with me when they gave us the wonderful results. Her hearing was absolutely perfect. The doctors at the House Institute didn't know what to say for they did not have an explanation. I told them I had the answer—"It's God." They replied, "Yes, it must be."

My father and I were ecstatic and filled with gratitude to God and Sara for this fantastic miracle. We drove immediately over to my husband's work to share the exciting news. Mike and I are so thankful that Ashley came into our lives and taught us so much, so quickly. She was three months old at the time of her healing. Today, Ashley is 18 years old with perfect hearing!

"And a little child shall lead them…"

Yes, God Continues to Heal Us

Linda Brown

*M*any individuals do not attend church on a regular basis, but when the holidays come around, they do like to come and pay their respects. God always tries to reach us when we give him the opportunity.

Linda Brown came to the Little Chapel in December 2002 with her sister-in-law, Susan Liberty Hall. Susan tries to never miss a service and she always brings a group with her. Many of her friends have received beautiful blessings and healings.

Linda was born and raised in Iowa. Her husband's work moved them to Arizona in 1979, after living a few years in California. Linda has three sons, but is no longer married.

She has always been a great believer in God, but never was exposed to the Holy Spirit healing someone. When God touched her at the Christmas service in the Little Chapel, it opened her heart to a new dimension and strengthened her belief. She learned quickly that prayer is the most powerful action anyone can take.

Linda promised God she would always be thankful to Him for her healing. She has kept her promise, and tells everyone God does heal today, just like He did over 2,000 years ago.

My sister-in-law brought me to the Little Chapel in December, 2002. We went early to get a good seat. The Christmas service is always overflowing, and even the extended chapel is filled to capacity.

It concerned me to get there too early because the pain in my knees was so severe, I didn't think I could sit that long for the service. The drive over there was very hard for me, and then I had to walk a small distance to the Little Chapel from where we parked. The pain bothered me so much; I almost left before the service began. Susan kept saying "Relax." She pleaded with me to stay, and said, "I know you're going to love this."

Sara looked so pretty as she came out on the stage. Her voice captured my attention, and I enjoyed listening to the entire sermon. When the healings began, she called out a healing for arthritis or pain in the knees. I raised my hand, but I didn't feel anything. She prayed over me, and said she would be back. I started feeling some heat, so I moved my leg up and down. When Sara came back, she said, "How does it feel now? The pain is gone, isn't it?" she said, smiling. Sara was right, the pain was gone. I replied, "Yes, yes, yes! It is gone!" I couldn't believe it—I was pain free.

The test of my healing was after the service, when we had to walk up to the main house for coffee and dessert. I made it all the way with my lighted candle and singing praises to God.

To this day, the pain has not returned, and I'm not expecting it to. We forget to be grateful every day for a pain-free body. We take things for granted until our bodies begin to break down with pain and suffering. Sometimes it takes this for God to get our attention.

He got my attention, and I'm grateful he did. My heart is full of joy for the healing of my knees. I can walk and drive my car without any pain. I'm so happy that I can get down on my knees now and praise God for His tender love and healing grace.

God's Unconditional Love is Our Greatest Blessing

Tim Brown
by Annie Brown

nnie Brown was born in Norwich, New York and lived in New York most of her young life. Tim was born in Seattle, Washington and moved with his family to Southern California when he was nine years of age.

Annie's work took her to Palm Springs, California when she met and married Tim. Tim had two boys, Matthew and Brian by a previous marriage. His wife had died of cancer and Annie was happy to take on the responsibility with him of raising the boys. Annie and Tim adopted a third boy, Jonathan, who is now a Christian music artist. Matthew and Brian are both married and have blessed Annie and Tim with four grandchildren.

Tim and Annie moved to Flagstaff, Arizona in 1993. They are both active in the Childhelp Chapter there. Annie and Tim have always believed in the power of prayer and Annie served in women's ministry and volunteer chaplain at the hospital over many years. When Tim was given the news he had cancer he allowed fear to creep in to his thinking. It was hard not to feel a little fearful because he had lost his first wife to cancer.

When he told Jill and Bill Babb about his problem, they immediately told him he must go to The Little Chapel. The power of prayer is so strong at every service and they knew he could be healed. They were right.

Tim and Annie are strong Christians and were open to the loving healing energy at The Little Chapel. They learned rather than fearing the worst to give power to divine possibility. God is greater than any condition or circumstance.

Every challenge becomes an opportunity for new growth and transformation and every blessing is a lesson in the power of prayer.

    In 2001, we began a journey no one ever is prepared for. After going to the doctors, for we thought was the flu, Tim was diagnosed with a bowel obstruction and they found a small tumor on his lung. As Christians, we reached out to our circle of friends to begin to pray.

After the first surgery it took weeks for many labs across the country, such as Stanford University and University of Arizona to finally diagnose Tim's cancer as Stage Four Metastaic Melanoma. (Melanoma undetected can present in forms of tumors in the body) We then travelled to MD Anderson in Houston, TX to meet with specialists in the Melanoma cancers. Once there, Tim's case was so unique, we found out he was the "case of the week." Not something you get very excited about at that point! Daily we updated our prayer warriors by e-mail. One of those precious prayer warriors was my long time dear friend, Jill Babb. She had passed on Tim's prayer request and story to Yvonne and Sara.

After testing the tumor in the lung, they concurred it was indeed the end stage of melanoma cancer. We met with the five specialists the last morning we were there. All 5 specialists told us that Tim had at the most, six months to a year to live. They recommended he be admitted and start a new type of radical chemotherapy that would most likely take him close to death, but he could at least be part of research for the future and that he might "get lucky" and get a few more months from doing it. Tim stood up (all 6'6" of him!) and politely told them all he had a golf tournament to play in next week and no thank you!

You can only imagine what that plane ride home was like. We have three boys; the youngest at the time was only 9 years old. Tim's older two boys (my step-sons) had lost their mom to cancer a few years previous. Tim was so brave and I will never forget his words "Annie, if the Lord is going to take me home, then I am ready. But if not, we will trust His plan."

I, of course, was not nearly that strong and at peace. I was filled with sadness and fear. However, as we settled back in at home, the prayers and support poured in. By now the prayers were coming from across the country and we felt incredibly blessed.

Jill and Bill Babb invited us to join them at a service at The Little Chapel to hear Sara speak and witness the beautiful healings that occur. We had heard so much about Sara and Yvonne and were anxious to go. It was an overwhelming and truly incredible time at the chapel. The Holy Spirit reigns there, and Jesus is most present. We felt that significantly. Tim felt a wave of peace and warmth envelope him as Sara began to call out the anointing of cancer at that service. He knew that the Holy Spirit was touching him and he opened his heart to receive all that God could possibly give him. He was healed!

We are now cancer free. Tim's case is for sure one of God's miracles. We are so humbled and overwhelmed by the idea that our Lord would choose to restore Timmy. As hopefully faithful servants, we write this story to pass on hope to those who feel hopeless against the monster of cancer. Our Lord is bigger than cancer...bigger than fear. Tim feels his time of total trust in God and the amazing healing prayers of Sara and those precious prayer warriors across the country gave him a second chance at life. We both never take for granted the precious gift of life that our Father in Heaven bestows upon us. Tim is a quiet gentle soul who shares his life for Jesus in his everyday walk. Be encouraged, be strong and know that His love is there for all of us—overflowing and abundant.

We will always be grateful to Jill and Bill for encouraging us to go to The Little Chapel so we could witness first hand the love of Jesus at work healing and blessing us and all those in attendance. We know without question miracles do happen, and God never misses a service at the chapel. Arizona is fortunate to have such a heavenly place to worship and to have Sara, a conduit for the glory of God, to do the healing of our physical bodies and help us to expand our soul growth.

Having Breakfast, Lunch, Dinner and Hors D' Oeuvres with God

Vera Brown

*I*f you ever want to see love in action, you must meet Vera Brown. She is always asking what she can do for you, and if you don't tell her something, she will commit a kind act for you anyway.

Vera owned her own beauty spa in California, until a few years ago when she retired. Many of the beautiful people in Hollywood would go to the spa on a regular basis. She made everyone feel good about themselves, and always had her door open to help solve any problem one might have with their complexion. She was genuinely interested in you as a person, and made you feel important.

If we truly believe something, we live it. She is quite a positive example for us to follow. She always brings love and light to the lives she touches. As you read her story, please allow the love and light to touch your heart.

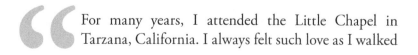

For many years, I attended the Little Chapel in Tarzana, California. I always felt such love as I walked through the doors there, but the feeling I got at the Little Chapel in Arizona was even greater. It almost took my breath away.

I have had numerous healings through Sara's ministry over the years. The first was about 20 years ago. One day, my thumb was stiff, and I couldn't move it at all. I had written a book, and knew plans were for me to go to several book signing events. I panicked about what to do.

I went to two of the top doctors in Los Angeles who were hand specialists. Both said I had carpel tunnel syndrome and needed surgery. One doctor put my hand in a splint and made an appointment for surgery.

Several days later, Sara came into my salon and said, 'What's wrong with your hand?' I told her, and she said I should have phoned her right away for prayers. I said, "Oh, no, Sara, there is nothing that can be done…I've seen the X-rays." She just looked at me and said, 'Oh, yes, there is something that can be done. Come with me to a quiet place and let's ask God for help."

She gently took my hand in hers and began to pray. The pain lessened, but it was still there. The next day she came by and prayed again. It felt so much better, and I could begin to move my thumb. The third time she prayed for me was the charm. I was so excited. My hand was perfect, and I could write and do whatever I needed to do. No surgery was necessary, of course.

That was the first of many healings. Sara is always there to pray for me, and has prayed through many highs and lows in my life. She was there when I went through hip surgery and knee surgery. Her prayers gave me such peace and removed all fear.

Several years ago, I received a healing of cancer through Sara. I am so grateful to God for all his many blessings, and for having Sara as part of my life. She has taught me so much about having faith and trust in God and not to limit Him.

Sara taught me to walk with God every day. I have breakfast, lunch, dinner and hors d'oeuvres with God, and I don't have to be in church or temple to do it. I talk to God all the time, and He speaks to me through my heart. I made a promise that I will always give Him the praise and thanks. Every day I feel a little closer to God.

Accepting the Gift of God's Love

Carter Budwell

*C*arter was born in Great Falls, Montana, raised in Richmond, Virginia, and now for the last 30 years has been living in Colorado. He has two boys, Carter and Jimmy, who he shares custody with his ex-wife.

He is a wonderful Christian and loves the Lord with all his heart. He struggled with getting a divorce, but feels he has received a healing resulting from the devastation he suffered from it at a service in Aspen when Sara spoke. The guilt was lifted and his heart was filled with love. Love is a gift, and he was happy to receive it in such a beautiful and tender way.

After I moved to Colorado, I met the woman I felt God wanted me to marry. I loved her very much, and didn't realize until after we were married she was bipolar. She suffered from alcoholism, drug abuse and mental problems. My heart broke to see the woman I loved go through all this, and do such destructive things to herself.

Two years ago, she asked me for a divorce. My first reaction was "No." We had two boys to raise and I wanted to keep our family together. I was full of anger, and I fought against the divorce. My friends encouraged me to get a divorce, and I finally gave in. I sold our home and business, and we have joint custody of our boys.

I heard that Sara O'Meara was speaking at our First Baptist Church in Aspen, and thought I'd go and ask for an inner healing. As I sat listening to the sermon, I began feeling a prickly feeling and then a warm flush. I knew God was touching me and helping me to let go.

I asked God to forgive me for anything I did to cause the failure of our marriage. His gentle touch that evening assured me He heard my prayer and that I was forgiven, and could go on with my life.

Every day I pray for my wife and I truly only want her to be well and happy. If God wants us to be together again as a family, then I am open for that. If we are to live in separate homes and raise our boys, then I am at peace with that. I only want to do what is best for all of us.

I am grateful to Sara for coming to Aspen and giving a service in our church. Since that evening, things that disturbed me are released, and I feel at peace about our situation for the first time. I am healed and the peace that I have in my heart now is miraculous.

God is Always Ready to Bless Us

Nick Bunick

*M*any of you have read the interesting and enlightening book *The Messengers* and are familiar with Nick Bunick. He has written three other wonderful books that I highly recommend: *In God's Truth, Time for Truth* and the latest book, *The Commitment*, released the summer of 2011.

Nick was born near Boston in one of the poorest areas in the United States. His parents, Russian immigrants, were orthodox Jews. He himself acknowledges a spiritual relationship with God, but does not practice a formal religion. He loves to tell people that "God doesn't belong to one religion, but embraces all teachings that share His messages." Nick believes that each of us is on our individual separate journeys to the same destination, to become at one with God. As we develop our spiritual relationship with God, we recognize that we are all brothers and sisters.

Lake Oswego, Oregon, is where Nick lives with his beautiful wife, Mary Jo, and their son Nicholas. He was a high profile businessman, owned several corporations and sat on the boards of others. In 1995, all that changed when the Angelic world intervened in his life and reminded him of his mission. Part of that mission was to found The Great Tomorrow as a nonprofit corporation committed to spiritual and humanitarian activities.

Sara and I had the good fortune of meeting Nick through mutual friends, and we now serve on the board of directors for The Great Tomorrow with him. He is a loyal supporter of Childhelp and the work we do for abused children.

" My lovely wife, Mary Jo, and I support the work being done for abused children through Childhelp and try to attend their fund-raising events whenever we can.

In October, 1997, we flew to Arizona to attend a Childhelp black-tie event honoring Princess Ann of England. The next day a group of us had brunch together, including one of Childhelp's favorite celebrity ambassadors, Cheryl Ladd, and her husband, Brian Russell. Brian had trouble with stiffness in his neck and asked Sara to pray with him. After we finished eating, Cheryl, Brian, Sara, Yvonne, Mary Jo and I went to the Chapel for special prayers. The Little Chapel is on the grounds where Sara and Yvonne live.

Sara led the prayers for Brian to receive a healing and he did receive one almost immediately. I had no mobility in my neck; I could not turn my head to the left or the right. I would have to move my entire body because my neck had no flexibility. X-rays showed that there were no spaces between the vertebrae in my neck, and that they looked like they were fused together. I assumed this had happened as a result of playing football too many years both in high school and college. When I shared this with Sara, she suggested that I also receive the healing in addition to Brian.

During the healing process, I felt totally calm, and did not experience either heat or cold, although Sara said she could see a green streak of light going from my skull down towards my back. Since that beautiful experience when I had the healing, I no longer have the problem of not having the ability to move my neck. In fact, I have had another multi-dimensional imaging (X-ray) since then that shows that there is now a space between my vertebrae. Indeed, God healed me that day with Sara being the conduit.

I have sent many to the Little Chapel for healings over these past few years and will continue to do so. I want others to receive the benefit of the wonderful energy and spirit that is shared at these services.

God is always ready to bless us when we are ready to receive. With everything that you touch, with everything that you feel, with everything that you see that brings you joy, you experience God.

They Never Doubted God Could do Anything and So He Did

Eleanor and Jug Carter by Robert Smith

E leanor and Jug Carter loved The Little Chapel and never missed a service until God took them home. They were the parents of several children and were blessed to have grandchildren and great grandchildren. They were fortunate to receive a number of healings in The Little Chapel, and many members of their family have also received healings.

It was a pleasure to watch them at a service enjoying every minute and praising the Lord for all the healings. Isn't it wonderful to know that God never thinks we are too old to receive a beautiful healing?

A proud son-in-law, Robert Smith, tells about how God touched the lives of Jug and Eleanor.

Jug was in his eighties when he asked God to heal his aging and weak eyes. He loved to read and play golf, and it was hard to do with his failing eyesight.

One Sunday in The Little Chapel, God touched his eyes and he was so grateful. He stood up and told Sara and the congregation that he felt the presence of the Lord and knew his eyes had been healed. Sara said, "Yes, God did hear your prayer and God is healing your eyes." He was one happy individual and he made everyone smile in the Chapel that morning.

Eleanor received two healings in her arthritic knee that she could hardly bend. Judy and I live in Hawaii and Judy's mom, Eleanor, came over to stay with us after her healing in The Little Chapel in Arizona.

We were so happy to greet her at the airport and see her walking so well. She took water aerobics classes during her visit, and was able to do some tough exercises. She even went with me on power walks up near the Kalalea Mountains.

Before her healing in The Little Chapel she could only limp, walk very slowly, and it was impossible to kneel. Anyone who knew our Granny knew she loved to pray on her knees. With eight children and thirty-some grandchildren, she had to pray a lot.

After that wonderful Sunday in The Little Chapel she had a skip in her walk and it was truly miraculous.

Mom and Dad are gone now, but they were a beautiful couple and wonderful examples for us all to follow. They never doubted God could do anything…and so He did.

I Went to Just Enjoy the Service But Left with Three Amazing Gifts

James Casey

Wadena, Minnesota is where James Casey was born and he was raised in Westford, Connecticut. He is a graduate of Central Connecticut State College.

James is the proud father of two grown sons, Shawn and Troy.

He moved to Arizona many years ago and is very active in his church, Scottsdale Airpark Rotary Club, North Scottsdale Chamber of Commerce and sits on the board of several foundations and organizations.

Marian Jamison brought him to The Little Chapel.

My significant other, Marian Jamison, had encouraged me to attend a service and I normally don't go to other churches. I'm very involved as an ambassador at my church and I'm extremely loyal but she said, "James, you need to come and experience this service." I said, "Okay, okay, I can take off a Sunday. One Sunday won't matter."

I wasn't going there because I *wanted* anything special or needed to be healed of some disease; I was just going to experience what Marian had shared with me.

A week before, I had been in the gym and I pulled something in my lower spine. I was hobbling, leaning a little crooked, and then two days later my knee pulled out. I was at a business function and all of a sudden I couldn't walk. I ended up going home early and kind of nursing it. I got a little better throughout the week but I still felt the pain.

As we drove to The Little Chapel, I didn't think about the pain I was feeling in my neck, back or leg. I was just excited to attend the service after all Marian had told me.

Walking through the doors of The Little Chapel was awesome. I knew immediately this was a blessed place filled with God's loving energy.

I was absorbed in the message and enjoyed listening to two men give their testimonies. I felt the Holy Spirit so strongly. After Sara spoke she started calling out different maladies and then she said, "There is somebody here with a neck problem." I thought yeah that's me, and I raised my hand. All of a sudden I realized my neck was fine.

Sara went on calling out other health challenges and she mentioned that someone had a back issue. Again, I raised my hand. She asked me to stand and when I did my back was perfect. I thought to myself, "Wow, what happened? Where did this come from? I didn't even ask or sign up for anything." I heard Sara say, "There's somebody here that has a bad leg – an issue with a left leg." I raised my hand and said, "Wow it's me again!" I felt great relief but I could still sense a little residual tightness, so Sara said, "On a scale of one to five where are you?" I replied, "About half of one." She asked, "*Now,* where are you?" I said, "All the pain has vanished – gone!"

Those hours in The Little Chapel were priceless. I didn't want the service to end or to have to leave the peaceful and loving environment. I went to just sit and enjoy the sermon, but left with three amazing gifts. I walked out of that blessed place with great awe of the miracles that God had bestowed upon me. I thank Marian for insisting I experience The Little Chapel, for I left a different, and pain free, man.

I Know God Wants to Heal All of Us

Maureen Christensen

aureen is a native Californian raised in Sacramento. She spent 25 years in Reno, Nevada before moving to Phoenix, Arizona.

She is divorced, but has a wonderful son from her marriage. She prayed for a solid year to have a son, and felt he was a gift from God.

Her son, Tom, was only 8 months old when she was first diagnosed with breast cancer. She couldn't believe that God would give him to her and then let her die. She begged the Lord to let her raise him to 21 years of age. Now, he is 28 and a doctor in his 3rd year of Orthopedic Residency at the University of Utah.

Maureen is a Licensed Marriage and Family Therapist with a private practice in Phoenix, Arizona. She has helped people for over 20 years with mental, emotional and health problems. She enjoys giving back to others what God has given to her—insight, wisdom, understanding, healing and a personal relationship with God. She spent most of her early professional years working as an RN in the Intensive Care Unit and Emergency Room at *UC*

Davis Sacramento Medical Center. In 1988 she received a Masters degree in Counseling. In 1998 she finished her doctorate in Health and Human Services.

Her hobbies are travel, snow skiing, hiking and attending retreats and conferences.

Maureen writes about her cancer journey, how the Lord healed her and how she glorified God through running Breast Cancer Support Groups for 15 years before moving to Phoenix, Arizona in 2003. She shares her most recent health crisis and how she was healed by Jesus through Sara O'Meara at The Little Chapel. She is a true light in this world and we are blessed to know her and have her be a part of The Little Chapel.

"I am the Lord that Healeth Thee, I am the Lord Thy Savior, I am greater than cancer, heart disease or any disease." These words have brought much comfort to me when I was diagnosed with breast cancer in 1982 at the age of 32. My son was only 8 months old. I wondered how this could be happening to me. God directed my path through the process of lumpectomy and radiation versus a mastectomy.

My physicians recommended a mastectomy but I begged God for direction and He gave it to me. I opened the Bible to Philippians 3:3 and this is what I read, "Beware of mad dogs, beware of cutters, you do not need a physical operation." I knew God had spoken directly to me and that I did not need the mastectomy.

As the cancer journey continued the Lord consoled and comforted me. In 1990 I had a recurrence of breast cancer. I was led by the Holy Spirit to attend a Bernie Siegel conference. He had us draw a picture of ourselves. It was this picture that led me to know I had more breast cancer. The irony is that I was given a "clean bill of health" just prior to the drawing. I was told not to come back for one year. Because of the drawing I knew I had more breast cancer even though my mammogram and ultrasound were normal. I insisted on a biopsy and to everyone's dismay it was more cancer. God works in various ways to prompt us and lead us to healing.

In 1998, I was diagnosed with thyroid cancer. Once again it was the prompting of the Holy Spirit that it was found. I had been on a retreat. We were asked to find a rock and give it a name. The word I gave my rock was indolent. The minute I said indolent I knew I had cancer somewhere in my body. The word "indolent" means hard and immovable. Within a short time after the retreat my doctor found a thyroid nodule and said it was hard and immovable. He wanted to watch it and I insisted on a biopsy. Sure enough it was cancer. I had a total thyroidectomy for papillary thyroid cancer.

On April 3, 2009, I had a follow up neck ultrasound that showed a mass where my thyroid had been removed. I was so scared and worried that I had more thyroid cancer.

On April 21, 2009, I found my way to Sara's healing service at The Little Chapel. I sat quietly in the back not knowing what to expect. Then Sara called out a healing of someone who had a lot of conflicting medical tests. She said this was due to the person being under extreme stress. I immediately raised my hand and she came right in front of my face. She said with determination and force "My darling you are healed." She said, "I am on to you and you are receiving a mighty healing from God." I began to smile, my face lit up and I knew she was right. People seemed to be smiling and there was a sense of knowing that this healing had taken place.

I left that night so happy and grateful to God and to Sara for being an instrument of God's healing power. I knew I needed to decrease the stress in my life. I needed to get my thyroid levels balanced.

Two weeks after the healing service, on May 6, 2009, I went for the scheduled biopsy of the 1.0 cm mass. They could not find a mass anywhere in my neck. They were very confused regarding what happened to the mass. I told them that I had gone to a healing service at The Little Chapel and I was healed. Praise God!

A second healing took place at The Little Chapel on May 28, 2009. Sara said someone had pain on the ball of the foot. I raised my hand reluctantly because I had already received the thyroid healing. But, no one claimed it so I figured it must be for me. I had so much pain from a plantar fasciitis of my left heel. Within two days, the pain was completely gone. I can wear high heels and sandals again.

Why did God choose to heal me? I guess it is because He wants to heal all of us. I had a lot of faith for the thyroid healing and very little faith for the healing of the fasciitis pain. But, God is the healer and He comes to those of little as well as those with great faith. Just come to Him, that's all He asks of us. For God says, "Come to me all of you who are weary and find life burdensome for I will give you rest."

We Should Never Give Up

Jo-Lyn Cleverly and Her Nephew, Nicholas

*J*o-Lyn was active in church as a child and loved it. Her mother played the organ and her dad sang. She lost her father in a car accident when she was very young, and her mother was left with four children under the age of nine to raise by herself. A Greek man swept her mother off her feet and they were married within a year. Lots of changes took place and lots of challenges presented themselves.

Through circumstances in her life, Jo-Lyn got away from attending church on a regular basis. She would attend services on Christmas, Easter and special occasions only. She knew she had guardian angels and her heart was always open to helping others.

Sara and I have known Jo-Lyn through Childhelp for many years. She has been a wonderful supporter and is always willing to help us help the abused and neglected children who cannot help themselves. She has more than one story to share with you…

66 After my father was killed in a car accident, my life took quite a different path. My mother and my new step dad had a child and we became a family like in the movie

My Big Fat Greek Wedding. Our family had a restaurant business, and there was always a lamb on a stick and lots of Greek people eating, eating, and *eating.*

My step dad turned out to be a pedophile. I feel that experience with him made me a stronger person because I survived and didn't let him conquer me. With the loss of both dads, it left a vacant spot in my heart.

When I married, I thought I would always have this man in my life to fill that vacancy. We had two children, Carly and Jack, and I thought my happiness would never end. When my marriage fell apart, I fell apart. I couldn't let go, and the grieving kept on and on. Until a wonderful therapist, Marylyn Murray, helped me a great deal and prayed with me every day.

It was Kathy Bowen who brought me to the Little Chapel. It was a candlelit Christmas service, and all I did was cry. I not only wanted an emotional healing, but I was there also for one of my dear nephews who was then only 10 years old.

I was setting the table for 25 members of my family who were coming over for Thanksgiving dinner when the phone rang. It was the Phoenix Police Dept. saying there had been an accident and they were trying to get in touch with my sister. I said, "Which sister?" I have three, and I said, "Is it Chareen?" They said, "Yes." I said, "Is it Nicholas?" and they said, "Yes." Chareen had already lost a little boy 17 years ago in a drowning accident with her best friend, and I feared the worst. He was in a coma, but not dead.

He was riding his bike on the bike path when a truck hit him going 35 miles per hour. His head hit the side of the windshield and shattered it, and then he went flying in the air and landed on top of his head. He had no broken bones in his body. The damage was all on his head. They replaced his skull with titanium plates.

My sister and I had been pregnant together and we were all so close. It broke our hearts to see Nicholas with tubes out of every orifice, his brain swollen and his spine draining blood. The hope for him making it was slim.

Our entire family united together and spent every day with him. We read to him, sang to him, talked to him and constantly told him how much we loved him. Every day we would look for a sign of life, praying he would wiggle a toe or a finger or make any movement.

Because I am a survivor, I thought I could handle anything. This was out of my hands, and only God could change this situation. We needed a miracle, and that is when Kathy Bowen said, "Come with me to a service in the Little Chapel."

Sara began the healing part of her service, and I cried through it all. She got my attention when she mentioned that someone was there who had tremendous pain in her heart for a 10 year old nephew who had been in an accident. She went on to say, "he is going to be okay." I thought, "She doesn't know what she is talking about." Again, she said, "The entire family is broken up over this little 10 year old boy, and he is going to be okay." I left the service confused and decided this was too much for me to handle or understand.

Sara sent me a couple of cards that truly touched my heart. She encouraged me to have faith and trust. She has helped me to get back with Jesus and I'm so grateful. I promised God that I would light a candle and pray more every day. I'm working on myself to not be so hard on myself and not give my power away to others. Nicholas is back home, to the delight of his family. He is in a school with a special education class and working hard.

I have learned we should never give up. The seemingly impossible situations are possible when we lean on God. I love The Little Chapel and wish everyone knew about it, and the great miracles that are happening there every service.

Faith is Key to Our Healing

Jim Cook

Jim was born in Maryville, Tennessee where he met and married his lovely wife, Carol, on June 2, 1965. They moved to Arizona in the Fall of 1967.

Jim and Carol are blessed with two wonderful daughters and one son. Velvet is married to Eric Jones and they have four children, Jake, Grant, Faith and Ben. Rebecca is a single mom of two boys, Keaton and Kedrick. Their son lives in North Carolina with his wife Dori and four children. The oldest is Caitlyn then Courtney, Jeremy and Josh.

Jim and Carol are active in Childhelp and one year they were co-chairs of our biggest fund raising event. The Childhelp Drive the Dream Gala is always in January and part of the Barrett Jackson Classic Car Show and Auction.

Carol and Jim Hebets brought them to the Little Chapel and they were thrilled to know about it. They already had great faith and were open to spiritual healing.

Sara always speaks about the importance of having faith when receiving and keeping a healing. External appearances may create fear and worry — but we should not give them any power. God desires us to continually live in faith and know that His love and guidance is always available for us. We should have faith in His goodness, and know that God is all we need.

Jim has had his faith tested many times, but has always looked at those times as great opportunities to grow stronger and closer to God. God's grace has gently led him through many times of uncertainty and continues to bless him abundantly and completely. He has learned to pray, listen and then act.

"When Jesus was walking with his disciples, a lady was filled with stories about the beautiful healings that Jesus performed. A lady who had been bleeding for twelve years reached out and touched His robe and received an instantaneous healing. Jesus turned to her and said she was healed because of her faith. When Jesus touched the eyes of several blind men, He said, "according to your faith it will be done unto you" and their sight was restored. Faith, faith and more faith is what we all need in our lives.

Last year when my wife, Carol, and I came to The Little Chapel we enjoyed every minute of it. We felt the presence of the Holy Spirit the moment we entered through the doors of the Chapel and His joy, peace and great love touched our hearts like we had never experienced before. Once you attend a service you are hooked, and never want to miss one after that.

I had a shoulder that was locked and I could not raise my elbow above my shoulder. It prevented me from reaching up and getting anything that was very high in cupboards. It made me frustrated when I had to always rely on others to do the simplest things.

Carol and I were sitting in The Little Chapel one Sunday morning, and after Sara's wonderful sermon the healings began. I was fascinated listening to the cancer healings and other major diseases when Sara suddenly said, "I feel someone has a problem with their shoulder."

I was hesitant to raise my hand, but finally I did and something unbelievable happened. My hand and arm went straight up over my head. I was so thrilled I wanted to shout out loud but I just leaned over to Carol and said, "I am healed." We both got tears in our eyes and began thanking God for His undying love. I've kept my faith, and I've kept my healing.

I pray that each of you who have read my story and the other stories in this book will let go of any fear that you are hanging on to and let God fill your hearts with His love and faith.

Wanting Only Eyes for God

Vita Cortese

*V*ita Cortese has been a close and dear friend since the early years of International Orphans, Inc. (now known as Childhelp®). She has served as treasurer on our Childhelp National Board of Directors since 1977. Vita has been an aunt as well as a surrogate mother to her brother Joe's four children since his wife died when the children were very young.

Vita was a part of Sara's prayer group in California and attended every service at the Little Chapel. Since the Little Chapel is in Arizona now, she comes about four times a year and always is willing to help meet and greet everyone. She has been touched by God several times at the services, over the phone, and even after a Childhelp meeting when she has needed a particular prayer for an ache or a pain that was bothering her.

Vita is the first to tell family and friends about how God heals others through Sara. She is so thankful for her healings, and she wants everyone she loves and knows to be open and receptive to the blessings God has for them. She has learned that God is not a God of fear, but of love.

I am a Catholic and was not taught in church about God healing people today like in the days of Jesus. Then I was invited to attend Sara's prayer group, and my eyes were opened along with my heart to a whole new way of believing. No fear was taught, just the love of God. We were told that God's love was the most powerful force, and could do anything if we let it. There were always great blessings and healings at every gathering.

Soon Sara had a Chapel connected to her home in California. I attended the dedication of it and chose to sit in the back row where I could see everyone throughout the service and watch God do His work. I never dreamt He would heal *me*—only others.

I was sitting there and for a moment I closed my eyes while absorbing the beautiful, powerful love that was all around the room. Sara mentioned that someone was being healed of a neck problem. I just sat there and looked around to see who was receiving that wonderful healing. Sara was very persistent and finally said it was someone in the back row and wanted them to accept this healing.

I am a very private person and hadn't told anyone, not even my sister, who is my closest friend, that for the past four or five months, I suffered with terrible pain in my neck and shoulder. I couldn't turn my head so I actually had to turn my whole body if I wanted to talk to someone on my right or left. It was so bad that in the morning getting out of bed I couldn't sit up and literally had to roll out of bed.

Here I was in Chapel, and everyone now would know my secret. But I didn't care, and was thrilled to feel the heat go through my entire body. The pain was gone and I was elated. The next morning I was able to jump out of bed with no problem and have ever since.

Another healing I received was not in the Chapel, but at our Childhelp office in Scottsdale, Arizona, a few years later. We were having a Board of Directors meeting and a ten-minute break was called. As I was walking toward the ladies lounge, I mentioned to Sara that I needed some extra prayers. I told her I was experiencing this darkness on the left side of my left eye, and it kept growing worse and worse to the point where I was just about losing my peripheral vision. She asked me to sit down, and she put her hand on my back and proceeded to pray. The heat was so strong, and I knew that was my sign from God that I was receiving another miracle. I now have peripheral vision and it's just wonderful. Praise God!

Every day I am trying to relax in God's love and let go of any negative thoughts so peace will fill my heart. I want my mind and body to stay healthy, so I can continue to do His work for the abused children through Childhelp USA. I know as I let go and let God have His way, the gentle and powerful love of God moves in and through me and in each moment I am being healed and renewed. I want only eyes for God.

I Love God's Wonderful Sense of Humor

Cris Cotone

*C*ris has a wonderful sense of humor that is such a terrific quality to have through life. If we can just laugh at ourselves once in a while, it helps. Sometimes we get bogged down with the negativity going on around us, and we forget to look at the positive things we have going on in our lives.

There is always something for which to be grateful. One blessing we all have is a loving God. There is nothing we have ever done or said, no error we have made, that can keep us from knowing and receiving God's healing love. Through grace we have the gift of love from God always.

Are we viewing a glass half empty or half full? Are we choosing to look at things in a negative light, or find the good in difficult situations? We all have times when we may not feel like smiling or laughing but the joy of God's spirit within can uplift us and carry us forward.

One day in May 2003, I went to the bathroom and urinated pure blood. I immediately went to see my gynecologist who recommended I go see a urologist. The urologist diagnosed me with bladder cancer. The doctor said he wanted me to be prepared for the worst.

He asked what my schedule was like the next few days. I said, "Why, do you want to have lunch?" He laughed and said, "Maybe after the operation." I liked his sense of humor.

In two days I was in the operating room. After the operation, the doctor said I was a lucky lady because it had not penetrated the bladder walls.

Three months later I had to go back for more tests. Bladder cancer is something that you live with, so you must have regular check ups. When the doctor entered the room I said, "Do you want to go to lunch?" That brought a smile to his face and made the feeling in the room less tense.

The tests that day came out great, which made the doctor and me very happy. Then he said, "I'm not working with women anymore." That really depressed me because our personalities clicked, and I was afraid another doctor would not have a sense of humor and that was important to me.

Four months later I went to the doctor he recommended. It wasn't that he was short but his energy and personality were just what I didn't want in a doctor. He was very quiet after he checked me. He said I had another tumor growing. I looked behind me and said, "You must be talking about someone else. You couldn't be talking about me. I have a hard time believing this, Doc."

He was very serious and said it was there, and for me to plan on being in the hospital for an operation in two weeks. I said to give me 30 days because I was going to try to get a healing in another way and I wouldn't need an operation. I told him I had been making conscious changes in my life and in my thinking this past month and I was not accepting this tumor in my body.

I knew in my heart somehow, someway, I was going to receive a complete healing. The doctor told me I was jeopardizing my bladder and my life but it was my choice to wait 30 days.

I immediately phoned my dear friends, George and Sedena Cappannelli, to tell them my news. They said I must go to the next Little Chapel service with them. They went on to tell me about the fantastic gift of healing Sara O'Meara has and that everyone in the audience at a service is blessed in some way. That sounded great to me.

I listened to the sermon that Sunday morning very carefully, and I liked the fact that Sara had a sense of humor along with her preaching. When the healings began she said there were four people in the room who had cancer. She asked us to raise our hands, and there were exactly four who did. As she walked toward me, I felt tremendous heat from my neck down my torso. It felt so good. It was definitely God giving me a thorough cleansing.

I couldn't stop thanking George and Sedena for telling me about this Holy place where God works through Sara to perform such beautiful miracles. My heart was so grateful.

I phoned Sara in a couple of weeks to tell her I was experiencing some pain on my right side around my bladder. She called me back on my cell phone right away. I was in my car, so she asked me to pull over to the side of the road so she could say a prayer for me. She prayed a powerful prayer, and then asked me to place my hand where the pain was. When I touched the painful spot it didn't hurt anymore. Sara said of course it didn't hurt because God had healed me. I was so thankful, and kept saying, "my cancer is gone, my cancer is gone." God had really healed me. I thanked Sara and then I hung up.

In a couple of weeks I began to question myself. Was I in denial of my cancer? Was there really another tumor? Maybe I just couldn't feel it and it was still there. I had to find out. I called the doctor and made an appointment to make sure everything was okay. When I saw him I told him I couldn't feel my tumor anymore and I thought it was gone. He said I needed to get into a hospital immediately and be operated because a tumor just doesn't disappear.

I pleaded with him to recheck me. He said absolutely not. I said, "What if you open me up and there is no tumor in there?" He kept reiterating, "You have a tumor!" I told him my insurance wouldn't cover all the expenses of the operation, and I didn't believe there was a tumor in my body now anyway. The doctor looked at me and said I was wasting his time for there was a tumor and I was taking a chance with my life to not have the operation.

One part of me felt sick, and the other part of me felt like laughing. I asked the doctor if he believed in miracles. Again, he said I was wasting his time. I said, "Okay, thank you very much for your time." As I was walking out of his office, I heard him say he was not going to charge me for the visit. Under my breath I managed to say, "thank you."

A friend of mine who is a nurse recommended another doctor for me to see. She said everyone loves him, and he has a great sense of humor. That sold me on him. It took me 30 more days before I could get an appointment with the new doctor.

I was happy when the day finally arrived for me to see the new doctor. Usually a nurse calls you in to see the doctor, but the doctor himself called my name and asked me in to his office. I felt he was down to earth and I immediately liked him.

I didn't take any of my past records of the cancer with me. He asked why I was there. I told him I was diagnosed with bladder cancer back in May and it was time for my check up. I explained my doctor was not seeing women anymore. I didn't mention the other doctor who wanted to operate on me.

After examining me, the doctor asked if I was sure I had an operation. He said usually people who have bladder cancer have scar tissue. He said I didn't have any scar tissue, and my bladder was perfect. Of course, it was perfect! God always does everything to perfection.

The doctors are still confused and in utter disbelief about what happened to my tumor. I love God's wonderful sense of humor! He has the best one of all.

God Heals Even the Irish

Marla Cunningham

*M*arla Cunningham is a pretty mother of three children; Cassidy, Courtney and Michael John. Her husband, Sean, was active on the Arizona State Board of Childhelp® for a number of years and does a golf tournament for our charity through his company CB Richard Ellis every year.

A few years ago, his mother and dad nominated Sara and I for the *Humanitarian Award* from the AMERICAN IRELAND FUND which we were fortunate enough to receive. They are a wonderful family and have a big heart for children. We are blessed to know and have them as part of our Childhelp® family. The following healing didn't happen in the Little Chapel, but at an Irish Gala.

My husband is all Irish and we never miss the Irish events in Arizona. We were sitting and talking at our table after dinner before the program started. I happened to see Sara and Yvonne at a nearby table, and went over to give them a hug and say, "Hi." There was an empty chair next to them so I sat down.

They asked all about the family and how everyone was feeling. I mentioned I had a little knee problem, and immediately they wanted to know all about it. I quickly told them my story.

I had such excruciating knee pain that it landed me in the hospital emergency room. I thought my knee was broken because it hurt so badly that I couldn't even lie down. They took X-rays and found it wasn't broken. They told me that if it wasn't better in a couple of weeks that I should go see a specialist.

Two weeks went by, then four weeks, then six months. Off and on, it was very painful, but I just ignored it. Now, here I was at the Gala and my knee didn't feel too bad. Yvonne asked if I would like Sara to pray for my knee (Sara never pushes her gift on anyone — she wants them to ask). I, of course, said, "Sure."

Sara placed her hand on my right knee and said a silent prayer. Within seconds my knee felt like it was on fire. I thanked her for the prayer, but said it was my left knee that hurt, so she placed her hand on the other knee and said another beautiful prayer. Both knees got a super charge from God. The heat was so strong coming through her hands and she said, "Your knee is healed now, but remember to thank the Lord every day for the marvelous healing that you were just given." It was an incredible experience, and she gave all the glory to God.

We finished chatting and I went back to my table to sit with my husband. I couldn't stop thinking about my knee. As I sat and watched the program, there was a feeling as if something was going right into my knee, like a fluid feeling, which expanded and bonded my knee. My knee felt like a new strong knee. I knew I was healed.

This is one Irish event Sean and I will never forget. We thank God every day for my healing and for His great love for everyone, including the Irish.

God Can Heal Us Anywhere if We Only Ask

Lana D'Amico

*L*ana D'Amico and her husband, Frank along with their two children, Sophia and Steven, moved from Canada to live in Arizona. Just recently they moved to Florida, after nearly 20 years in Arizona. While living in Arizona, Lana and Frank loved to come to The Little Chapel, never dreaming they would ever need a healing. Both have received many blessings, but the following is about Lana and one specific beautiful healing.

"Coming from Canada, our family enjoyed skiing. A few years ago, I felt my boot rubbing against my leg to the point it began to hurt, and I had to stop skiing. I went to the doctor and was told I needed to have surgery on a small vein. After the surgery, my foot swelled up and there was an ulcerated hole on my leg that kept oozing liquid. This went on for a long time, and I got tired of wearing black slacks for fear of staining. I kept going back to the doctor for two years, but nothing seemed to help.

Finally at the beginning of 2001, Frank and I were sitting in The Little Chapel and Sara began calling out the different healings. She said someone is having trouble with an ankle and a leg. I looked up and said, "That's me," and raised my hand. Sara verified that God had healed me and I was so thrilled and grateful.

My ankle felt warm and the oozing had stopped. All the way home I kept saying, "I can't believe it—I had a miracle!" We had seen others healed at the services many times but for it to happen to me blew me away.

The next day I went to the doctor and he was surprised to learn that the oozing had stopped from that last Friday to Monday. He could not believe that the hole had closed up. "Yes," he said, "it was a miracle!"

I worked in a beauty shop in Arizona and all day long I shared my miracle. I will never forget how good God was to me and I want others to know God can help them also. Soon I will begin working in Florida, and will be happy to spread the good news here. I know Sara is only a phone call away and God can heal us anywhere, if we only ask.

Celebrating God's Love Everyday

Lynn D'Argenzio

*L*ynn, Enrico, and their daughter are a God-loving family. They give credit to God and his beautiful angels for getting them to the Little Chapel. They have been enjoying the Arizona sun for many wonderful years. Before that, they lived in California where they met in church and married. They feel that meeting in church made their relationship very special, and they are truly a happy couple and grateful for all their many blessings.

I know you will enjoy reading about her wonderful experience.

We all look forward to vacation and I couldn't wait for mine to start the next day. A co-worker and I had completed an early morning appointment and decided to find a restaurant to have lunch. We were waiting at a traffic light when we were hit hard in the back — rear-ended. It was a tremendous jolt and I felt my whole body just snap. I guess they call it whiplash.

After we exchanged phone numbers with the other people in the car, we drove back to work. When I got out of the car at work, my legs kind of buckled under me and I could hardly walk. I am a designer and customers were waiting to see me. I tried to talk to them, but I felt myself getting woozier and woozier, and I knew I couldn't continue.

I managed to drive myself home, and my husband, Enrico, insisted that I go see a doctor. The next day I went to the emergency room and they took X-rays. They told me to put ice on my back, take painkillers and I'd be fine. I wasn't fine, and as time progressed, I started to have such severe pain in my lower back that I could hardly walk. I had to shuffle along. It even hurt to sit.

I kept saying that I wasn't going to accept this pain, but somehow I couldn't do it alone. I needed more prayers — stronger prayers — to help this pain leave. There were ice and cold packs, ice and cold packs and lots of pain pills. I thought I was going to become an addict or something.

Then I started with therapy. I would start to feel better, but by the time I got home from therapy it would start all over again. Next came the injections at the base of my spine. In addition to that, they were doing MRIs, and each one was worse than the last. One MRI showed I had something wrong with my brain—that maybe I had a stroke.

The neurologist I was seeing was not compassionate, and every visit I would end up crying and feeling worse. I started seeing a doctor who does energy healing. He helped a great deal but it took Sara to make me completely perfect. Sara was the conduit for God to give me a complete healing at a service I shall never forget.

During the healing part of the service, Sara said someone was there with a back problem. I raised my hand so she came over and started to pray over me. She said the light of God was all over me, and that I was getting a healing. I started to feel warm and the heat made the base of my spine tingle.

After the service, Sara invited me to go up on stage with her for extra prayers, and the next thing I knew I was flat out on the floor. The power of the Holy Spirit came over me and it was unbelievable. I have never ever felt so much humility and love.

Several of us went out to celebrate after the service, and we have been celebrating ever since. I gladly gave my testimony in The Little Chapel in January 2001. I feel terrific, and I'm so thankful to God, His angels, Sara and all the others who helped me become healthy again.

Sara and Yvonne and their organization, Childhelp®, do so much to help the abused and neglected children. When I received my healing, I promised God I would tithe more to the children and I always will keep my promise.

Even the Angels are Smiling

Fred Decatur

*S*ometimes when Sara and I travel to visit the different Childhelp® programs throughout the United States, we find that our tiredness mostly comes from going to and from our destinations, and praise God—He brought us two wonderful drivers; one in Washington, DC, and one in Los Angeles. This has made our lives so much better. Because our work is for charity, these drivers see to it that the cost is about the same as a taxi, and even sometimes less. On one of our trips to Los Angeles, our driver, Fred Decatur, received a wonderful healing. He is so grateful for his magnificent healing, he tells all of his customers about it. I'm certain that brings smiles to all the angels in heaven to see a heart so appreciative for God's healing touch. Fred is also our devoted driver now whenever we're in Los Angeles—which is quite often.

The hotel where I work as a driver told me there were a couple of VIPs coming to town. No one wants to pick up VIPs because they don't want to "goof up." The manager asked me to pick them up as I was a senior driver and should be able to do the job.

At this time, I was being treated at Kaiser for diabetes, arthritis, and many other things. The doctor had asked me to come in and see him that very afternoon. He looked straight at me and said, "We've received the results of your last tests, and to make it as easy for you as we can, we've got crutches and a wheelchair for you to take with you today." My eyes started watering and I could feel the tears begin to fall down my cheeks. He went on to explain that my arthritis and diabetes have combined to cause bone to rub against bone, and there was nothing they could do. He told me to go home.

When I picked up Sara and Yvonne later that day, I didn't take my crutches because I was too embarrassed. The ladies had so much luggage, I thought they must be in the garment business. Maybe famous designers?

They were very friendly and easy to talk to, so I told them my story. Sara said, "May I pray for you before we leave?"

The morning I was to take them back to the airport, Sara came out with the luggage and Yvonne stayed behind to take care of the bill. Sara got in the back seat and put her hands on my shoulders. Her hands were as hot as a stove. She started praying and telling God that I was a nice man, which really impressed me. She went on talking to God like you would talk to your father and ask him for things. I thought I was beginning to have a heart attack and I was afraid to move. She was taking her good old time back there, talking to God, while I was burning up.

When Yvonne came to the car, Sara finished her prayer, and I was happy. I was nervous, hot, and didn't know what to think. As I was unloading the luggage at the airport, Sara asked how I felt. I told her I felt "great." She asked, "Then why are you limping?" "I've been limping for about 5 years, and I forgot not to limp," I answered. She assured me the heat I felt came from the Holy Spirit, and because I was healed, I would never limp again. I found surprisingly she was absolutely right, that I really could walk perfectly.

About 10 days later, I got a call from Kaiser and they said they just figured out what they were going to do with me. They wanted to see me immediately. I did go to see them, but I left my wheelchair and crutches at home. As I sat on the table in the doctor's office, I tried to explain I didn't need them anymore, and I had been doing all sorts of things since I last saw him. The doctor wanted to know what had happened, and I said, "Doc, I don't know how to tell you this. This lady that I drive, named Sara, prayed for me when I took her to the airport, and I've been perfect ever since. Like a 21 year-old." He asked, "Who is Sara?" I told him that she and another lady came in town for 3 or 4 days and went back to Arizona. "That's all I know about her."

I knew it was hard for the doctor to believe me. A nurse came in and the two of them treated me like a spectacle for about an hour. The doctor asked, "Where is the water that was on your knees? We're supposed to draw that off today." I said, "I don't know." He asked another doctor to come and question me, and they kept saying, "Are you telling us the truth?" "Absolute truth," I kept saying.

They had me come in every 10 days and would ask how I felt. I always would say, "Great!" One day a Chinese doctor came in the room, and after I told him my story, he smiled and said he knew the power of prayer and what it can do. He was so happy for me. Every time I go to Kaiser now, people point and whisper, "There he is."

My Iranian heart doctor said up in the mountains of Iran they believe in the power of prayer. She, too, was thrilled with my many healings.

When I go to my golf club, I walk and no one helps me up and down the stairs. They are all amazed I'm no longer using my crutches or wheelchair and my golf game improved! Because of my recovery, I feel I have made believers out of people who didn't believe. I tell my story to everyone who rides in my car.

"When I was asked to give my testimony at The Little Chapel, I was so excited and proud. My plane from California to Arizona arrived early, so I went straight to the Chapel to pray and meditate before anyone else arrived. I had never experienced such peace and my head felt so clear. I thanked God for giving me the opportunity to tell all these people in Arizona about the healing I received in California, sitting right in my own car.

Since the big California earthquake in the early 90's, I had suffered from a constant ringing in my ears. I had been buried under my furniture in my home, and I was lucky to be alive. Whenever I would fly, I would have to wear earplugs. When I flew back to California that wonderful Sunday afternoon after giving my testimony, I didn't have to wear my earplugs. Thanks to God and Sara, I had received another beautiful healing.

Every day I say a silent prayer to God and Sara for being the conduit for my healing. I agree with my daughter when she says prayer is so much more powerful than medicine. I am a living example!

Crying is a Blessing

Elena Didier

*E*very month, dear Elena looks forward to the service in the Little Chapel. We all love to shed a tear when it is for the right reasons, but none of us want to experience unhappy situations that make us cry. Elena Didier, born and raised in Canada and now living in Arizona, couldn't cry if good or bad things happened. The following is her story.

"Blessed was the day that Lana D'Amico introduced me to the Little Chapel and to the spiritual truth that is taught there. I am always thanking God for the joy and peace I find in the Little Chapel, and I am always so happy to witness the many miracles.

I can still remember the first Sunday I attended a service. The Little Chapel was overflowing, so Lana and I sat on the steps of the stage and our husbands stood on the side up front. After the healings, Ralna English sang the most beautiful rendition of "You'll Never Walk Alone." The moment she began to sing, my heart started to pound, and I received the miracle of tears.

On July 1ˢᵗ, 1987, my oldest sister, Angie, died in my arms while I was singing that song. Since that sad afternoon, I was never able to shed a tear. I felt I had an obligation to the family to be strong like the rock of Gibraltar.

I was sexually molested between the ages of 3 and 5. My father had taken full responsibility of one of his nephews, and he loved having him live with us because our family was all girls. The sun rose and set on Frankie. I kept my secret about being molested by him because I knew no one would believe me. I realize this made me have very low self-esteem, and a great fear of men.

I married an ex-seminarian at 19 years of age. He did not want children, so there was no consummation of our marriage for three years. Hard to believe, but true. He did not believe in birth control, because of his religious beliefs, and me being the green Italian goody-two-shoes, I said this would be fine. Big mistake! The one good thing that came out of it was that I learned to speak impeccable French because he was of French-Canadian background. My family was furious that I wanted a divorce. I could write a book about what I went through during this time.

I married again, to a wonderful man, in 1977. Over the years, I tried to be everyone's nurse and support by flying all over the country to meet someone's needs. My husband was diagnosed with prostate cancer in 1991, and had major surgery in January of 1992. Complications? Yes. Did I face them alone with him? Yes. Did I cry? No.

I have had at least 12 operations of my own. Some of them were major. It amazes me how everyone looks at me and judges me as seeming to not having a care in the world. Maybe it's because I want them to think this. My life has been a roller coaster with great heights and depths that were quite a challenge. Sometimes you need to release your emotions, but I just couldn't for such a long period of time.

Sunday, May 4th, 2003 was a blessed milestone in my life. Sara put her hands on me and I felt a warm flush come over my face. I was so overcome with sobbing that I could not speak. I know

now I received the miracle of release. I truly believe that many of my physical problems have been the result of the deep-seated emotional pain I kept hidden for all these years. I had to learn to "let go and let God."

I'm so grateful for the miracles of tears — tears that have eluded me for many, *many* years. To all of you reading my story, and who are plagued with anxiety attacks/stress; it's okay to cry. Let go of the past and the pain. God will heal you and remove the ache in your heart if you let Him.

Every day I thank God for Lana for taking me to the Little Chapel, and for Sara for being the wonderful instrument of God and the Holy Spirit. I am so happy I can cry.

Thank You God for Transforming My Challenges into Positive Victories

Betty Donald

etty was born in Louisiana, and moved around a lot in her younger years. She became a stewardess in the early sixties and flew in and out of Arizona until she decided to move there permanently in the nineties. She is divorced, but has successfully raised a son and an adopted daughter who are always in her prayers along with, Amanda, her granddaughter.

Sometimes *change* is hard for us. When we don't want the change it is difficult for us to accept. Nobody can take anything from us that is rightfully ours. That which belongs to us will always return at the right time. If something does not come back to us, then it isn't meant to be. We must let go and get on with our lives. Something better will come along if we let it.

God always wants the best for each of us but He never forces anything on us. He gave us free will. When we release the resistance to change, new things can come into our lives. Old hurts and painful memories stay with us until we let them go and make room for new happy memories. No one can disturb you or make you unhappy or happy unless you let them. Betty learned this great lesson through coming to The Little Chapel.

> The healing atmosphere of love was overwhelming as I walked through the doors of the church. My negative side began to dissolve with all the positive energy around the room. I immediately felt at peace. As I looked around I saw all these bright, shinny and happy faces. Happy because they were there to be blessed and many were praying for a healing — a beautiful miracle.

"The Holy Spirit never misses a service," one lady said to me as I sat down next to her. That gave me great comfort because I did want a healing of my broken heart that I have hung on to for over thirty years. As I approach turning seventy, I began to look at the negative side of that. I always could find the negative side of things.

It was the Christmas service and all about the life of our Lord Jesus. As I listened to the sermon I realized what I was doing to my life. I asked God to help me be positive and to let go of anything that kept me from growing spiritually because my desire was to have a closer relationship with Him. I could see and feel how strong Sara believed and that touched my soul and changed my thinking and how I now believe. I want to live on a higher vibration of love and light and not wallow in darkness and negativity.

We all had coffee and dessert together after the service. Sara walked by me and asked how I felt. Before I could reply — she said, "Oh, your heart was healed and it feels much lighter now." She was *so* correct. My energy was so much better leaving the service than when I had arrived.

After a few days I went to the graduation of my daughter-in-law, and I was seated right next to my ex-husband for lunch. I was calm, cool and had no negative feelings towards him. It was a true miracle after thirty years we were able to talk to one another for the first time without getting into an argument.

God also gave me another healing. I am completely off medicine for acid reflux and I can even drink coffee now without it bothering me.

Each day I now recognize the presence of God within me and within every circumstance of my life. Thanks to God I am transformed. Turning seventy is going to be the beginning of a new me. I want to eat right, think right and put my positive attitude into action.

Nothing is Impossible When We Look to God...Unless We Think it is

Joseph Donvito

Joseph Donvito served in the military as a medic and trained in battlefield surgery and crisis response. He is a Chaplain and had witnessed many healings take place. Throughout his life, he had been fortunate to witness healings either in his own life or in the lives of others, all as a result of a belief in God. He is married and has a son and two wonderful daughters.

Joseph was introduced to The Little Chapel and Sara O'Meara through a friend. Attending his first service, and watching God's Healing Power work through Sara to heal people, he knew he had found His spiritual home. Sara has helped him and his family and he is forever grateful for the miracles that have occurred because of Sara's prayer work.

Joseph is a true prayer warrior. He faithfully joins a small prayer group the night before the Little Chapel service to pray for every one who will attend the next day. Lifting every one up in prayer and filling the room with love and light is such a vital part of a healing service. His sincere prayers are from a heart filled with love and are powerful.

" When Sara calls out the healings for people, don't be afraid to claim those healings. Don't think they are for someone else because they are for YOU!

When I was in the service I suffered injuries to my spine and was told by doctors that I would never be able to walk unless I used either crutches or a cane. I heard these words but did not believe them because I believed in a Higher Power that says I am healed. I share this with you because at one particular Little Chapel service I had excruciating pain in my back. It felt like an ice pick was poking into my spine. Sara called out a healing for back pain but I didn't want to get up in case the healing was meant for someone else.

I didn't want to embarrass Sara or myself but a friend, Kathy Bowen, kept prodding me to get up and accept the healing. So I finally stood up and claimed the healing of my spine. The pain was gone in that moment and has never returned.

I am so thankful for the healing work that Sara does on God's behalf and forever grateful for the healings of my family and for me. When Sara calls out a healing, stand up and claim it, open your heart and receive God's Healing Power! "

Our God is a Miracle-Working God

Jerry Doty

*J*erry was born and raised in Battle Creek, Michigan. He married Janice in 1975 and they moved to Arizona in 1979. They are blessed with four wonderful children and three grandchildren. He is happily retired and enjoying his family and his favorite hobby, music.

Jerry and his lovely wife, Janice, are such a great team. He does all the sound for the Chapel services and she is back stage right by his side smiling and spreading joy and laughter to everyone before they take part in the service.

Jerry and Janice never miss a service and neither does the Holy Spirit. Sara always says there will be no healings if the Holy Spirit fails to attend the Service, for God does the healing and uses her as the conduit.

"I've been active in church for over 27 years but The Little Chapel is my family. I love everyone who attends and all those who participate in the program every month. The Little Chapel is truly a place where God and His angels are present. So many individuals in this world are desperate to experience the love and compassion of God. We are blessed to have The Little Chapel in Arizona where all who enter are touched in a special way.

I have been dealing with depression since my childhood. Have you ever been in a secluded place — maybe the woods or out in the desert and you hear a rustling in the bushes and instantly you are petrified with fear? You just know it's a rattlesnake or it's somebody that's going to jump out and hurt you. The adrenalin flows and you are in a frozen place. Well, if you've ever experienced that then you've experienced what I used to live with every day of my life.

With depression, your brain is sending the wrong signals to your emotions and it effects how you see and perceive things. An example might be if your pastor walked by reading his notes and studying them for the next sermon, you might make a comment to your family how wonderful it is that he spends so much time studying to bring you a good message. If that happened to me, I'd be upset and would wonder what I did to him that he purposefully looked at his papers just to avoid looking at me and saying, "Hi." Depression convinces you that people don't like you and that life is like a big party and you're not invited. I got so I wouldn't discuss it even with my lovely wife with whom I share everything.

I am thankful that I finally found doctors who had the right medications for me and how this has helped me to have a somewhat normal and happy life. You can never miss taking your medication. Once I ran out of my medication and in two days I'd gone back into a massive depression. Another time, I was just tired of taking the medication and within days I spiraled into a depression you can't even imagine. I became suicidal and laid on my bed with a pile of pills and cried out to God for help. I asked Him to give me a reason not to take my life and end it all. God did listen and reminded me of my dear wife and family who depend on me. He said, "Jerry, just trust Me, for I have something special for you." I put the pills back into the bottles and took my medication.

During The Little Chapel services, I am in the back room working on the technical end of things. I hear the service but I'm so busy paying attention to the camera angles and making sure the audio is in balance that I don't digest the service until later. I edit each sermon and put it on a CD and DVD. I get to listen to each service three or four times during the process and I love it.

One Sunday at The Little Chapel, Sara was calling out different healings and she said someone is being healed from depression. I heard her say that and said to myself, "I'll take that healing" and went on with my work. I really didn't think any more about it. After the service I packed up the equipment and said my good-byes. Two days later I started to feel a little weird and my mind was kind of foggy. I prayed and asked God what was happening to me. He brought back to my mind the last Chapel service when Sara mentioned that someone was being healed of depression. He reminded me that I said quietly, "I'll take that healing."

He heard my whisper and in my heart I knew He had healed me. I realized I was taking medication for something I no longer had. No wonder my mind was foggy. I quit taking ALL medication immediately. I had the faith that God healed me but I was a little afraid to trust completely, so I kept the pills in my dresser drawer for a couple of months. God had such patience with me until I learned to fully trust Him.

To this day, years later, I don't suffer from any form of depression. Every night I thank God for touching me in such a profound way. Remember, God sees your heart and hears your every prayer and desire. He wants us all to be happy and healed and I'm so grateful. Our God is a miracle-working God.

You are Never the Same Once God Touches You

Sharon Dupont-Mccord

Sharon Dupont-McCord is the wonderful lady who found our home for us in Paradise Valley, Arizona, in August 1994. It is truly paradise, on 6 sprawling acres for it has lots of green grass, trees and a large building that is just right for The Little Chapel.

Sharon has become a devoted friend whom we love dearly. She has served on the Arizona Board of Directors for Childhelp® and has a beautiful heart for others. She has nearly always attended the Chapel services since day-one.

I am blessed with good health, so I always went to The Little Chapel to hear the sermons and watch others receive great healings. Little did I dream one day I, too, would need some help.

A few years ago, my husband, Bob, and I were taking our daughter and granddaughter to the Nutcracker ballet. We were on the freeway, having a fun time visiting, when all of a sudden the car in front of us came to a screeching, abrupt halt. A truck had dropped a mattress on the highway in front of them. Everyone was going regular speed limit, but we hit the car in front of us, and the air bags deployed. I now understand why they have a sign near the windshield saying that they are really dangerous. My head shattered the front windshield. It all happened so fast; we were stunned as we looked at each other. We were shocked by it all, but happy to see we were okay.

My head had shattered the window in spite of the airbag. A smoky substance filled the car and we could barely see. Everything was just a big blur as we noticed the police, ambulance, and fire trucks arriving. As we got out of the car, I felt the pain in my arm and shoulder as I had hit my head. We wanted so much to divert our little granddaughter's attention because she had her heart set on going to the Nutcracker. We declined going in the ambulance to the hospital. When we left, the pains in my shoulder, arm and part of my head became worse. The pain continued for several days but I kept thinking it would go away. One morning, the pain in my shoulder had gotten so bad it made me sick to my stomach.

Chapel day came and at the end of the service, I was watching all the interesting healings. Sara said, "Someone is receiving a healing of their arm and shoulder." I thought for a moment, "Could I be the one?" I was rather reluctant to raise my hand, but I wanted to get some relief from the pain, so I did. Sara walked over to me, and placed her hand on my shoulder. She said a prayer and then asked me to raise my arm up high. I wanted to say I couldn't, but I thought maybe my shoulder was healed, so I should try. I raised it a little bit at first, and then went farther and farther and farther. All of a sudden, it felt great, and I knew God had taken the pain away through Sara.

The Little Chapel has meant everything to me the past several years, and I always feel such comfort and love sitting and listening to the sermons. I am deeply grateful that I, too, can say God touched me and took away my pain. You are never the same, no matter how minor the healing is. God is always willing to help us, if we just ask Him, and then let go and let God do what He knows best.

The Power of His Love is Awesome

Sheila M. Elmer

*S*heila was born and lived in England most of her life. She has experienced both great tragedy and triumph over the years. Shelia managed to overcome the difficult times in her life and prefers not to dwell on them. As is her way, she holds her head high and quietly moves on. In 1990, after her fourth husband died, she moved to Arizona.

Sheila works 96 hours a week as a caregiver. She is a faithful Christian and refuses to work on Sunday. She never complains, and loves The Lord with all her heart.

"I heard about The Little Chapel through Jim and Dean Glaves, two very dear friends. Bringing me to The Little Chapel was the best gift they could have given me.

I suffered with degenerative arthritis in my neck and back for years. I couldn't sleep without taking three Advil® every night. When I heard about the different healings that had happened in The Little Chapel, I was anxious to attend a service.

The minute I walked through the doors of The Little Chapel I felt the presence of God. It was so powerful, I could hardly stand up. Great peace came over me.

When I looked up, I saw a life size beautiful marble statue of Jesus, I felt a little uncomfortable and memories began to flood my mind. I was a former Catholic when I lived in England. Many times I would go to church and pray at the foot of the Virgin Mary. It was so emotional for me I would begin to sob and cry uncontrollably resulting in my having to leave the church, which broke my heart.

I decided to move my seat in The Little Chapel so I couldn't see the statue of Jesus; so that my mind could concentrate on the message of the sermon. I felt so good through the service. I just knew God was going to heal me and use Sara as the conduit. The desire of my heart was to be pain free from my arthritis. I prayed so hard for God to touch me.

He heard my prayers, and I am so grateful. Sara saw God's beautiful light all around me as I was receiving my healing. I felt like I was being lifted up and out of my body. I was in the presence of The Lord and I didn't want to leave Him. The power of His love was awesome.

Sara came by me twice during the healing part of the service, but didn't see me raise my hand to tell her I had received the desire of my heart, a healing of my arthritis.

A nice lady sitting next to me at the service encouraged me to stay after and ask Sara for special prayer. I stayed and found myself on the floor of The Chapel when Sara prayed over me. The power of The Lord was so great, I could literally not stay on my feet; it knocked me to the ground. What a morning April 16, 2004 was for me. I shall treasure it forever. I have not had one little pain since that outstanding service.

God Blesses a Family Who Looks to Him

Nancy Engemann

The next story is truly a family affair. Nancy Engemann was a member of Sara's prayer group in California in 1987. She strongly believed in God's miracles and was always open to receive one.

Nancy is an attractive blond and wants to enjoy life every moment of every day. After raising two lovely daughters, Susan and Carrie, she spent a lot of time in Italy. Becoming a grandmother has brought her back to California. Her daughter Susan has 2 children–Mia and Callie and Carrie has a daughter, Ashley.

God loves it when a family is so open to receive His blessings. Nancy has given her family the greatest gift she could ever give—a belief in God to be open and receptive to the truth that sets us free. Nancy has received so many blessings and miracles over the years through the Little Chapel, but I have selected an unusual one to share with you. After her story are stories about other members of her family who have received unbelievable miracles.

I suffered for years with bunions and always had to buy two pair of shoes, one in size 7 and the other a half size larger. One day while I was driving on my way to purchase new shoes, I stopped the car and phoned Sara—who was also in her car. I explained my problem to Sara and said I thought it was too expensive and wasteful to have to buy 2 pair of the same shoes. I wanted a healing.

Sara pulled off to the side of the road and prayed with me. By the time I arrived at the shoe store, I had received my healing. I was able to buy several styles of shoes instead shoes in different sizes.

An outstanding healing happened for my father, Paul. He was first diagnosed with prostate cancer and then it spread throughout his entire body. When he learned he had bone cancer, they placed him in the intensive care unit at *MD Anderson Center* in Houston, Texas, with no hope for survival.

My father didn't believe in "all this miracle stuff", but my mother did. She phoned me and I phoned Sara. Sara started praying immediately for a miracle. She asked us to arrange for a phone to be brought into intensive care to hold it up to my dad's ear for him to hear Sara's prayer. To the shock of everyone, my dad received a healing, and even gave a testimony at one of the services a few months later. It has been almost over 25 years now.

My mother Peggy believed in miracles because she had received one a few years before. She used to have mini-strokes. One day she had a stroke while driving and ran into a telephone pole. Amazing as it was, she walked away without a scratch. My mother asked Sara to pray for her to not have any more strokes, and she has never had one after that.

My daughter, Susan, was born with a leg and foot that turned inward. We never thought much about it until she became a teenager and wanted to go to a dance where all the girls would be wearing heels. It was impossible for her to wear heels, so I phoned

Sara for an appointment.

The next night, Susan and I drove to see Sara at her home. She greeted us warmly and then we sat and talked for a while. Sara asked Susan if she would like her to pray with her. Susan was young and didn't know what to expect. To her amazement, she received an instantaneous healing. God not only made a little girl happy, but also touched her soul, lifted her thinking to a new dimension and strengthened her faith. She was able to wear heels to her prom and has been able to wear them ever since.

Several years later, Susan met a nice young man, Derek, and fell in love. They decided to get married even though he had lost his job and had to work at night doing odd jobs just to bring in some money. She worked in the daytime so the schedule was a little hard on the newlyweds.

They attended The Little Chapel regularly, and asked Sara to pray for Derek to find a new job. Months went by but they never lost faith. He had sent out his resume to many companies but nothing was happening for him. Sara kept encouraging me "trust God." Know that God hears your prayers, He knows your needs, and He will provide a job for Derek that will be perfect.

The months kept slipping by and finally Derek received a phone call and got a job offer from a company he had not even thought about. God did answer his prayers.

Derek also received a healing on his hip. He loves to play golf, but after playing a game he would always suffer with such pain in his hip he could hardly drive home. At one of the Little Chapel Sunday services, he felt heat all through his body, but he still had pain in his hip every morning. He continued to pray and his hip started improving. By the end of the month, he played 18 holes of golf and had no pain. The pain has never returned.

Susan and Derek have no doubt about the wonderful way God can perform miracles. They had tried to have a baby for some time but it didn't happen. They realized they had forgotten to ask God for help. They prayed every night, Sara prayed every night and again God answered their prayers.

Susan got pregnant and they were so happy. On a routine visit to the doctor, he told her something was not right with the baby. She phoned Sara right away and asked for prayers. Sara told her there would be nothing wrong the next time she returned to the doctor. Sara was correct. When Susan returned to the doctor for more tests, they couldn't find anything wrong. Susan and Derek have a beautiful, healthy, baby girl named Mia — thanks to God!

My other daughter, Carrie, had two tumors the size of oranges over each ovary and didn't have a period for four months. Sara prayed for Carrie and when she went back to the hospital for another ultrasound, they were all gone! The next day she started her period.

God has been so good to my family and I feel truly blessed. Many of my friends have also received healings through Sara's gift, so I'm always on my knees giving thanks. When we get on our knees and pray with a sincere, loving heart, that is when He lifts us up to greater heights and beautiful blessings.

My Day Starts and Ends on My Knees

Beverly Owen Fasciocco

Beverly is the lovely daughter of our dear friend, Gloria Sutherland. Beverly and Gloria love The Little Chapel, and both have received wonderful healings.

Beverly was born in Connecticut, but spent most of her life in California. After the big earthquake in California in the early nineties, Beverly, her husband, Leo, and their two children moved to Gilbert, Arizona.

She is very spiritual and her great joy is to volunteer her time at St. Anne's Catholic Church. She is a beautiful example of living a Christ-like life.

I am so grateful for my many blessings. My mother and I had attended the chapel services many times in California, and when we all moved to Arizona we started attending the services in the new Little Chapel.

About ten years ago in December, I went to our family doctor. He found a mass in my uterus. He referred me to have an ultra sound. This confirmed the mass. In one month I was to see an OB-GYN and have another ultra sound. Meanwhile, my mother and I went to the December service at The Little Chapel.

The December service is at night in the middle of the week and is very, *very* special. The whole service was so moving. I felt the power of the Holy Spirit and kept praising God for His healing touch. A peaceful, loving, calmness came over me like I had never quite felt before. I thanked God for answering my prayers because I knew my mass had dissolved. Sara smiled as she saw the light upon me and confirmed what my heart already knew. Yes, I had received a healing, and we all praised and thanked The Lord.

On the way home my mother and I kept thanking God for The Little Chapel and for Sara's wonderful gift that continues to bless so many souls.

In January, I returned for the ultra sound. The mass was gone. The OB-GYN couldn't find it either when he took another ultra sound.

My promise every day to God is to try my best to be faithful to Him. My day starts and ends on my knees with a grateful heart.

Trusting and Thanking God

Mary Grace Ferrante

*M*ary Grace was born in New York City and moved to Phoenix, Arizona seven years ago. She works as a coordinator for volunteers and enjoys spending her free time reading, walking and swimming.

Mary suffered with several physical problems, so a dear friend recommended a few years ago that she should attend a Little Chapel service. She believed in spiritual healings so she was quick to say, "yes," she would happily attend.

Over the years she has received many beautiful blessings and a wonderful healing for which she will always be eternally grateful.

"I had been attending the services in The Little Chapel for a couple of years. Every service was a treat and I received many personal blessings and witnessed so many others receive unbelievable healings. If you attend The Little Chapel services, there is no way you won't believe in a higher power and in miracles. The healing power of love is always strong in The Little Chapel and at every service many outstanding healings occur.

In July 2003, a doctor prescribed a strong antibiotic that actually caused a serious infection of my gastro-intestinal tract called *"C. dificile."* It is known to be nasty and have long lasting effects. I suffered 11 days and nights of diarrhea. I was seriously dehydrated and lost 10 pounds. I continued to lose weight at a rapid pace. Soon I had lost over 25 pounds, 15% of my weight, and had severe intestinal pain. The doctors considered surgery on the gall bladder to alleviate some of the discomfort.

I was given other medications to counteract the *C. dificile*, and they in turn, caused other side effects. My body was weak, depleted of nutrients. I could eat and digest very little. I was unable to work for many weeks.

I came to The Little Chapel in October and November of 2003 asking for a healing of this and other maladies. In November, Sara called out a healing for someone who had been given "the wrong medicine." No one raised their hand. I didn't feel anything so I hesitated to raise my hand. Sara asked again, and I slowly raised my hand saying I wasn't sure but maybe it was me since a medication I had taken had harmful effects on my body.

Sara said, "You received the wrong medication?" I said, "Yes." In that moment, with my right hand raised, I felt a warm tingling from my fingertips down my arm and down the center of my body. Sara confirmed I was healed, and that I would be completely free of pain. My pain is gone, my weight is back, and I am so happy to feel good and be able to eat normally. The scheduled surgery has been cancelled.

I seem to be having progressive healings on my right ear (sinusitis) and lung problems. God knows the right timing for everything, and I'm depending on Him. I am just trusting and thanking God for all He has done for me.

I promised God that after my healing I would devote my time and energy to love and serve Him daily with joy in my heart. I intend to keep that promise.

More Time to Do More Work for God

Rhonda Fleming

Rhonda Fleming is such a gorgeous lady and has a wonderful presence about her. She has been a dear and loyal friend for many years. Rhonda started her movie career as a teenager and has starred in hundreds of films.

She became a Christian at 18, and always wanted to do more with her life than just be a beautiful, successful movie and TV star. Her purpose has been realized by the positive effects of her many philanthropic efforts. She and her husband, Darol, also open their home every other month for a prayer group, with the exception of a short summer hiatus.

She truly loves the Lord and has built a Chapel at our Childhelp® Villages on the West Coast and several meditation rooms at our different offices and Advocacy Centers. Her heart is very generous, and we are proud to have her as a part of our Childhelp® family as a National Celebrity Ambassador.

" I have had many blessings and healings through Sara's ministry. Sometimes I just phone up and ask for prayers, for they are so uplifting.

The Little Chapel in California was extremely peaceful, and I always loved to attend the Sunday Services. One day, I was limping on a sore and swollen toe when I arrived. During the healing part of the service, Sara kneeled down by me and placed her hand on the toe and gave a powerful prayer. She asked me then to stand up and walk down the aisle. I did with no pain. We walked up and down the aisle together a couple of times, and I was delighted that the pain was entirely gone. It never returned.

Another time I was to have a lumpectomy and I was very fearful about it. Sara prayed for me over the phone and she kept reminding me to give my fear to God and rest in His love. Love was going to heal me, not fear. The next morning, I surrounded myself with love and light. Everything went well and it was benign though the doctor suspected otherwise. Thank God and thank Sara for the prayers.

My late husband, Ted, was very ill, and in and out of the hospital for several years. Sara was willing to continually pray for him, and he was able to stay with us a lot longer than the doctors thought he would. Ted knew it was God's call, and he was grateful for the additional time he was given to be with all of us.

I have been saved and healed so many times. It's by His grace that I'm here today. I feel He had more work for me to do; more souls to touch and bring to His light and love. God brought a wonderful Christian man, Darol Carlson, into my life a few years ago and our home is open for prayer meetings and our hearts are open for His love and guidance always.

Sara is a mighty prayer warrior, and the Lord uses her as a conduit for such marvelous healings. I'm honored to be a part of this book that will touch many lives, and I pray that my words will help you to know that all things are possible with God. "

Being Wiser About the Use of My Time

Elizabeth Frankel

lizabeth Frankel was a neighbor of Sara's in California. She is a busy married lady with children, and runs her own business as well as running an active home life. She volunteers a great deal of her time working with the elderly and underprivileged children. She loves to tell anyone who will listen about her healing. She has given her testimony in the Little Chapel in California and Arizona and is happy to include her story in this book.

" My right leg was seriously injured when I had my second child. The nerves were damaged during the Cesarean. As time went by, my leg got worse and worse. The pain was unbearable. For nine years, I lived on narcotics every night. Even with all the pills, I would moan, groan and cry all night. My husband was a saint!

A new neighbor, Susan Abrahamson, moved in next door and we became close friends. When Susan realized the pain I was in, she said I must meet Sara and let her pray for me. I looked at her kind of funny because at the time I wasn't acting very Christian-like. I told her I wanted nothing to do with anything like that.

The next time I saw Susan my leg was killing me. I'd been to doctor after doctor, one specialist after another, and no one could help me. My last ditch effort was going to be Stanford University.

Susan asked me to please call Sara before I left for Stanford. She assured me she was nice and felt certain she could help me. I looked at her for a moment and thought, "What the heck! I'm in such pain; why not give it a try? Besides, she lived just 2 miles away."

"OK, Susan, I promise I'll call her," I said.

The time almost arrived for me to go to Stanford and I hadn't kept my promise to Susan. I love Susan and didn't want to break my commitment to her, so I phoned Sara. She sounded pretty nice on the phone, so it wasn't so bad. She asked for me to come by her home so she could pray for me in person.

I gathered up my MRIs, my scans, my medical folder, and off I went. I took it all in the house with my cane, and Sara looked at me kind of like, "What in the world is she doing with all that stuff?" My thinking was that she was going to analyze all this medical material and get down to brass tacks and start praying over it. That was the only thing I could figure out.

She looked at me sweetly, took my hand and said, "Why don't we just put these aside and talk, and then let's pray." She prayed and I listened. That was hard for me because I'm always the one talking. It was great. I went back home, feeling a little better. It went well, I thought.

The next Chapel service, Susan wanted me to attend, but my mom was at the house and we had other guests staying with us, so I used that for an excuse. I was very tired and stayed in bed all morning. My husband came upstairs to get me because it was past time to take everyone out for brunch. I said, "Honey, I just need to rest. Please go on without me."

It was wonderful to relax and rest. I had not been able to do that in years. I didn't have any clue that I was being healed. Susan had been praying for me at the Chapel service, and Sara told her I was being healed.

A couple of days after that, a friend and I drove up to Big Bear. I had not been driving very much, but seemed to be feeling better now, so I decided I could drive up the mountain. After we arrived at the house, I climbed a spiral staircase and didn't think anything about it. I'd forgotten completely this had not been possible for me to do before. I helped carry in some wood and then decided we should wash all the curtains. We took every curtain in the house down, washed them, and then hung them back up.

As we were driving back down the mountain for home, my friend said, "You know, I'm never going with you again, Elizabeth. You almost killed me with all your activities."

When I got home, it hadn't even dawned on me that I was not taking narcotics at night to sleep. I don't know why, I just didn't think about it. I guess I just felt like a new person. I can't describe it.

The phone rang, and it was Sara. She said, "Elizabeth, how are you feeling?" I said, "I feel fine." She said, "Are your legs hurting? Are you having any problems with your leg?" I touched my leg. "No, it's not hurting."

She said, "I want you to get down on your right knee and get up by yourself without holding on to anything. Get down and get up." I did. I did it two times. I did it three times and let out a scream.

My husband, Marshall, was upstairs and I yelled for him to come down quickly. "My leg is completely healed! Come see for yourself." Sara told me I had been healed last Sunday. Susan had gone to The Little Chapel for me, and God answered her prayers. WOW!

It had been healed for days and I was just walking around doing my thing. I never stopped to think about it. A true blessing that I didn't even realize. I began calling Sara "Sister Sara."

Later, I was returning home from a trip to Washington, DC, and while sleeping on the plane, I had my legs crossed. Somehow I threw a blood clot from my knee through my lung and through my heart. I went to one hospital and then I was going to go to Stanford, since the X-rays proved I had serious problems, the doctors were gravely concerned and suggested I go to a renowned specialist.

Before leaving for Stanford, I called "Sister Sara," for another problem and once again went by her home to pray with her. This time I was not reluctant. Instead, I was most anxious to land on her doorstep.

After I got to Stanford, they ran a lot of tests on me. I was resting in a bed with a friend standing by visiting with me when the door opened and in walked several of the professors. One put his hand on me and said, "We don't know why but you have been given a second chance. Someone a lot more powerful than all of us doctors has had His hand on your shoulder. Make good use of your time." Once again, God used Sara to heal me.

I did promise God I would try to be wiser about the use of my time. Spending time telling others about my healing is well spent and my joy. I haven't had to use my cane to walk since 1991. I do keep it in the closet at home just as a reminder of this great healing and how good God truly is.

I also promised God to work on becoming a better person by being more compassionate, kinder and more giving to others. God has blessed me physically and monetarily and I am happy that I'm fortunate enough to give to needy children and the elderly. God has touched my heart to help them and I will always follow His lead.

Be Open to Receive His Miracles with a Loving and Grateful Heart

Carol Franza

*C*arol was born in New Orleans and raised in Atlanta, Georgia. She moved to Arizona in 1999 and attended Scottsdale Artist School. She is divorced and has three grown children — Justin Matthew, Devon Reed and Laurel Elise. She attends McDowell Christian Church on the weekends when there is no chapel service. Ron Head is a good friend and invited her to the Little Chapel. She has always loved Jesus since she was a small child.

Carol remembers reading in the Bible that Jesus said, "If you have the faith of a grain of a mustard seed nothing shall be impossible to you" and those words gave her great comfort through the years. It wasn't until she came to The Little Chapel that her simple faith was transformed into knowledge. In the chapel, she saw how faith in God and his healing love produced great miracles. It is God's deepest desire to heal us so we can do all the things we were brought here to do. God wants us to complete the desires of our hearts. We each have a mission to fulfill and it is His joy to help us reach our goals and succeed beyond our most fantastic dreams.

" Every time I enter the doors of The Little Chapel, I feel the presence of God. I have received so many blessings, but my last healing is the one I want to share with you.

As the Holy Spirit began to work through Sara, after her sermon one Sunday morning, I felt tremendous love move all around me and over my entire body. I had asked for a healing of my right lower back and the right side of my neck. As I felt the Holy Spirit working on my body I found it impossible to stay connected with the earth or with Sara or with anything that was going on around me. Sara's voice was like a distant whisper and I couldn't respond to her.

I did feel a release in my lower back. I had a compressed vertebrae and it felt like a guitar string vibrating. This event went on for several minutes. I wanted to stay in that love vibration, but that was not to be. I shall always cherish those moments as well as my healing.

The three nights that followed the service I was awakened during the middle of the night and my body was stretching. It wasn't something that I was doing; God was adjusting me. He was stretching my body. I have never had any pain from my back or neck again.

Sometimes God starts His healing process on us while we are driving to the Little Chapel and sometimes He continues healing us long after the service. Our part is to be open to receive His miracles with a loving and grateful heart.

Many times now as I sit in the chapel praying I hear Sara repeating the exact words that are going through my mind. I think that is God letting me know that He is hearing my prayers.

One day I was very upset about a family member. The service was ending and I was really begging God to hear my prayers. Sara was exiting and turned around and looked right into my eyes and said, "God hears your prayers." Those words went straight to my heart for I knew He had heard me, and I completely relaxed and gave it all over to God.

The most miraculous thing to me is that despite all of my faults, God is always there for me, taking care of me and loving me. His unconditional love is always available to heal our bodies and our hearts and transform our challenges into victories.

One Life Can Have a Beautiful Ripple Effect on So Many Others

Marde Gideon

Marde was born and raised in Amarillo, Texas. He lived in Arizona from 1988 to the fall of 2003 when he returned home to Texas for personal reasons. He learned about The Little Chapel through Salli Stronglight. She attends the Little Chapel regularly. The services opened his spiritual eyes to healing and just how wonderful God truly is. Marde liked to just come and sit in the Chapel and feel God's love. He said it was so strong and powerful and made him feel good.

Marde drove a cab in Arizona and told everyone he could about The Little Chapel. He never came alone on Sunday and felt everyone he brought received a blessing and a healing of some kind. It is fabulous to see how God can touch one life and how that life touches another and another, and what a beautiful ripple effect one life can have on the world.

Have you ever had a severe back pain? Well, I had an injured back for over 26 years, and suffered with extreme pain every day. Some days were harder than others, but each day was a real challenge.

Over the years, I have had many fine Christians pray over me. It helped for a little bit, a couple of weeks maybe, but the pain would always come back. My friend, Salli, told me about The Little Chapel and Sara. I was skeptical at first, but I thought it might help me for a while.

The Sunday I attended the service I had great pain and pressure in my lower back. As the healings began, I felt the weirdest sensation. The pain just left my back and went out both sides of my body. Sara kept saying, "God is telling me several backs are being healed."

I began to lean and twist my body to see if the pain would return. It didn't, so I finally raised my hand. When I did, I realized the carpel tunnel had been healed in my hand, so I told Sara about that. Then I said, "Oh, by the way, my back was healed also." She said, "You decided to claim it now, huh?" I told her I had the pain for 26 years, and it was hard for me to believe it was truly healed by God and would never return. She said, "You think 26 years is too long for God?" I said, "Oh, no!" I did want the healing and began thanking our Lord Jesus for both miracles. That night I woke up 7 or 8 times expecting pain. I think the shock of not having any pain woke me up. I kept thanking God all night long.

Sara talked a lot about forgiveness in her sermon. That is a big obstacle for us to overcome. It can be a block for us to not receive a healing, so I work on forgiving others every day. I don't want my pain to return, so I try not to think painful thoughts about others. That day will always stand out in my memories. It was one of my greatest experiences of all times.

The Little Chapel changed my life, and I want to ask all of you who are reading this book to keep Sara, and the others who help in the Chapel work, in your prayers. We need to all pray for each other. Sincere prayers from the heart can produce miracles.

Every day is a gift from God and how we spend our time makes the difference in our lives. I'm still driving a cab in Texas, and telling everyone about our wonderful Jesus and God. I tell them if they ever go to Scottsdale, Arizona, they must go see Sara and the Little Chapel. It will change their lives. It did mine.

The Smallest Challenge Can Be Our Biggest Blessing

Susan Goraj

*C*hicago, Illinois was where Susan was born and she moved to Phoenix, Arizona in 1989. She studied ballet from 5 years old until 19. Susan began her musical career at age 24. Jerry and Susan have been married for over 24 years and have three sons, Michael, Jeremy, and Joshua. Julia is their youngest. Susan met Jerry when he joined the band in 1984 and they performed together until 1989.

It was her son, Michael, who first convinced her to go to The Little Chapel. Carol and Jim Hebets kept encouraging her to attend and finally brought her to the Little Chapel and she is so grateful for many reasons. She tries to never miss a service for she feels she learns so much from listening to the sermons, and then witnessing the healings that occur.

Like plants that need sunshine and nutrients to flourish, she feels she replenishes her mind, body and spirit when she comes to The Little Chapel. It is such a joy to watch Susan strive for a deeper spiritual understanding about situations in life. God continues to nudge her in the direction of her highest good.

For the past twenty years my work has required me to carry heavy banquet trays. About two years ago, I began to feel the repercussions in my lower right thumb joint and palm. It progressively got worse to the point that when I spent a night working, the pain flared up for days and I couldn't put any pressure on it at all. This affected my job and I found myself twisting my hand off the arthritic side every time I had to carry a tray, which brought on a different pain in my wrist — not good.

I was abundantly blessed the first time I attended The Little Chapel. It was the Easter service on Tuesday evening, April 21, 2009. I came not expecting a healing, and not because I didn't think I was worthy or that I didn't believe in this sort of thing, it's just that I didn't think, period!

The wonderful healings began after Sara spoke and I was so interested in all the blessings that were happening that evening. I was praising and thanking God for His great love for each of us. When I heard Sara say a hand was being healed, my hand shot up in a heartbeat! I just knew deep in my soul it was meant for me.

Sara walked right up to me and asked me to tell everyone about it. I was happy to share my story and I began to point to the spot, but when I touched it, the pain was gone! I wiggled and prodded and pressed and banged on my thumb and nothing. It was out of there. I began to cry and cry and couldn't stop. Receiving this healing meant so much to me. It may seem like such a small healing, but to me it was big. It affected my work and that affected my family, so my little thumb was a big problem for all of us.

Many times I feel the pain of bone on bone in my thumb, and instantly I thank God for my healing. The pain goes away as fast as it comes when I release it all to God. I thank Jesus for being our perfect example of unconditional love.

The smallest challenge can lead us to bigger and greater things for our lives. Whatever brings us to a closer relationship with God is worth it. The Little Chapel has touched my whole family in such a profound way. I thank my little thumb for the pain it gave me because that challenge became my greatest blessing.

Learning to Trust God with My Life

Taryn Gosch

aryn was born in Fairfax County, Virginia and lived all of her young life on the East coast. When her grandfather, Bob Sigholtz, married Sara O'Meara they moved to California, where Sara resided and started a new life. Sara was delighted to inherit a daughter.

Later, Taryn and my daughter, Dionne, followed Sara's son Chuck to ASU, and became little sisters to his fraternity.

Taryn married Karl Gosch in January 1995 and they have a daughter, Sara Catherine, named after Sara. Taryn and Karl are active in The Little Chapel. Karl is an usher and Taryn sends out the tapes of the services to those who request them. They have learned that God is always willing to help us through our challenges. We all have them but it is our attitude about them and how we handle our situations that make the difference in our lives.

Obstacles are given to us for our spiritual growth. God can take every problem, every wrong choice that we make and turn it into a beautiful blessing if we look to Him. It is always our choice; He never forces His love and guidance.

> My journey thus far has been one of many hurdles, but I realize now as I grow older we must embrace the journey, search for the daily miracles and be thankful for God's unconditional love for each of us.

My parents were divorced when I was 8 years old and my sweet mother raised me. When I was 12 years old, I lost my mother to cancer that devastated me beyond belief. As I reflect back on my life at that time, I realize how much I've grown spiritually. If I had known God on a more intimate, deeper level, my journey perhaps would have taken such a different path. I don't regret what I've been through because every experience has taught me a great deal, and I feel better equipped in so many ways to help others on their path.

After my mother died, my grandfather adopted me. My father had remarried and had a new family, and did not want me. My grandfather provided all the things parents should for a child, a loving home, clothes, food and a good education.

My grandfather, Papa Bob, married Sara O'Meara during my last year of high school. I not only was blessed with a wonderful new mother, but two fabulous brothers, John and Chuck, and an exceptional extended family, the Feddersons. Life would never be the same!

To express what Sara has brought into my life would be difficult because she has brought so much it would fill the entire book. She is the reason I know God the way I do and I will be forever grateful for that gift. Sara, my grandfather, and God have made me what I am today. All I want to do is serve God the best I can.

My healing was one of the mind, body and spirit. It actually happened in The Little Chapel in California. I was sitting in one of Sara's services and I was really praying hard for my spirit to be healed. I was in a bad place of sadness and despair, not knowing which direction to go in my life.

I wanted to be in the center of God's will for my life, and I felt I wasn't there yet. A wave of heat engulfed my body and I began to shake and cry uncontrollably. There was no question God's hand was upon me and I was engulfed with His love. I was so overwhelmed with joy, and I raised my hand to acknowledge the healing. Sara looked my way and saw God's light going through me, and told me to hold on to the healing. This truly changed my life and I began a whole new relationship with God. My main goal for my life now is to stay on the highest spiritual path I possibly can.

I am married to a kind, spiritual man, and we have been blessed with an amazingly spiritual daughter who loves God and is so aware of Him at such a young age. I continue to feel blessed with a wonderful and supportive family.

I have so much love for all the hurting and broken people that find their way to The Little Chapel by God's gentle guiding. I have witnessed many of God's healing miracles, one after the other, using Sara as His faithful and obedient servant. Anyone who enters The Little Chapel is touched in a way, whether it is physical or emotional, and really are never the same again. My prayer for each of you fortunate enough to be led to read this very special book is that you will be touched in a way that will change your life for the better.

I pray you will trust God with your life. Sometimes we question certain challenges we have to go through, but I have learned that if we hang on and stay faithful to God, His ways are always better for us than we could ever plan for ourselves.

Walking Freely with No Pain

Gerald Gruver

erald Gruver was first introduced to The Little Chapel by his lovely friend, Hope Riveron. One day, Hope told Gerald that she had dislocated her shoulder a while back, and the doctors told her she must have an operation. She told the doctors that she didn't want people operating on her. "There is a better way to handle this than going through surgery and having all that extra suffering," she said. Hope went to The Little Chapel and she received a progressive healing. Each day her shoulder got a little better.

Gerald and Hope met at a New Year's Eve party that he gave in his home, and they have been the best of friends ever since. Gerald and Hope were married on April 16, 2004.

I worked with a partner in the antique and decorating business in Boston and Cape Cod for about thirty years. We also went on the road and displayed our wares at about fifty antique shows a year, traveling as far as Virginia Beach, Virginia.

It was not an easy life being on the road all the time plus running an open shop twelve hours a day. All the tension and frustration over the years just about did me in. After spending several weeks in the hospital and a fortune on medications, I decided it was time to try something different.

My partner retired in 1984, and we sold the business and I moved to San Francisco, California. After a couple of years I took a job with *Bank of America*® in the credit card department. Although the salary was much less, I did not have all the tension and pressure I had been under in the past. Eight years later my department was transferred to Phoenix, Arizona.

On New Year's Eve of 1999, a friend brought a guest to my party and introduced me to Hope Riveron. We seemed to click right away and have been together ever since.

I had been suffering with rheumatoid arthritis for the past 15 years, and in spite of all the operations and medications it took 30-45 minutes in a hot shower every morning to get my stiff joints moving. The pain in my lower back and right hip was so severe I could not stand up straight and walking was difficult. I used a cane, walker and wheelchair to get around most of the time.

When Hope realized how much I was suffering, she told me about The Little Chapel and asked me to come to a service with her. I said, "yes" and that Sunday, September 16, 2001 will remain an outstanding memory in my heart and mind for the rest of my life.

As I walked through the doors of The Little Chapel, I felt I was walking into the home of an old friend. It gave me a warm feeling, like when you meet someone you haven't seen for a long time, and then you have fellowship together. It was such a peaceful feeling, and I thank God for it.

After Sara spoke, the healings began. She was calling out healings and I was fascinated by it all. She said, "There are two people here today who have rheumatoid arthritis, and one of them is suffering with a lot of pain in their back." Thank God I knew that was me right off the bat. I'd been suffering long enough and it was time to get rid of it. So, I just shot my hand right up in the air, and she saw it. She went to someone else first, and I was glad because it gave me a little time to do some recuperating.

When Sara came to me she said, "You're the one who has a lot of pain in your back." I said, "yes" and stood up. She walked over to me and I felt a very warm sensation on top of my head, and it traveled down my spine and into my hips. The pain I came in with just seemed to melt away. I said to Sara, "Oh thank God, it feels so good to stand up straight without pain."

After the service, Ralna English, from the *Lawrence Welk Show*, came over to me and gave me a big hug. She said, "You received a wonderful blessing today. Don't let anyone take it away from you."

The next day I was back to work and several of my co-workers noticed a big change in me. I told them about the wonderful healing I had over the weekend and they were so happy for me. In the middle of the week I had an appointment with my rheumatologist, and he was amazed. I told him there was only one answer for it. God had touched my body and healed it. He said he believed in that, and I said, "I'm glad to hear that because most doctors don't."

I had been going to doctors and taking prescription drugs for so many years. It's good that there are doctors to let us know what our ailments are, but it is better to know the Great Physician who can heal our infirmities when no one else can. I am so thankful to my Heavenly Father for what He has done for me.

Thanks to God and Sara, I walk freely without pain. I still get a little twinge once in a while just to remind me how it used to be. It keeps me humble and appreciative to God. I am much stronger in my faith now and I am thankful for each new day He gives me.

Having Faith the Size of a Mustard Seed Brings Us Miracles

Diane Harris

Diane was born in London, England, to an Orthodox Jewish family. Even though she would go to Temple, she had a fascination about Jesus. From a very early age, she would watch all the Easter movies and cry like a baby when Jesus was crucified. She would ask her family over and over again, 'What's this all about? Can you give me any answers?' Her questions were never really responded to.

When she got old enough at school, she took New Testament Religious Knowledge class. She learned about Jesus, and oh boy, did He win her over. From the time she was nine years old, she took Jesus in her heart and believed and accepted Him as the Son of God.

In March 2002, I was sitting in The Little Chapel enjoying every minute of the sermon. Since I was a young adult, I had suffered with extremely bad migraines. Those of you who have had a migraine know how sick they can make you feel.

I loved it when the healings began, and people were so thrilled and happy when Jesus, through Sara, touched them and blessed them in a profound way. Sara came over to me and told me she saw a bright, beautiful light behind me. I knew that through the love of Jesus and the faith that I had, I was healed. It was a true miracle, and I haven't had a migraine since.

Jesus healed me, and I'm Jewish. He doesn't care what you are if you believe. From Judaism came Christianity. We're all the same; we are all God's children. I'm a Jew and I found Jesus. It is not as rare as it used to be. It doesn't really matter what race, religion or creed you are. Jesus really loves all of us. I want to share with everyone and anyone who will listen what God has done for me. I want to never fail to help others. God helps us, and we should always help each other. If you have faith, you too can have a healing. Jesus said, "all we need is to have faith the size of a mustard seed."

The Choice is Always Ours

Tami Harris

*B*orn in East Chicago, Indiana, Tami received her degree in Nursing at Purdue University. She has one son, Dan Wheeler, and daughter-in-law, Paige, and 2 wonderful grandchildren. She was married for 30 years and lost her husband 3 days after Dan and Paige were married.

She married Avery Harris on September 9, 2000. She retired after 40 years as a Nurse and now enjoys volunteering for the Scottsdale Police Department and is very active in her church. She currently is the Director of the *Scottsdale Rose Garden* and loves to travel the world. She adores The Little Chapel and glows with excitement when she talks about her healing experience.

She is proud to be an ambassador for God and wants to help others to realize how good and loving He is.

"Sometimes things change and we wonder why. Many times things change because God wants us to be somewhere else at that particular time. That happened to me the night I received my healing.

The Little Chapel is closed every June, July and August and begins again in September. I had looked forward to attending the first service for the year. Usually the services are on Sunday morning with the exception of the Christmas one. This September was going to be in the evening and my daughter-in-law phoned and asked me to baby sit that very night. I love to spend time with my granddaughter, so of course, I said, "yes." A couple of days before the service, my daughter-in-law called and said something came up and I didn't have to baby sit after all. I was free to attend the service at the Chapel.

It was my first time to attend, so I didn't know what to expect. My husband and I arrived an hour early because I was told it would be crowded. Everyone was very friendly so we felt welcomed. I enjoyed the music and the sermon and then the healings began. Sara named several healings and then she said someone had a very complicated back problem and was in constant pain.

I'm looking around the room and my husband nudges me, "I think it's you," he said. He was praying hard that it was me. He hated to see me in constant pain from scoliosis, which I had been born with. Over the years I had tried several different medicines and gone through a lot of therapies. I had rehab physical occupations, chiropractic acupuncture and many more. Nothing relieved me from my pain.

As Sara came to our row she stopped and looked at me and motioned for me to stand up and step out in the aisle. I made it to the aisle and then she told me to walk back to the door where we entered the chapel. She said by the time I would walk to the door and back I would be healed of all my pain. I thought I might as well try it because nothing else had worked and I really needed a miracle. I slowly inched my way down the aisle to the door and turned around. As I started walking back to the front of the chapel, I began to ask myself, "Where is the pain?" I always had pain, but I couldn't feel any pain whatsoever. By the time I reached Sara, the tears were streaming down my cheeks.

That was the first time in my life I was pain free. I'm deeply grateful for the wonderful healing. I'm also grateful for the pain I had to endure all those years because the pain brought me to The Little Chapel and a closer walk with Him.

The Little Chapel is blessed to have Sara who allows the Holy Spirit to heal through her. From the moment you enter the door of the chapel you feel the presence of God and the healing angels. As we allow ourselves to let go and trust God miracles can and do occur. His love is our greatest blessing and is always available for us through every experience in life if we are open to accept it. The choice is always ours.

I Am So Grateful to be Healthy, Happy, Whole and Humming

Linda Harrisong

*L*inda was born in Iola, Kansas and raised in Coffeyville, Kansas. Her family was very active in this little town, and church was an important part of their lives.

In 1994 Linda and her immediate family moved to Arizona. She is very proud of her adult children and the grandchildren are the light of her life.

She is a friend of a mutual friend, Victoria Liljenquist, who brought her to The Little Chapel. Coming to the Chapel has given her such joy and inner peace like she has never experienced before. Jesus showed by example that perfect love brings perfect joy.

"My friend, Victoria, kept urging me to go to a Little Chapel service and I am so grateful she did. I will always have a special place in my heart for her because The Little Chapel has opened my eyes to the beautiful truth that sets us free. The atmosphere in the room is truly Divine love, Divine harmony which is a haven for God to lift us up to a higher vibration where healings can and do occur. I realize how powerful God's love is, and I am working on having a greater capacity to love myself and others. One of the bonuses about loving yourself is that you get to feel good.

After the service in December 2009, I felt a full body renewal from the top of my head to the bottom of my feet. I had a cyst on my lower back from a childhood injury and the pain was completely taken away. My lungs cleared up and I could breathe freely. The energy was so fantastic in the room I never wanted to leave. I felt like a different person and I continue to feel great. I had been healed of every ailment.

How fortunate we are to have The Little Chapel in Arizona and Sara as our teacher and a conduit for His healing. Every morning I thank God for my many blessings and say, "I am so grateful to be healthy, happy, whole and humming."

Each Experience is a Tool to Grow By

Ron Head

*R*on was born and raised in San Mateo, California. He is the father of two fine boys—Ryan and David. He grew up in the sixties, which was quite a challenge, but he gives God the credit for helping him through those rough years. He loves all sports especially golf, tennis and swimming. He is a wonderful artist.

Over twenty years ago, he moved to Phoenix, Arizona and never plans to leave. Ron started attending the services in The Little Chapel over eleven years ago. He has had so many healings and blessings over the years and feels he was a completely different person before coming to the chapel. He has learned so much through the sermons. He now knows how vital it is to handle things with love. When his son, David, phoned and shared his problems, Ron was able to answer his son in a kind and loving way.

Ron believes God prepared his heart to be able to handle this situation correctly. Before coming to The Little Chapel he would not have asked his son, "What can I do to help?" Through this experience Ron and David have become closer and they have truly learned that God is our help in every need.

Mother Teresa once said, "It is not the magnitude of our actions but the amount of love that is put into them that matters." When we are a channel of love and light, great things do happen.

" I am honored to share my testimony because my heart desires to tell everyone about how great God is. He continues to bless me and when I attend a service in The Little Chapel I see God touching the lives that are there. Everyone prays for each other and the atmosphere is positive and loving. To see God's love in action is awesome.

A large part of the blessings I have received from The Little Chapel have been through the wonderful people who attend, especially Sara and Yvonne. As you walk through the doors of The Little Chapel you feel a holy presence. I have been coming to the chapel for years to hear the profound messages and I feel the healings are a bonus for me. God has healed my physical body many times and my contact with the Holy Spirit has improved so much that I feel this is by far the greatest healing I have had. Sara's messages and prayers have helped me so much in my walk with God. It is almost unbelievable.

There is always something going on in my life that requires prayer. Whether I'm concerned with finance or romance, social standing or health issues, nothing works without God. If my walk with God is strong I enjoy life and I enjoy the challenges that come with it When I listen for God's plans and approach life with compassion for others life has a wonderful meaning for me. I believe that whether I have cancer or have just won the lottery, my purpose in life is to know God and His will for me. Sometimes God gets my attention with a situation that I find miserable until I remember His presence and guidance in my life. With the knowing that God is with me I can continue to move down my life's path. The Little Chapel helps me remember that a loving God is always with me.

The first physical healing I had at The Little Chapel was a few years ago when I had been suffering with tendonitis for several months and having no improvement. During the healing portion of the service, Sara walked down the aisle of the church and stopped by me and laid her hands on my arm. An immediate warmth spread up my arm and by the next day my arm was almost completely pain free. Every day it kept improving and every day I kept thanking God for his healing love. There is no pain now.

One night before The Little Chapel service, I had a flare up of my Crohn's disease and I phoned Sara for some extra prayers. As she began to pray for me, I felt a peace surround me. By the time The Little Chapel services started the next day I was feeling much better, and everyday I continue to improve. There was a progressive healing for which I am very grateful. I learned how to depend on God more each day.

My favorite healing was not for me but for my son, David. A few years ago David got into some trouble with drugs and the law. He had been arrested for possession and dealing in the selling of marijuana and was facing ten years in a state prison. We had an attorney, been to court where he pleaded not guilty and were waiting for the next court date. I asked Sara to say some of her special prayers for David and also asked my many prayerful friends. I was most concerned for my son and the path he had chosen for himself. An intelligent and gentle young man was destroying his life with the choices he was making. However, Sara told me, "God will see David through this. The outcome will not be what you think. Watch God at work here."

Prayers do work. David started making some wise choices. He re-enrolled at Arizona State University (ASU). He also began attending AA meetings. He started to talk about God and soon he was invited to go on a Men's Spiritual Retreat for a weekend. When he returned he came to me and said he wanted to change his plea to guilty on the drug charges. He had been moved by God during the weekend retreat to acknowledge his wrongdoing and wanted to throw himself at the mercy of the court and God's protection.

David then told his attorney what he wanted to do and the attorney thought he had a good chance of getting out of the charges and recommend he not change his plea. Against his attorney's advice and with trepidation, David faced the judge as he spoke from his heart and told him the truth. He said he had done some wrong and didn't want to waste the state's money on the court anymore, so he was changing his plea to guilty and waiving all his rights.

The judge was so impressed with David's honesty that he gave him two years probation and no jail time, and the assurance he would clear his record if he continued to turn his life around. The judge had been on the bench for over twenty years and only three other people had ever pled guilty before him.

Yes, when we listen to God's guidance and do what is right, God will help us through our challenges. He sees our hearts and knows if we are sincere. He doesn't promise that getting back on the right path for our life is always easy, but He does promise to hold our hand and help us every step of the way if we let Him.

David has continued to change his life. He has graduated from ASU and is now attending grad school. He is active in AA and his story and his commitment have helped several other young men change their lives. He is happy and continues to trust God. When we look to God our choices change and our lives improve.

God is a great teacher. Here in this school of life I am working on my thoughts and actions daily. As I grow spiritually my health improves. My life has struggles, but I know each problem has a solution. Obstacles are really a gift for us to learn something. When we learn the lesson the obstacles are removed and we are free to move on to other things. Every day I pray to be a better student and a better example for others to follow.

God wants us to love Him, love ourselves and others, and then we will be truly happy. That's what we are taught in The Little Chapel: A heart filled with love has no limitations.

Listening to God Has Made My Heart Happy

Nadine Healy

Those who receive a healing in The Little Chapel are thrilled beyond words. When they are asked to give a testimony, so often they are afraid to get in front of the microphone and tell everyone about their outstanding experience. Part of the healing process is to give glory to Him, and they are missing the boat when they don't. Nadine Healy is always very happy to tell everyone about the miracles in her life.

I am a "snowbird" and spend the cold winter months in the Arizona desert. I spend the other months in Minneapolis, or in my home on the lake in Wisconsin.

In the summer of 1999, while enjoying my home on the lake, I was diagnosed with pneumonia. I've never been "*sick*" sick. I've had things wrong with me, but never had to go from the bed to the couch to the chair all day and every day. I couldn't seem to get better.

My ex-husband, John, came up to help me. The neighbor told him they could hear me coughing all night. John said, "While I am here, I'm going to sell your house." I said "Good" and told him the neighbor next door had expressed an interest, but I was too sick to follow through. After I told him what I wanted for it, he walked across the yard to my neighbor's and soon came back with a counter-offer. We went back and forth and finally my first miracle happened—my neighbor bought my house.

I had been on 7 different antibiotics and it was time to go back to Arizona. I thought I'd spend a week resting in Vail first. I was exhausted when I reached the condo and couldn't even go out and get food until the next day. It was cold, and snow was on the ground. I said, "I'm outta here!" I had paid for a week and stayed only two nights.

I couldn't wait to get to Arizona and to the first Chapel service. It's funny how your prayers go from lovingly saying things to God to begging. I got to the Chapel and tried not to cough too much during the service. When the healings began, Sara looked at me and remarked that she saw the light of God upon me. I coughed my last cough. The cure was instant. I just immediately felt better. The next day I listened to my body and rested most of the time. By Tuesday, I was back to feeling like my old self. Miracle #2!

I always receive great blessings when I attend a service in The Little Chapel, but another healing didn't occur until about three years later. For about a year, my shoulder gave me great pain, and for about 6 months, my right knee hurt so badly, I thought I might have to have knee surgery.

Sitting in the Little Chapel one bright and sunny morning, I asked God to heal my shoulder and knee. It was like a spray of energy that shot out from Sara and went to me and to several others who were sitting around me. We all felt the power, and I knew instantly I had received two more miracles.

My promise to God is to always follow His lead. Instead of me making all the decisions for my life alone, I try to be still every day for a period of time, to listen to God. His direction for my life is always better. I've always gone to church and believed in God, but now I know God in a real way, deep in my heart.

I only wish we could have a Little Chapel everywhere to reach more people. The feeling of God's love is so strong there. People need to experience that, and to learn God's truth through Sara. She teaches us how to live a more Christ-like life. She puts it out there, and the choice is ours. I've made my choice and my heart is happy.

"Reporting for Duty" Everyday with Open Hearts for His Guidance

Carol and Jim Hebets

Carol and Jim Hebets are dear friends of both Sara's and mine. In fact, we consider them our extended family. Their hearts only want to do what is right, and what is God's way. They have raised five children and are now enjoying six adorable grandchildren. They all reside in Arizona.

Most couples go through difficult times, but in many cases your marriage can be even better after the storm blows over. Carol and Jim are a strong couple who have a tremendous mission ahead. God took advantage of their personal problems to get their attention. When they got on their knees about their marriage, God lifted them both up to a higher way of thinking and living.

Every morning they thank God for their new life and they say they are, "reporting for duty" and are willing to do whatever God asks them to do.

We would suspect that most of us in our marriages, even those of us who have wonderfully healthy marriages, have moments of crisis, moments of fear, or doubt or anxiousness; moments of a lack of trust in ourselves and our spouses, moments when we blame, moments when we attack, moments when we lose our self-esteem, or never had self-esteem.

We had gone through it all. God had to throw a brick in our lives before we woke up to the fact that we needed Him to take charge. We were making a mess of things. Both of us kept blaming each other instead of trusting each other. We were separated for 8 weeks and it looked pretty grim for us to ever get back together.

I, Carol, came to The Little Chapel first. Sara received an interesting message for me that day, and it was very, *very* revealing to me. I thought Jim and I were through, and would be going our separate ways. The message made me stop and rethink everything. It opened the door a crack that there may be hope for our marriage.

At the same time, I, Jim, was blessed to have two dear friends, John Lang and John Politan, take me on as their personal challenge. They invited me to participate in a biblical portrait of a marriage. I realized many things, especially how important it was to love my wife unconditionally. As I examined the story of our lives, I had to honestly admit to myself that I had failed over and over again in giving my wife the single thing that she cherished the most, and that was my love, absent any conditions. And you know what the trouble was? My humanness, my weakness, my own insecurities, prevented me from being that kind of a loving husband.

After Carol got her message from the Holy Spirit through Sara at The Little Chapel, and I started meeting with my two friends, we decided to see each other over Thanksgiving. We still had old challenges and began bickering back and forth. I begged God to find a way for me to let her know that I did now, and would forever more, love her unconditionally. The sacrifice God asked me to make was to show up in our church on a weekday morning, and I literally had to humble myself and lay prostrate on the floor and surrender my life to God. This was a Catholic church with a grammar school next door, so the kids were flowing in and out.

Those husbands, wives and children who knew our family saw me lying on the ground, and I had to keep asking God to provide the courage that I lacked. I was humiliated, but I knew in my heart the only way that would work for me was if I could surrender my ego in such a supreme way as to lie there prostrate on the ground asking Him to take control of me for ever more. I was scared, humbled and humiliated, but I was also filled with courage, love, grace and faith that only God could provide.

I knew He wanted us to live a holy and Christian life together, and to raise our children that way. We both knew God was with us, and wanting us to work out our problems. We began living together again, and John Lang and John Politan met with us for 4 ½ months every Monday night. We learned through these classes of four people, that if we didn't have the answers, God did.

We went to the Christmas Little Chapel service, and Sara had a wonderful message for us. We were to open our hearts because God had a mission for us to accomplish together. She said we must trust. We both began to question, but then we remembered a service when Sara said, "When you are given a miracle or another chance, hang on to it. If you say it's not going to work, or it didn't happen to me, you let it go." The light of God was over us as she spoke to us, and in our hearts we felt the words she said were true. One by one, as the weeks followed, miracle after miracle began to occur. Not only did our marriage heal, but also other miracles began to happen.

I, Jim, had unrelenting pain in my back for about three months. Even though I was in a lot of pain, I was determined to attend the next Chapel service. The Chapel was full by the time we arrived, so we had to sit on the steps of the stage. There we sat on the ground and in a strange, awkward position to see Sara. My back was killing me all through the service, until the healings began. Sara looked down at me and asked if my back was bothering me, and I said, "Yes." She said the Holy Spirit was all around me, and instantly, and only by the grace of God, I was healed. The pain has never returned.

Even more profound was a healing I received on my tooth. Sara and Yvonne, Carol and I were to fly to California and go to the Childhelp® Village in Beaumont. I bit down on something hard on a tooth that had a small crack in it, and completely fractured it. For an hour, the pain wouldn't go away. I took no medicine, and decided we should phone the ladies and pass on our regrets that we wouldn't be able to go the next day.

Sara answered the phone and said, "Let's pray." I had forgotten to look to God for the answer, and I guess He had intended for us to go, because all my pain left and never returned. She asked in her prayers for the pain to leave until I could get to a dentist, and it did immediately. Several days later, when I finally went to the dentist, he said it was virtually impossible that I never felt pain. The nerve was completely exposed.

Both Carol and I loved visiting the Childhelp® Village and seeing the children who had previously been abused and neglected now in a safe haven. We are now a part of the Childhelp® family, and proud to be in service for God's work in this way. Once you see their little faces, you are hooked.

One more miracle in our family and this time it was our son, Jamie. Jamie plays baseball and had broken his arm just before the playoffs for the school championships. The doctors said his arm would take six weeks to heal. He was extremely disappointed. Carol called Sara to pray with Jamie on the phone. Sara declared that he would play in the playoff regardless of what the doctors had said. He got a new X-ray made after praying, and the fracture was still there. One of the mornings, on the way to school, he told his mother, Carol, how upset he was, and angry with God for not answering his prayers. That evening, Jamie and I had a long talk about God, Jesus and how to pray and how to stay positive and accept God's answer to our prayers. Be thankful and grateful to God for all that we have and trust Him for our future wants and needs. Sometimes we have to step out on faith.

The doctor removed Jamie's cast, and told him he shouldn't play baseball for six more weeks. He asked his mom to take him to see another doctor, and he told him the same thing. When the finals came in 2 ½ weeks, Jamie decided to step out on faith and play. His team won, and his arm did not hurt.

We are truly a grateful family for all the miracles God has bestowed upon us. We wake up every morning and thank God we have the privilege of opening our hearts for His guidance and showing up for duty to do His work. Out of every problem or obstacle there can be a beautiful ending. We are living proof. God changed our entire family through the teachings and healings that we have witnessed in The Little Chapel.

Thanking God for the Privilege of Helping Others

J.R. Hebets

*Y*ou just read the testimony of Jim and Carol Hebets. J.R. is Jim Hebets' nephew. J.R.'s father was Jim's younger brother who died when J.R. was only 3½ years old. Jim has always been like a second father to him. Jim and Carol took Sara and me and our children on a cruise to the coast of Italy this past summer. They brought their son, Jamie, and their nephew, J.R. along also. It was a private yacht, so we were together all of the time. It was our joy getting to know these young men. They are both such good souls, and always looking for ways to help others.

J.R. helped a friend, Amy Sharp, to receive a healing through Sara. He has also opened the door for many others. He has learned at a young age how great God is, and loves to share this knowledge with anyone who is searching and seeking to find answers about life. What a beautiful soul!

J.R. is a student in Biola University in Irvine, California. He will soon be a Youth Minister.

I remember the first time I went to The Little Chapel in Arizona. I live in California, and was with Amy in San Diego when she received a healing over the phone. I hadn't met Sara in person yet, so it was my big day. I needed a healing this time.

I am a personal trainer, and I do a lot of activities. When I train my clients, I push them to the limit. I climb the stairs with them, run across the whole gym and do whatever I ask them to do.

I got a minor fracture on my shin, and as I sat in the Chapel that Sunday, I asked God to heal it. I was sitting right under the air conditioner where all the cool air was coming in, and yet I was burning up. It felt the same way when Amy was getting her healing. It didn't sink in that I got a healing until I got up to leave and my shin was not hurting. One minute it was hurting and the next minute it was fine. WOW!

After the service, Sara prayed with me about getting closer to God. I liked to party too much and I wanted to be a good example for my cousin, Jamie. Her prayers made me feel incredible. The stress lifted, and I felt a hundred times better. Ever since that day, my life has been better and better and better.

During our outstanding trip to Italy, I received another blessing from God. Jamie and I were on a Seadoo® and I hit a big wave that made me fly up in the air. As I landed, my chest hit the steering wheel and I smacked my chin real hard. I thought I just bruised my chin, but as I got off the Seadoo® and back on to the boat, I saw that my chin was bleeding. My first thought was I would have to go see a doctor and get stitches in my chin because it was a pretty deep cut.

It was time for lunch and my jaw began to really hurt. My jaw hurt so much that my Aunt Kathy encouraged me to ask Sara to pray for me. That night, Sara did pray for my chin and jaw and when I removed the bandage, the cut had stopped bleeding and was no longer an open wound. The jaw felt fine and I was able to eat dinner with no problem. I received another healing. Nothing hurt after that. This was truly an awesome trip.

When I returned home to California, I learned about a friend who was having a hard time about life and God. He used to teach Bible study, but when several friends died suddenly, he began questioning things. He was a tough Marine, but this all made him crumble.

He had broken his knees, so one day at the beach when everyone around us was surfing and he couldn't, I told him about Sara. He said he didn't know about all this. I knew I would have to push him into contacting her. I took him up to the beach house where Carol and Jim Hebets (my aunt and uncle) were staying, and asked Carol to call Sara. I stayed in the room with him as Sara began praying over the phone. That same familiar feeling came into the room, and he was totally healed. He was able to jump up and run outside. Nothing hurt after that, and still to this day he feels wonderful.

I'm open for God to use me anytime and anywhere. I give thanks for the privilege of helping others. It is a gift from God and gives my life a new meaning.

Putting God in the Pilot's Chair

Mary Hoffman

Sara was asked to speak in the Renaissance Unity Church in Warner, Michigan. Marianne Williamson speaks quite often in the church, and when she made the announcement about Sara speaking, she encouraged everyone to come. Marianne is a friend of Sara and me. When Marianne highly endorses someone, people listen. Mary Hoffman felt in her heart it was important for her to attend the service.

Mary had been in a relationship that was not a healthy, positive one and she needed prayers around the circumstance. She was meditating about it before the service, and felt a great release on a deep soul level. When Mary heard Sara speak, it helped her to accept her healing completely. She realized what a hold fear had on her. When we allow God's truth and love in our hearts all fear dissolves.

I'm a student of *A Course in Miracles* and I love and respect how it has touched and changed Marianne Williamson's life, as it has mine. I truly trust her judgment about people. When Marianne told how she admired Sara and the healing work God does through her, I knew in my heart I couldn't miss her service.

I had been dealing with a poor relationship for months. I completely blamed him for everything. I felt it was due to his ignorance, unkindness and sickness that we were having problems. All I could see were his huge faults.

One morning before the service, during my time of prayer and meditation, I was suddenly enlightened to the fact that I was equally or more responsible for these problems, misunderstandings, and the deep unhappiness we were experiencing. I realized I also had some issues to work on for us to have a healthy relationship.

At the service where Sara spoke, I felt the Holy Spirit giving me lots of love and relief. I felt my sanity coming back because I realized that I had been blaming everyone but myself. I had allowed fear to dominate me for many months.

I promised God, as I sat in the church that day, that I would work on being positive and let go of the fear in my heart. I also promised to put God first in my life. Sara said, "Don't let anyone take your healing away from you." These words were so helpful to me. I'm determined to keep my healing, and thank God daily for hearing my prayers and helping me to turn my life around.

I was stuck in the lower emotions of everything negative and the "poor me" mentality. Sara helped me accept a higher level of thinking and living. I'm in a wonderful life-changing group now, and all my relationships have greatly improved. I finally placed God in the pilot's chair.

We Got Our Miracle

John Hopkins

ohn is Sara O'Meara's son and I had the privilege of being at the hospital when he was born. I am his proud Godmother and John has always been like a son to me. He is a gentle, loving soul and his essence is pure. John has two children, Ashleigh and John Charles. He is happily married to Celeste and they all live in Scottsdale, Arizona.

John is an usher at the Chapel services and has witnessed many outstanding miracles over the years. He knew to call on God immediately when he had his accident. When we look to God and put our trust in Him, all things are possible.

" It was an ordinary Sunday afternoon at the Hopkins house. The children were watching cartoons, and I was working on my weekend projects. I had been trimming the olive tree in the front lawn for two weekends in a row. One more branch to go. I called for my wife to help hold the rope, and I began to saw the branch. In an instant I went from the top of the 12 foot high ladder to a loud "thud!" on the ground. I landed in a fetal position on the gravel, a few inches away from a concrete half wall.

My wife ran inside to call 911, not letting on to the children what had just happened. She came back outside with the cordless phone to try to communicate with the emergency operator what my symptoms were. By the time she reached me, I was sitting up and was holding and rubbing my left shoulder, complaining that it ached. Not more than two minutes went by before I heard the sirens coming and then the paramedics arrived.

They sat me up on the half wall and took my vitals. By this time, the children had heard the commotion and were outside asking what was wrong. We told them I was hurt and the paramedics were here to help me. A paramedic told me they would have to immobilize me (much like a car accident victim) to take me to the hospital for x-rays. A friend watched the children, and off we went to the ER.

As usual, the ER was busy and took down all my information. About 30 minutes went by, and then it was my turn for the x-ray. A few minutes after the x-ray, the nurse and the doctor raced into the room to announce that my C-4 vertebrae had been broken, and they would have to transport me via ambulance to the trauma hospital 20-30 minutes away.

My wife phoned my mother to tell her what had happened. She was in Aspen, where she goes twice a year specifically to write The Little Chapel services. She immediately acknowledged how proud she was of our faith, and knew God held me in the palm of His hands. She said she would catch the next plane back to Phoenix, but to trust God all will be well.

Upon arriving at the trauma hospital, they performed a CAT scan to confirm the break. Then a neurosurgeon came to describe what he thought were the best options. Option #1 was to have me wear a "halo", which is a metal ring placed around your head and screwed into your skull approximately 3 millimeters, to stop any mobility from the shoulders up. The doctor said I might have to wear it for up to six months.

Option #2 was to have surgery to fuse the broken vertebrae to the next vertebrae. Risky, but a few months of rehab would give me back 80% mobility. I joked with the doctor by saying, "I can't wear a halo. I'm in sales!"

The doctor said, "We'll have to perform an MRI to really see the extent of the damage to the spinal cord." Then he left. During our wait for the MRI, which was an unbelievable four hours, my head was burning up. It was bright red and beading sweat, while my feet were numb from being so cold. I put my socks on and wrapped my feet in several blankets. During this time is when God was performing His true miracle on me. We had everyone praying; my mother was now on a plane back from Aspen, and Godmother Yvonne was driving down to be with me from Flagstaff.

I believe that the four hours we were waiting for the MRI was God's work because the MRI room was literally two doors down from where we were standing in the ER. Every time I would ask a nurse about the status of the MRI, they would reply that they would call the MRI room and no one was there

But God knew what He was doing. Finally, the MRI technician came to wheel me down to the room. The MRI was performed and by now the time was 7 pm, which meant no more visitors because I was now being placed in the intensive care unit. My wife went in the elevator determined to find the doctor to get his diagnosis. She couldn't locate him, but she ran into Yvonne and Emma, who has been my mother's housekeeper for 40 years now and helped raise me and my brother Chuck. Then, all of a sudden, they saw the doctor walking past the other hallway. They asked the status of John Hopkins — the "broken neck" victim.

The doctor smiled and scratched his head (literally) and said, "I've never quite seen anything like this. The break was a horizontal line and it was clean, fell right back into place, no crushing of the bones. There is no edema (swelling). Frankly I think we can send him home in a couple of days with a neck brace."

All three of them smiled and Yvonne declared, "We've got our miracle!" Later, in my recovery room a nurse added, "You must have done something good in your life to escape this tragedy!" I did recover quickly and I've always given credit to God for His miracle. I had 100% faith that God would take care of me.

People with neck braces must have some kind of "bond" because during my recovery, when I would go out to a restaurant, they would ask, "What happened to you?" The most memorable was when a man in a wheelchair, who was a *paraplegic* asked me and I replied, "I broke my C-4. The man looked down and said, "So did I." A miracle indeed!

Even the Pain in One Little Finger Matters to God

Linda Jacobson

*L*inda came to Arizona thirty years ago. The sunshine felt good to her after living in Denver, Colorado a good part of her life. She has two children, Alana and Joseph, who are in college. Joseph is studying in Rio where Linda does a lot of business. She imports crystals from Brazil, and sells them here in America.

Linda has been fascinated for years with individuals who have been blessed with the gift of healing. She has read all Kathryn Kuhlman's books, seen her videos, and has studied everything she could about her. She never doubted God could heal anything.

We always like to hear about unusual and outstanding miracles. God delights in answering our prayers even for one of our little fingers. His joy is to have us pain free and healthy.

> The joint on my right middle finger was impaled by a cactus sticker over a year ago. It has been an interesting challenge in experiencing what one little finger can cause you to go through.

I came to The Little Chapel with a friend many years ago. I have strongly believed in miracles for years, and knew all about the wonderful gift Kathryn Kuhlman had. Sara had a healing of cancer through Kathryn, so I was excited to meet her and learn more about the healing work she was doing at the Little Chapel.

The Chapel is so beautiful and peaceful. The first time I attended, it felt so good to be in the presence of like-minded people. The energy and power in the room was heavenly. Her message was right on, and I was sorry when it ended. Then the healings began, and I could hardly contain myself. It was such a beautiful morning; I was on cloud nine all day.

I have received many healings, but I want to share with you one in particular. Sometimes we hesitate to bother God with minor irritations, but God is always willing to heal us if we ask.

One Sunday morning during her service, my finger was in such great pain, I asked God to heal it. I had surgery and had taken a lot of therapy, but nothing worked. The joint was locked stiff. I had not been able to touch my finger to my palm. As the healing began that Sunday, I made a fist and pushed my finger down to the palm. I felt a light 'pop' in the joint, and the pain was gone. Sara walked by where we were sitting and said she saw my finger in a capsule of golden white light. Extreme heat shot through my body and I couldn't stop crying.

The finger is small, but the miracle was great. It touched my heart so deeply to think God would be interested in healing such a minor problem. My promise to God was to never doubt, always ask and trust in the way He answers our prayers. His way is always the best. I want to be an example for others and be more Christ-like every day. I'm so grateful that I found Sara and The Little Chapel.

Trusting in God for a Healing

Gloria C. Javier

Gloria C. Javier was born and raised in Manila, Philippines. Coming from the Philippines, she was quite familiar with all kinds of methods of healing. Her daughter-in-law is also named Gloria, and she works in the Childhelp Corporate office in Scottsdale, Arizona.

Gloria C. had heard a lot about Childhelp and The Little Chapel from her daughter-in-law. She thought that the healing work being done through Sara in The Little Chapel sounded wonderful. It never entered her mind to ask for a healing for herself. It took her loving daughter-in-law, Gloria P., to open the door for her to go to The Little Chapel and receive a beautiful gift from God.

" I moved from the Philippines to Los Angeles, California in 1993. In the fall of 2002, I went to Arizona to visit my son and daughter-in-law and their wonderful family. I had been having severe pain in my neck for quite a while and finally couldn't turn my neck on either side. Gloria P. kept looking at me and finally asked what was wrong with my neck. When I told her how long I had been suffering she said, "I'm taking you to The Little Chapel." The service was in two weeks and I was scheduled to stay longer, so I was in luck.

We were both happy when Chapel day came around. I decided to not take any medication to relieve my neck pain before we left the house. I was going to trust God for a healing. We never said a word to each other until after the service. I told Gloria P. that when Sara was calling out healings for necks, I took it. Immediately the heat started from my neck down through my body. I thought it was just the Arizona weather at first.

When I returned to Los Angeles, I went to see my doctor. I told him my neck pain was gone and I was not taking any more medication. The doctor just smiled, and began to examine me. He was surprised, but happy to confirm my neck was fine.

When I flew to the Philippines a few months later to visit my family, I told them all about Sara and The Little Chapel. If any of them ever come to Arizona, I know they will want to attend a service. I am so grateful to God and thankful to Sara for my healing.

To Quote Winston Churchill – "Never, Never, Never, Give Up"

Judy Jensen

*J*udy was born in Phoenix, Arizona and raised in Parker, Arizona. She attended Arizona State University and in 1971, right after college, she moved to Honolulu, Hawaii. It was there that she met the handsome, talented singer Dick Jensen. They had two wonderful children. Their daughter, Summer is thirty-three and their son Brandon is now thirty.

While living in Hawaii, Judy spent a lot of time in the winter and summer months at her second home in Aspen, Colorado where she met Jean Trousdale. Sara stays with Jean in Aspen when she writes her sermons for The Little Chapel. Sara was asked to do some healing services in a church in Aspen while she was visiting Jean. Jean told Judy about the special service and Judy said she would love to attend. She enjoyed every word Sara spoke and saw how God was using Sara not only to preach the word but heal hearts and bodies. She couldn't believe all the wonderful healings that took place.

Judy never had the desire to live in Arizona again but God began to change her heart as her parents were getting older and having more medical problems. Hawaii was a 6½ hour flight to Arizona. She moved back to Arizona in October of 2000 and her parents passed away in 2003 and 2004. As we know, sometimes we cannot foresee the hand of God, but if we are faithful he will direct our paths.

Jean told Judy when she was going to move back to Arizona to be sure and attend The Little Chapel. From the first time she went to The Little Chapel she knew that this was where she could feel the presence of God. She attended The Little Chapel services on a regular basis until she moved to Los Angeles in 2011 where her children are now both living.

Judy works for Childhelp® and is such an asset to our organization. She has a positive attitude and all of our volunteers enjoy working with her.

> My deep desire is that my testimony will touch the hearts of all those who read this story and want a miracle.

I'm so grateful God sent Jesus into the world to remind us of His unconditional love and compassion. God's love and truth are the only things that permanently change hearts. It is that tender but powerful love that heals our minds and bodies.

I have lived in mansions and I've experienced not knowing where my next meal was coming from. I have been hurt deeply, and have also experience great love. Through my hills and valleys over the years, God has always held my hand. What a comfort to know that God is always with us, and will give us the guidance we need when we sincerely ask for His wisdom about our circumstances. He has always met my needs, and I know He always will as long as I look to Him. I have received many blessings, but now I want to share with all of you one of my physical healings.

I was helping to unload things from a truck to a room at The *Biltmore Hotel* where Childhelp® was having an event when I injured my left shoulder. I thought maybe I just strained it so I took some Advil® and I kept on working even though it was quite painful. My shoulder continued to hurt for months. Sometimes in the mornings I could not even lift my arm shoulder high without intense pain. I travel quite a lot for Childhelp®, and the pain got worse every time I put my luggage in the overhead bin. I finally decided to go to the doctor and find out what was wrong. I had an MRI and found out that I had a torn rotator cuff. The doctor suggested physical therapy, but said I would need surgery. He also said that I could take a cortisone shot but it would only be temporary. I declined. I'm left handed and it was my left shoulder that was injured so I couldn't imagine 6-8 weeks of not being able to use my arm and I didn't have time for surgery because it was such a busy time at work. I decided to wait and live with the aches and pains. I could not sleep through the night as every time I moved the wrong way the pain was so severe it would wake me up.

Then my special blessing came in The Little Chapel. I prefer to sit in the back of The Chapel because then I can see God working His miracles on the entire congregation. God's loving energy was so strong and many were being touched and healed that evening. Suddenly Sara called out a healing for a left shoulder. I knew in my heart that healing was for me and I took it. It didn't happen instantly but I knew that God was going to heal me and once again show me his love and power. It was a progressive healing. Each day it seemed to get better and better. One month later I woke up and the pain was completely gone. The surgery was no longer necessary. I was so excited I couldn't wait to tell everyone, especially Sara. This was a true miracle as the doctor had told me that a torn rotator cuff does not heal.

I know I have to be careful with my arm because I do have a weakness there. It is just like after you have pneumonia you have a weakness in your lungs. But I have no pain at all. To God be the Glory.

God wants to help us all have good, healthy bodies. He wants us to have our minds at peace at all times and above all to have faith. Miracles not only heal our bodies and hearts but also build our faith in God. When you know the unconditional love of God it is easy to love others.

Obstacles Give Us Our Greatest Opportunities for Spiritual Growth

Denise Johnston

enise Johnston is like another daughter in our family. She is such a loving and wonderful spirit, and has grown in her spirit through "soul surgery" like so many of us have. Sometimes we put ourselves through so much heartache because of the choices we make. But when we look to God, He helps us through our difficult times, and He knows these challenges can make us stronger. Obstacles provide our greatest opportunities for spiritual growth.

I have always worked hard and have the good fortune of being extremely successful in my career. My challenges have been in my personal life.

When I was in my mid-thirties, I met and fell in love with a man that I thought was my soul mate. We were so compatible and did everything together. We had so many fun times, and I thought they would never end. But the years began to tick away and he never wanted to think about marriage. I wanted to get married and start a family. It had been four years so we decided to spend some time apart, and do some deep soul searching. It was extremely painful for me. I wanted a commitment, but he didn't. You must both want it to make it work and work right.

After about 6 weeks of traveling to New York and Europe, I was back home in California. The Little Chapel service in Arizona was the next Sunday. I truly wanted to attend because my heart was broken, and I desperately needed prayers.

As I sat in the Chapel, I prayed so hard that we would get back together. As Sara began the healings she said there were two women who had broken hearts, and they were about relationships. She came to me first and said, "You have been trying so hard to let go, and God wants you to let go. He has something so much better for you right now. He knows how much you love this man and how dear this person is to your heart, but if you let go, He will bring so much more to your soul, to your life." I was happy to know good things were coming, but crushed that my romance was a big, "NO."

He tried to get back together with me but I knew deep within, it was only a matter of time and my heart would be broken again. My friends were terrific and very supportive. God keeps bringing me many blessings and I am so grateful. My lesson is to let go and let God bring him to me.

I also have had a couple of physical healings. One was my spine. I had whiplash and was unable to turn my neck in any direction. I was told at a Chapel service that I was receiving a progressive healing. The next day when I got out of bed I knew, without question, that I had a healing.

Through my healings of physical aches and pains, and heartaches, I have learned how much God loves us. He always wants the best for us, so why should we try to change it? I pray for more wisdom and enlightenment every day so I will make better choices for my life. I ask God to speak to my heart, and I made a promise that I will always listen.

God Gave Me Another Chance to Live and Complete My Mission

Ron Jones

on Jones was born in Centerville, Iowa and lived there until the age of eleven when his family moved to Southern California. He graduated in 1978 from the University of San Francisco. He and his lovely wife, Mary, have two children. Their son Stephen is married to Valerie and they have three children: Jacob, Alexis and Maya.

Ron and Mary have a daughter Valerie who is mentally challenged. In 1979 they all moved to Phoenix, Arizona because they could receive better benefits for her. They are very active in their church here in Arizona.

I am a walking testimony of the power of loving prayers. Two and half years ago I was in the Banner Desert ICU on life support and not expected to live. Obviously the doctors and nurses were wrong because I am still here.

Let me give you a little bit of history to put it in perspective. The story really starts about two and half years ago. I had a PET scan that revealed a few spots on my left lung. The doctor said, "No problem, I think it's just valley fever." Let's do a biopsy on one of the spots because it's easy to get to. It turned out to be cancerous. I had lung cancer. I was a heavy smoker for fifty years but other than that there's no reason I can think of that I should get cancer. The doctor said, "No problem, we will just cut off the bottom half of your lung and everything will be fine."

The operation was on the 11th of June 2008 and it went nicely. I was apparently bragging that I was going to have the fastest recovery ever from lung surgery. A few days later my world started to come apart. My body began to shut down. My lungs collapsed. I got pneumonia. My kidneys quit working and they had to put me on dialysis. I developed a thing called Tachy-Brady (*Bradycardia-Tachycardia*) Syndrome in my heart. If you are not familiar with that, it's kind of interesting. Your heart can either go real fast or real slow. Real fast is not a problem because that can be handled. However, when it is real slow it could stop and you would die. My heart doctor said, "No this is a pause." I said, "Well maybe to you it's a pause, but I think that it is a stop so do something." I was on a ventilator and had lots of people praying for me. For a week and a half I was really out in "la-la land". I was out long enough that the breathing tube damaged my vocal cords and my epiglottis (that part of our anatomy that keeps us from drowning when we drink water). They actually had to teach me how to drink again and that's an interesting experience. Typically all the liquids had to be thickened.

On the 4th of July, I was released. Mary decided that this was my new birthday. I get at least two birthdays a year now, which is fine as long as my age doesn't go up. I love all the presents though. With God's help, I left the hospital under my own power walking upright. I felt God on one side and my wife was on the other side. My recovery progressed and towards the end of the year, one of my doctors prescribed Coumadin. It has a side effect called purple toe syndrome and mine were a beautiful shade of purple. Also, one of the effects of Coumadin is kidney failure. I was in and out of the hospital a couple of times trying to figure out what was going on. The kidneys didn't actually fail at that time but they were weakened.

In January of 2009, I had difficulty breathing so I went to the hospital and found out I was on the verge of a heart attack. The doctors wanted to do an angiogram but couldn't because iodine literally kills kidneys. If you are healthy and your kidneys are in good shape then you won't have a problem but mine were not good. The doctor said, "Well, look you can live without your kidneys but you can't live without your heart." We decided to go ahead and do the angiogram, have open-heart surgery, and have a quadruple bypass. My doctor was the best in town and things worked out pretty good. However, my kidneys failed and had to go on dialysis permanently.

When I attended a service at The Little Chapel, I filled out a prayer request card with about seven things on it. After the sermon was finished, Sara began the healings and I kept raising my hands for every thing. It got to the point that when Sara would call out a certain healing everyone would look at me to see if I was going to raise my hand.

After that service, around the beginning of June, amazingly my kidney output started to increase. It kept getting a little better so the doctor gave me some medicine that he thought might help as well. The test results kept improving and things kept getting better and better.

Finally, my kidney doctor and my dialysis nurse had to admit that maybe they could consider taking me off of dialysis—something unheard of with my condition. It is common knowledge in the medical field that once a person goes on dialysis you have three choices: stay on dialysis, get a transplant or die. Now let us add a fourth option, a healing from God.

I feel great and my blood tests keep improving. I have been off dialysis for several months. My doctors and nurses are not sure how to handle that! One of my doctors keeps telling me how lucky I am. I keep telling him that God healed me in The Little Chapel, but he just walks away, shaking his head in disbelief.

Our God is such an awesome God, and it overwhelms me sometimes when I think of what He has done for me.

My wife and I stated a ministry called Grafted Branch ministries under the all nations Anglican banner. It will be necessary for me travel a lot now, so I'm certain God healed my kidneys so I can complete my mission. I tell everyone who will listen about The Little Chapel—about the healings that happen at every service and about my fantastic over the top healing.

Thank You God for Putting My Cancer to Sleep

Leah Key

*L*eah is a beautiful southern lady. She is happily married to Jim, and they have one daughter and three grandchildren. The little ones all call her "Queenie."

She modeled for many years, but now enjoys giving her time, energy and talent to charities. She has been very supportive of the Childhelp events in Tennessee. She even chaired a garden event for Childhelp one spring. Leah is always happy to tell others what God did for her.

In 1990, I was diagnosed with breast cancer. I received treatment and thought everything was fine and my life went back to normal.

Then, in 1997, I was diagnosed with tumors in my spine and ribs called metastatic bone-cancer. Prior to that I was being treated for rheumatoid arthritis. The doctors had not diagnosed me properly, so by the time they determined it was cancer, it had spread to the base of my skull, my hips, and across my back, and my back was broken. They had to do all kinds of X-rays and blood work on me.

I have the greatest respect for my oncologist, but he certainly doesn't sugarcoat anything. He looked right at me that day and told me that he didn't know how long I had to live, but he would start treatment. I have often thought that he could have used a little course in bedside manners, but I am not sure they teach that anymore.

Anyway, from there I went home and thought, "Am I going to die or am I going to fight for my life? What am I going to do here?" I must tell you that there were times that death would have been welcome because I was terribly sick. I didn't want to eat. My sweet husband would practically spoon-feed me and plead with me to try to eat. Gradually, my strength began to come back.

A lot of people were praying for me. We have a healing service at my church in Knoxville, and my husband, Jim, would take me. Spring soon came and Linda Willey told me that Sara and Yvonne would be coming into Knoxville for a Childhelp event. Linda and Dick were giving a party at their home, and she said if I could get someone to bring me over she would get Sara to pray for me.

Sara did meet with me and told me all about her fabulous healing through Kathryn Kuhlman. She prayed with me then, and many times after that over the phone. Her prayers would always lift my spirits and give me the encouragement to fight to live.

I did get a little better, and then Linda asked me to go to The Little Chapel in Arizona in May 2000. I had heard so much about The Little Chapel that I was happy to have the opportunity to attend a service. I loved every word of the sermon and loved the healing part even better because I received a healing.

As I sat quietly listening and seeing the different healings happening around me, I suddenly felt warm all over. I had a wonderful, peaceful feeling inside that I could not explain. That day—especially those precious moments in the Chapel — I will always treasure, and I thank God for His healing touch.

When we returned to Knoxville, Tennessee, I couldn't wait to go back to the doctor the next Monday. I had blood work done and X-rays taken. My heart was pounding, and I was wondering "What is he going to tell me today?" For the past 2 years, he would put the X-rays up on the screen, and he would make me look at them, and then explain what was happening. This morning he said, "Let me give you a hug!" I thought, "My God, I'm dying!" I just knew I was dying, or there truly had been a miracle.

We went into his office and sat down and he looked at me and said, "You know, I don't understand this. According to my medical book you are supposed to be dead." I said, "But I'm very much alive...I'm here." He said, "I know that, and it's just as though your cancer has gone to sleep." I was simply numb realizing I had been healed.

I knew without any doubt I had received a healing that day in The Little Chapel. I went directly home and got on my knees and thanked God. I am so thankful for Sara's wonderful gift that she so freely shares with everyone. May everyone who reads this book open their hearts up to God's tender love and blessings.

Letting Go of Negative Thinking Allows the Miracles To Begin

Carole Klein

The lovely Carole Klein is a neighbor of Ralna English, and they have become dear friends. Ralna asked her to join the Phoenix Chapter of Childhelp®, and they have spent quite a lot of time together. When The Little Chapel was going to open in Arizona in the fall of 1995, Ralna asked Carole to attend the service. She knew Carole hadn't been feeling well and told her that God uses Sara as a conduit for healing people. Carole thought she had tried everything. God and her belief in Jesus had been part of her life for years but she had never been to a healing service. Now, she never wants to miss one.

I am blessed to have five grandchildren and love them all so much. My daughter-in-law, when pregnant, was having repeated kidney infections which the doctors couldn't alleviate. She received a beautiful healing through Sara's prayers. Lori began improving immediately and has never again had any problems. She gave birth to a healthy boy.

Sometimes our health issues appear out of nowhere. That is what happened to me. After some years of high stress, my life had calmed down. Yet, unexpectedly, I started to have some weakness and body pains. Ignoring these for a number of months didn't seem to cure the condition. Fear that perhaps something more serious could be wrong sent me to a physician.

After a number of tests, they found a cyst in my thyroid, a body systemic infection due to sinus and something abnormal in my blood work. No adequate diagnosis could be made, and therefore, various present-day medications were prescribed to see if reduction of symptoms could occur.

My body went haywire and just rebelled. My heart started going crazy, my heels were throbbing, my blood pressure shot up to an unbelievable range. I stopped taking all medication. The doctor thought my body would adjust, but it didn't. I went from doctor to doctor, and tried various treatments, but nothing seemed to work.

I had begun attending The Little Chapel services, and one beautiful Sunday morning I prayed that God would touch me and release me from all this pain. The healings at the Chapel began and soon I heard Sara describing my condition, even indicating that no doctor could come up with an adequate method of treatment. She asked who it was, for she wanted to give them a message.

I raised my hand. Sara looked right at me and said, "Do you believe that God has touched you now? Your condition, regardless of what physicians say, will be healed if you depend on Him. God is the Great Physician!" My middle name should be "Thomas" as I have struggled with doubt all my life. I wanted to believe but questioned that God would really do this for me.

Sara kept saying such positive things to me and told me not to be concerned, because over the next few months a complete healing would occur. A deep peace came over me like I had never felt before, and I knew her words were correct. The doubts left, and the healing began. God's almighty hand had truly given me His healing touch and in a very short time, all the symptoms that had plagued me for almost a year, disappeared.

A few years ago, I did a study from the Bible on healing and it struck me that every healing I read about was a healing of action. Jesus requested a positive action to accompany the healing. "Stretch out your hand." "Stand up." "Go to the temple." Whatever the request, there always appeared to be an action of faith required. Faith and trust is now what I hold in my heart, and what a difference that has made for my life.

Doubt and fear put blocks in the way for God to reach us. God never forces us to accept His love. We choose to accept instead of fear and doubt. When we choose to remove all the negative thoughts, the miracles can and will begin!

I Was an Atheist Until My Shell Was Cracked and Shifted into a Spiritual Direction

Dr. Robert Koppen

*I*t is always an extra good feeling when a doctor acknowledges the "Great Physician." Many know they can do only so much and the real healing is in the hands of God. People and God make a terrific team when they work together.

This story is about a wonderful physician who grew up without the knowledge of God in his home. The Sundays that he spent in The Little Chapel have turned his life, and his wife's life, upside down. He is a new person and gives God all the credit.

> I am Dr. Robert Koppen and I was one of those "bad, unbelieving physicians" starting out. I was registered as a medical specialist and thought I knew it all. I had absorbed the latest medical science and *knew* that nothing that couldn't be proved by science had any meaning.

In 1977, I met a special man, Ronald Beesley, who was my first spiritual teacher. He started working a little in America but he was practicing mainly in England. He was good. He cracked my shell. After studying a week with him, he gave me a wonderful blessing. He said, "While you came in an atheist, God has touched you, and from now on you will be one of his own and walk with the angels, side by side." I was deeply moved.

I enjoyed shifting into a spiritual direction but certainly was not in any state of surrender. I saw Jesus just as an inspiring teacher at the time, and felt the Holy Spirit was a concept for people who grew up in the Roman Catholic Church. It still had no meaning for me.

In 1985, I was receiving a healing treatment from a lady who suddenly brought through the energy of Jesus, and I was asked if I was ready to start consciously participating in His work. I was so moved I fell on my knees and cried. It still took me 13 more years from that moment to The Little Chapel service in November to accept what Jesus asked me to do.

Sara said right at the beginning of the healing service, "There is a man here, who has never really accepted the Holy Spirit, and the Holy Spirit is ready to give him a great gift, but he has to accept it. Who are you?" Sara kept repeating it. She never gives up when she knows she has been given a message from the Holy Spirit. It took poor Sara two minutes to make me raise my hand.

I thought I walked in the Chapel feeling fine. My body was working, and I was just enjoying being in the energy and seeing others get healed. Sara kept pleading, and I kept ignoring what I was feeling. Finally, I raised my hand and an immense light flooded me, and I couldn't stop crying. I didn't hear anything else she said. I later received the tape from the service and recognized my voice. It took me 21 years and two minutes to receive this wonderful blessing.

Since that November service I feel greater joy. It is less work when people who are really down come to me. I make them leave feeling up. A lot of subtle things have changed. People I give treatments to tell me that there is more energy.

This concept of the Holy Spirit being the gift of God to those who are ready to move to the next level of surrender now has a deeper meaning for me. I am inspired each time I attend a service at The Little Chapel by seeing how beautifully and fully the Holy Spirit uses Sara. It is impossible to feel the high energy Sara generates and not be touched and transformed by it.

My Life is Changing Everyday as I Put Positive Thoughts into Action

Jill Sheridan Leatherbury

Jill had a fairy tale life growing up in Shadey, Maryland. Her family has always been a great support to her, and she has learned to appreciate them more and more over the years. Her first marriage was quite a challenge because of abuse, but she was blessed with four children—Jordan, Jeremie, Isaac and Arianne. She is now remarried to a wonderful man named Don and they are one big happy family.

Jill is very open to receiving healings and has been touched in some way at every Little Chapel service she has attended. She promised God to be a light in this world for Him. Her heart feels strongly that she is to devote her time and energy towards helping others who find themselves in an impossible situation to get out and start over. She learned she had to be strong and trust God every step of her personal journey. It wasn't easy, and there still is a lot of work to do. She wants to help and teach others to stand up for themselves and encourage them to do what is best for them and everyone involved. We are all precious to God and should live in a loving nurturing environment. Anything less should not be acceptable.

Jill feels that music has played a big part in her healing of abuse. She plays the piano, sings and writes music as well as teaches piano to children and adults. She lives by the Edgar Cayce quote, "Do the best that you know to do and the rest will follow." This strengthens her, as she never gives up when things seem insurmountable and has always given her best under the circumstances in which she found herself. When the time felt right to make a change for her and her family, she did. She is turning her heartaches into blessings not only for herself but also for others.

" I attend the *Logos Center Church*. The people who belong follow the teachings of Jesus Christ and the glory of God through readings from Edgar Cayce and other wonderful studies.

One Sunday over a year ago, my Pranic healing buddy, Richard Renn, announced he would attend, "The Little Chapel." I thought, "Who would miss a Sunday at the *Logos Center?*" I wondered what could be so special. Richard mentioned that healings took place at every service and, oh, did I ever need some healing! I knew I had to go to The Little Chapel and meet this healing lady.

At this time, I was continually dealing with my abusive former husband. I had escaped from his abuse almost three years before and moved to "court appointed" Scottsdale, Arizona with my two youngest children, Arianne and Isaac. My ex-partner's abuse to the children and me included physical but capitalized in mental and emotional mistreatment. He illegally held two of our teenage sons, Jordan and Jeremie, in Tampa, Florida. Both boys enjoyed the freedom of the neighborhood and, unfortunately, Jeremie involved himself in drugs. In May 2009, my oldest son, Jordan, came to Arizona to live with me along with my two youngest children and my husband Don.

I held a lot of resentment and weight on my shoulders. So much so, that my left arm became useless. It was numb and I was unable to lift it above 5 o'clock as the pain was excruciating. It felt like a bone was frozen. One day a butter dish slipped from my hand and broke into many pieces. I finally realized how God was trying to get my attention. I had let my faith in Him slip away along with the butter dish.

In August 2009, a friend gave me the phone number of The Little Chapel. She told me to call and get on the mailing list for the chapel services. As excited as Christmas morning, I made the call the next day.

Instead of a recording, I heard a sweet voice on the other end. "Hello?" Oh dear, I realized I had the private phone number.

"Um, yes, is this The Little Chapel?"

"Yes."

I cringed. "Is this the Healing Lady?"

Now I am 50 years old and I didn't know the Healing Lady's name. I felt like a child in the presence of Jesus suddenly and accepted that this was a meant to be moment. Talk about humble.

"Yes," she said gently. "What do you want?"

I answered with "I just want to be on your mailing list."

The Healing Lady on the phone said, "What do you really want?" I thought, "Wow! Thank you God." I finally found The Little Chapel and Sara O'Meara, God's messenger.

"Well, you know how nothing is a coincidence, I must tell you about my son, Jeremie."

The Healing Lady listened to synopsis of my son who remains in an abusive relationship with my ex-husband. I relayed that I was going to Tampa to pick him up.

"Does he want to go with you?" she asked.

Sadly, I answered, "No, he is 16 and free to roam in Tampa and now dealing in drugs. I know I need to raise my son and he should be with the rest of his family."

The Healing Lady said, "I am being told it's time for him to be with you." My heart wanted to cry. "I am also being told he won't resent you for it."

This wonderful angel of God spoke to me as I held on to my moment with the rest of her beautiful message. At the end, we blessed each other and now I was on TLC mailing list.

As I pushed "end" on my cell phone I looked within and thanked God for the Healing Lady. I still didn't have a real name but made certain to bless the realm she had lit up with those wonderful spirit guides—her magnificent angels.

The next day, I stood in line at the airport with my brother to depart for Tampa. I was dropping my suitcase on everyone's feet and apologizing for an arm that I had damaged with my negative consciousness. All I could think of was my wonderful encounter with the Healing Lady and her inspiration from God. But I received a strong reminder that I'd better get back on the right track and focus more on God and my meditations.

Once on board the plane, I settled in with my laptop and began another chapter of the book I am writing. A sudden bliss came over me, and I noticed the presence of two guardian angels. I felt they were the Healing Lady's guardian angels! A connection was made and I felt they were assuring me of God's love and strength to help me on the trip to pick up Jeremie.

Understanding "Thy will be done", I returned to Arizona without Jeremie, but I gained greater understanding and trust. Sara had said Jeremie would one day come home and live with me.

One afternoon, while at home with my wonderful ten year old daughter, I could see the place at the tip of my shoulder where the pain originated in my arm. She reached over and poked it. The pain was horrible and the feeling of healing and the knowledge of God's light through Sara's channeling struck my mind. I lifted my arm high! My daughter gasped.

"Arianne! Look! I'm healed!" The instantaneous healing was God's doing and I knew it was my gift.

As a former gymnast and dancer I wanted to show my daughter and myself I was healed. I did cartwheels in the back yard with ease and danced through the rafters of the attic with joy. God was showing me once again to never give up, have faith, trust and let Him be in control. When I gave God my problems, my healing was instantaneous.

I stopped dwelling on the past and all the negative feelings, and became grateful for what I had now. God brought a wonderful new spouse, Don, in my life, and my oldest son made the choice to come live with all of us in Arizona. I had to know in my heart that God was still working with Jeremie, surrounding my son with loving prayers daily. I put all my trust in God to touch his heart and bring him home with me where he belonged.

The first healing service I attended was in September 2009 and I received another healing. I felt a shiver and then heat go down my body. I was instantly without pain.

In the October service I had the same experience on my lower back. I never want to miss those powerful healing services. I cherish every moment I'm in that holy place. It is amazing to watch God in action.

Before going to sleep on the evening of January 15, 2010, I laid on my bed with both arms above my head. My left arm felt perfect but my right arm had pain around the shoulder bone. I asked God to please heal it at the next chapel service. Then I fell asleep.

I had a dream that was so vivid. In the dream Sara came to me after a chapel service. God used her as a conduit to heal my shoulder. God has her working even at night. When I woke up I had no pain. God was so gracious to heal me even before the January service at The Little Chapel. Praise God and thank you, Sara. My heart is so full of love and gratitude.

Another miracle happened in January when my son, Jeremie, finally came home to live with us in Arizona. Our whole family is so delighted!

In April our family was blessed with yet another wonderful miracle. My brother, John Henry, who had previously chosen a life of alcohol and drugs was touched by God a few years ago and he quit using drugs. He became a more loving person but still drank. He could only visit us for three days at a time because that's how long he could last with my rules of "no drinking."

John lives in South Beach, Florida and Don and I flew him to Arizona to attend the April 2010 Little Chapel service. It was an evening service and my brother could feel the presence of the Holy Spirit the minute he walked through the doors of the chapel. After hearing Sara speak, he agreed with us how special she was, how much God's love shines within her and through her to others.

After John returned home to Florida he phoned me. He explained how the evening in The Little Chapel affected him and wished he were still in Scottsdale. He felt like he was in a dream. He lost his desire to drink and had the will power to cure himself. That phone call was the beginning of another miracle.

In a few days John phoned again and was so excited. "I wanted you to know your healing lady is real. She's the real thing!" Of course, he was preaching to the choir. John said Sara's face appeared before him while he was riding his bike to work. She kept saying, "Why won't you let me heal you?" He admitted he was ashamed to need a healing for his drinking problem. I was so happy and proud of him. I feel he has much to contribute to this world. He made the choice to accept his healing and our entire family is thrilled beyond words.

I'm grateful for having a mother who was a beautiful example for me to follow. She taught me about God's great love & light and that God was always ready to help us but we must ask. My family helped me and my children escape from a life of abuse. A very good friend took us in her home for eight months until we moved to Arizona. My wonderful brother, Robert Leatherbury and sister-in-law, Linda Shuttleworth bought a house for us in Scottsdale and helped us get started with a new life. Not everyone is so fortunate and I feel very blessed.

My husband, Don, is truly an angel and was sent to help me begin "Bridge from Abuse Foundation." Together we plan to publish my book and make a film to help others who are being abused. I was so happy to learn that the healing lady — Sara O'Meara and her friend Yvonne Fedderson started the Childhelp® organization over 50 years ago to help abused and neglected children. Like the ladies, I was also an actress in Hollywood but in the 80's.

In closing, I want to ask all of you to never treat anyone with disrespect. The damage that occurs goes deep within and only God can heal those scars. We must remember that God loves each of us unconditionally and His love can heal and change anything.

We must make the choice and take the first step. God will hold our hand and lead us when we are ready to follow. He never promised it would be easy, but with Him all things are possible.

With God There is Always a Way

David LeMieux

David was born and raised in Montana where he now resides. He has eight fantastic siblings and he was also blessed to have amazing parents. His dad was an attorney and his mom was a homemaker.

He had a wonderful childhood filled with horses, dogs, milk cows and beef cows. His family was active and always going weekend backpacking, horseback riding or taking trips to their little cabin in the mountains.

David was raised Catholic and still frequently attends hometown services on Sunday. He was a high-energy kid, always running from one place to another and asking lots of questions with great curiosity about life and how things were made. He was a leader on the high school basketball and cross-country state championship teams. His curiosity about life and the world we live in extended through engineering school where he earned his BS and MS degrees.

David's first professional job was a great experience but all work—often working 100 hour weeks, but taking vacation time to hike, backpack, kayak or snowboard, depending on the season.

He was in great shape and strong when he contracted Lyme disease. He didn't know what was wrong with him for 14 years.

Our human problems are really God's opportunities to reach us and help us to a higher way of thinking and living. When we have a severe health problem or things aren't going the way we would like to have them go in our lives, this gives God the golden opportunity to reach us and set us on a path that is much more to our liking; a path that will bring us the inner peace and happiness we desire in our lives. We will always have hills and valleys, but that's how we learn. Every valley can be an opportunity to grow in some way spiritually. Our low times can be high times for our greatest spiritual growth.

It was hard for me to believe that I had Lyme disease. Despite seeing numerous doctors and undergoing seemingly endless tests, after 14 years of a downward spiraling illness I was finally diagnosed. The diagnosis wasn't a cure; the past 4 years have consisted of nearly continuously increasing dosages of antibiotics until my body no longer responded. There was nothing else my doctor could do, so I switched to natural approaches but after 6 months on these treatments I was still getting worse.

Then I began looking for people with the gift of healing as I had witnessed people become instantly well through their prayers when I was in college. My lymph massage therapist suggested a healer known as "John of God" in Brazil and she loaned me a book about him. I was just beginning to read it when my Aunt phoned me to talk and I flatly told her of my plans to travel to Brazil to see a healer that I didn't know anything about except for short videos on the internet that were rather disturbing to watch. She responded, "Before you go to Brazil you should consider going to Arizona to The Little Chapel." That sounded so much better to me because it was more what I was searching for so before we hung up I'd booked tickets for both of us. I was going to Arizona in just 10 days.

I didn't know what to expect from the healing session at The Little Chapel, but I did expect to be healed. I was praying earnestly; praying for a healing and praying to become closer to God. I was so ill and filled with unstoppable pain the night we arrived. I thought I was going to have to ask my Aunt to take me to the hospital. I felt I couldn't even make it to The Little Chapel service. I prayed God would help me endure the pain at least to walk into the chapel.

I made it to the chapel and listened intently to Sara's sermon about the incomprehensible depth of God's love for *each* of us and I remember her saying, "Almost as wonderful as God's healing gift is the feeling of his loving touch on your soul."

When the healing session started the very first question Sara asked was if anyone had problems with their right leg. Well I've had Lyme disease for 18 years and it was killing me but I wasn't being choosy about how the Holy Spirit heals people because I also had problems with my right leg. My Lyme disease actually started in my right leg. I raised my hand immediately.

When Sara pointed to me I stood up and went right to her. Then I walked around and felt a sudden strength in my right leg. Everything started changing. My head was swimming. I felt a warm band extending from my left shoulder to my right shoulder and from my face to my abdomen. The experience seemed to make time stop for me and Sara was off praying for other people's healing, but she told me, "Sir, God has touched you; you are healed!"

No mistake. I knew I was healed. Let me say that again: after 18 years I was healed. Little did I know that God healing me was also like a door opening within me and it opened me to experience the loving touch of God. Oh, how amazing! The band across my chest and down my center line formed a "cross" that burned heat to the core of me. Though I can't describe how, it had a feeling of luminescence and all around my heart (3-dimensionally), my heart was surrounded by pure bright white light. It was warm, amazing love but I don't know words to describe how wonderful God's loving touch really feels.

When I returned home to Montana I took my mother and father to a favorite mountain with a special waterfall to thank God in prayer for my healing. We all prayed in thanksgiving. As we were getting in the car to leave, I told them to drive on. I wanted to walk and continue to praise God. My Father called out to my Mother, "Look! Look! Can you believe what we're seeing?" My Mother, thinking she'd missed a sunset or beautiful peak of a mountain looked up and all around and said, "Where? Where?" My Father excitingly exclaimed, "No way down the road. It's David. He's running all the way down the mountain!" Yes, it was I, David, who had always been in pain, running like a racehorse. My legs were sailing down that hill, at last free from illness.

I am in awe of this entire experience. Since leaving The Little Chapel, I've continued to feel the touch of God, which I feel even as I write this nearly 2 weeks later. It's sort of like Sara got me hooked up to a battery charger and I've been on God's "trickle charge" ever since. It's not always a trickle either, just two days ago I had a sudden experience of millions of needles going through me from my head and neck and then extending down my chest, arms and legs. It was like a physiological circuits overload being zapped by electricity and when I thought it was over I was hit in the head by another round of needles. Although I can't describe it otherwise, it wasn't painful and lasted less than 10 seconds. Every time I express gratitude to God over and over again for my healing, it seems the experience redefines itself.

Lately I've been feeling like the lucky-starfish in an old story: An ocean storm is blowing to shore and an old man at the edge of the shore is facing the crashing waves and driving wind. This storm has created an unusual ocean current that washes thousands of starfish up on the beach where they would surely die. The old man is methodically picking them up one-by-one and chucking them back into the sea. Observing this scene—the magnitude of the storm and all the starfish on the beach—a young man goes down onto the beach and approaches the old man saying "Sir, it's no use there are so many of them. What you are doing it doesn't matter." The old man replied without slowing down as he picked up another starfish to throw it back into the sea, "It mattered to that one." So I am like a lucky-starfish and it mattered to me. I think through God's love we can each be a lucky-starfish and he is just waiting for us to *ask for* and to *accept* his gifts.

So often when we think about achieving something we consider how to get started. I heard something I liked not too long ago, "Don't start, just do" and that was how it all began with booking my airline tickets. I just thought I'm going to *go*, I'm going to *ask* and I'm going to *accept* my healing. Now, all I can do is give thanks to God for my healing.

Since I wrote this story, my Mom and Dad attended the next Little Chapel with me and both of them were healed as well. We are all more grateful than words can adequately express.

God Answers a Loving Grandmother's Prayers

Mary Lou Luvisa

*I*t is beautiful how God loves to answer prayers for the precious little ones. Sara and I have spent all of our adult lives caring for abused and neglected children, so they have a special place in our hearts.

When Mary Lou asked for prayers for her grandson, Cooper, Sara immediately started praying for him. Cooper's grandmother wants to glorify God for His love, and for His action for her grandson.

" I want to tell you about one of the three lights of my life—my little grandson, Cooper. We all have our own daily meditations and prayers in our communications with God, but I don't think there is anything that brings us to our deep need to communicate with Him than when we find a child in need. We all want children, especially our own, to have the happiest childhood possible. My testimony here is centered on that child, who at the time was three years old.

He lives in San Diego with his father (my son), mother and older brother, whom he idolizes. One Sunday morning, we took off for a day of seeing SeaWorld®, and it was evident from the time we were in the parking lot that Cooper was limping. His mother thought it might be from the pair of boots he was wearing that were hand-me-downs from another child. He consented to being carried that day, which was quite unusual, but by Wednesday we took him to the pediatrician because he wasn't getting any better. The doctor didn't have X-ray capabilities in his office; so, it was the next day before X-rays were done. At 4:00 PM that afternoon, the pediatrician called and stated the radiologist read the X-rays and they were quite concerned. The X-ray showed the femur had collapsed. They suspected a massive infection and blood work needed to be done immediately.

Our thoughts ran back and forth between "Is it cancer? Is it a terrible blood infection that can't be cured with anything but surgery?" Fortunately, no infection was found in the blood stream, and other tests ruled out any abnormal growth. For some reason, the blood supply was not being fed to that particular area, and the initial diagnosis was Perthis Disease. It happens in pediatrics or sometimes older people get it in the hip. Later the diagnosis became idiopathic vascular necrosis, which is another way of saying, "We don't know why the blood supply is not getting there."

In order for the area to heal itself, it had to be kept immobile, and of course, with a little guy this had to be a cast to prevent him from walking. Here's how Cooper taught us to accept what we have and to live for the present. Already I felt God was touching this child. He was a typical rough and tumble 3 year old, and he was showing us what to do. He participated with the antics and the joking about the cast. When he came home, my other grandson, Kyl, and I were shocked. How was Cooper going to function with the cast? Again, Cooper put us at ease. His father put him on the couch in a half-sitting/half-lying position, and he would politely ask for things to be handed to him if he couldn't reach them. Later he wanted to be placed on the floor where he could play with his toys. We gradually began to relax and feel that this could work. He was unable to turn over at night, so his mother slept with him turning him every 45 minutes.

All the while, we kept hoping he was going to heal. He remained in a cast for 7 weeks. During this time he gradually became stronger. He was able to get himself up the stairs to where his bedroom was. He never complained. He directed all his energies to what he was going to do and how he would fill his day. The week before his cast was removed, he looked up at his daddy and said, "Daddy, this cast sucks!"

Cooper attended a Lutheran preschool, and was kept in their daily prayers. After the December Chapel service Sara continued praying fervently for him. She stated that Cooper would get progressively stronger and stronger and to trust God. I felt the presence of Jesus in the Chapel and knew her prayers were powerful. It reminded me of the Bible stories I read as a child, and it gave me faith that Cooper would be healed.

After 7 weeks, the X-rays showed that there had been improvement. The cast was removed. Cooper was so happy to take a bath that he had two baths a day. He is now out of the brace and has no limp. We still try to keep him from jumping, but he is able to "pop wheelies" on his bike and do all the other things four-year-olds can do.

The X-rays are done every two months, and show a very slow, but steady improvement. As Sara has said many times, it is up to God whether he heals instantly or progressively. Every day we pray and every day Cooper improves. God does know what He is doing, and we trust Him with our lives, and especially with Cooper's life.

Standing Tall in My Posture and in My Heart as Well

Brenda Macchiaroli

renda Macchiaroli is a frequent visitor to The Little Chapel in Arizona. She is a gentle spirit who loves Jesus. She is blessed with a wonderful gift of singing and writing music, and enjoys using her talent in church choirs.

Brenda has had five children of her own, and one adorable grandson, Lucas. She has also given her time and talent to helping the abused and neglected children through Childhelp. Her heart is overflowing with goodness and love.

Sometimes it is hard for us to accept the ways of God, but we know so little about our souls, and God knows everything. I believe we must trust and have faith that one day we will understand why certain things happen to us.

I lost a son when he was only 2 ½ years old. He was our only child at the time, and we were devastated. He had croup that turned into pneumonia. As we left the hospital, we felt the presence of God so strong. We knew our little Michael was being taken up to Heaven where he would be loved by all the angels.

Three days before he crossed over, we went to church and he asked, "Mom did God build this?" When we visited the Grand Canyon a couple of months before, he said, "Did God make all of this?" God created so many beautiful things for us to enjoy and He inspires us to do many great things, like the Little Chapel. He gave Sara this vision so we could all benefit from it.

I always enjoy the sermons, and the healings are the frosting on the cake. Each one sweeter and better than the last. All of them so special. One Sunday Sara said, "Someone has an upper back problem and they are receiving their healing now." I looked around the room to see who was raising their hand. No one had yet, so I barely put my finger up and hoped that she wouldn't see me. I wanted the healing, but I was embarrassed to admit it in front of everyone. I was afraid that it wasn't for me. Isn't that silly?

Sara came to the end of the row where I was sitting and said, "Brenda it is for you. Are you going to accept it?" I kept looking at the floor, but she was persistent. All of a sudden I could put my hands on the back of the pew and I could stand tall. She had me get up and walk and it felt great. I still have that healing. I am very grateful today, not just because I'm standing tall in my posture, but in my heart as well.

At another service, Sara gave me a strong message. She said I was thinking about a large music project, but I lacked focus. This was correct. I am finally doing something about it now.

Going to The Little Chapel has made me realize how much God cares about us. He wants us healthy, happy and focused on what we are doing with our lives. We all have a mission, a reason for being here. I want to complete my mission, don't you?

I believe my son, Michael, completed his mission quickly, but some of us have more work to complete before we return to our Heavenly home. I have learned that time is precious and should not be wasted, so I have made a promise to focus on my work now, and I am determined to complete my mission with God's guidance and love.

Replacing Anger with Love

Carol Manetta

C arol was born and raised in Detroit, Michigan. Just recently she moved to Paradise Valley, Arizona and is so happy to be living near The Little Chapel. Elizabeth Brazilian first brought her to a service and, with Carol's background, she loved and enjoyed every minute of it.

Carol is an Angel Therapy Practitioner. Our heavenly angels are always at The Little Chapel, helping us and loving us.

Most of my life, I've had difficulty with my lungs. Years ago I saw the radiology results that showed a great deal of scar tissue from pleurisy. I have suffered with asthma and chronic bronchitis for years. Every morning when I awakened I had a great deal of coughing and clearing.

I began praying and asking God why I was suffering so much with all this. One day while I was meditating, it became very clear to me that I was holding on to a great deal of anger. When we don't forgive and let go of anger it can manifest in our bodies and make us sick.

I had a long-standing grudge against some people, so I began working on releasing that anger immediately. I forgave those people and I forgave myself for holding that grudge. I prayed for them and began surrounding them with God's love and light. I must admit it made me feel better when I began this process.

The next Sunday morning was The Little Chapel service. When I woke up that morning, I was incredibly happy. Years ago I was a professional dancer, and that morning I put on some classical music and danced and danced. My lungs were absolutely clear. No more coughing!

After Sara spoke that Sunday morning, she asked if there were people with breathing problems. I raised my hand and she walked up to me with a smile on her face. She said she had a vision of me being healed while she was praying Saturday evening. I thanked her for her tender prayers and for confirming my wonderful healing.

If any of you who are reading this story have anger in your heart, please release it. Why hang on to something that will make you sick? Replace the anger with love and I know you will feel the difference. Everyday I thank God for working through Sara and giving me breath and joy in my heart to dance.

Develop Trust and Faith in God Now

Augustine Mastropolo

Savannah, Georgia was the birthplace of Augustine, but at age one his family moved to New York. He received a BS in Computer Science and did some graduate work in cognitive psychology. He has been happily married to Marianne for thirteen years and she was the one to learn about The Little Chapel through mutual friends of ours.

He is so happy and grateful to God for his beautiful healing. It changed his life and opened his heart to love on a much deeper level. Our capacity to love is the only thing we take with us when we graduate to heaven.

> My heart is so full of love and gratitude for The Little Chapel, and for all the powerful prayers Sara has poured out over me during January through July 2009.

I will summarize my situation as it unfolded from January to July and provide some background information. It appears that I had a heart attack due to job stress on January 21, 2009. Two cardiologists developed four theories to explain the root cause but none of them can be backed up with scientific evidence. Since the diagnostic tests were inconsistent, they now label this cardiomyopathy. It is apparent that a healing was progressing during this time that confused the cardiologists. For me there are many levels of messages and meaning surrounding this ordeal.

I have been physically active working out at a gym doing an intense aerobic class twice a week as well as walking, light weight lifting, core and stretching exercises. I eat a mostly healthy diet, don't smoke or drink (only red wine for health), have low blood pressure, low cholesterol and no family history of heart disease. I do have one risk factor; a job that is extremely stressful (equivalent to an air traffic controller), as a Technical Project Manager for a large bank.

I believe it was a culmination of stress in January that caused my "heart attack." I was under extreme pressure and a close worker died of stroke (he was 33), which was probably a trigger for me. Of course, I had no overt symptoms (except for a slight shortness of breath) on January 21. It was coincidental that my echocardiogram was scheduled for January 22. On February 3rd, I was given a report that showed myocardial infarction, ejection fraction (Ef) 40-45%, hypokinesis of apex, septum, and left ventricle. This news caught me off guard and to use the word "shock" would not come close to describing my state of mind.

A series of tests produced confusing information about my heart. A nuclear stress test on February 9th confirmed septum damage but the Ef was almost normal. An angiogram on February 12th showed "no coronary disease" or blockages but an Ef of 40-45%. The cardiac MRI on February 24th report was ambiguous. Two cardiologists developed four theories as to what happened. They are: coronary artery spasm (brought on by stress), Takotsubo syndrome (stress), micro-capillary blockages and viral attack on the heart.

Since the cardiologists could not explain what was happening they began to use the label of idiopathic cardiomyopathy to label my condition. As we know the power of prayer and healing was at work during this period and was confounding the medical tests and doctors. Each time I talked with Sara, she assured me that I would be coming out of this okay. But I have to learn the deeper meaning of faith as I usually lean toward the scientific worldly answers.

I have to declare that all of the health and medical problems that I have had in the past are miniscule as compared to the word "heart attack." I now know what someone goes through when they are given the diagnosis of heart attack or cancer. I believe that I was being taught a lesson about trust; trust in God. On a deeper level, I would have to rely on faith and trust each day.

On March 17, I had another echocardiogram. The technician told me she did not see any damage and that the heart's pumping (ejection fraction) looked normal. The report a few weeks later confirmed this and produced a sensation of exhilaration for me. I would be able to resume my regular normal life again.

The concept that I could die was driven home during this ordeal. Each night as I went to sleep, I had great fear that I would never wake up, sometimes forcing me to stay awake longer than I should.

Doctors and medical tests are not perfect and I will never know the cause of my problem. Heart attacks can happen to people who don't fit the usual profile. Heart attacks can be "silent" and the heart can be damaged without ever knowing it. It's better to develop trust and faith in God now, without having to go through a life-changing experience.

Maybe God calls on and sends messages to people in ways we don't understand. I must trust God now as I have gone back to the high-stress job several months ago and need His protection. I have increased my prayer life significantly. As I learn to give over my stress and problems to Him I sleep more peacefully.

God is always ready to help us, protect us, and guide us to a higher way of living when we look to Him for our answers. When we let go of fear and fill our hearts with love, our lives change for the better.

I'm thankful for my life-threatening experience because it turned my life upside down and completely changed my priorities. Attending The Little Chapel services is a must now. Every day I ask for the unconditional love of God to fill, renew and guide me. The work I am doing on myself is not a goal; it is a process — a lifetime process. I am enjoying the process.

He Heals Us Out of Our Earthly Ways to His Higher Way of Thinking

Mary Ellen Mckee

Mary Ellen and Bob McKee have enjoyed over 30 years together. Bob had three children from a previous marriage and they now have eight fabulous grandchildren.

Mary Ellen is a happy person and tries to always find the good in people and the good in circumstances we have to go through. It bothers her when people blame God for obstacles or hard lessons in life but are quick to take all the credit when things go right. She acknowledges that she may struggle sometimes with being quick to judge others, but continues working on this daily.

She was taught as a child that it is more blessed to give than receive, so she is always thinking of ways to give and help others. She came to The Little Chapel for a loved one, but eventually it was her time to receive the blessing of healing.

Mary Ellen and Bob live across the street from Carol and Jim Hebets in Phoenix, Arizona. Carol is always open and ready to talk to people about the Little Chapel wherever she happens to be—even while jogging.

I like to do everything fast, so I'm always speeding out the door when I go power walking. Carol was also going for a walk down her driveway and yelled to me, "What are you doing?" I said, "Oh, going for my walk. I have to hurry, meat in the oven, dinner time is coming soon." She said, "Well, I know you walk faster than I do, so I'm not going to hold you up." I said, "You know what, I am really out of energy today, so it doesn't really matter. I really don't want to walk fast. Let's just walk together."

We did a 2 mile circle around our neighborhood, talking all the way about family and friends. I told her that I would really like to help my brother. I went on to tell her about his heart. She then informed me all about The Little Chapel and asked me to go to the next service and encouraged me to bring my brother.

I phoned my brother, Craig, and told him about my conversation with Carol. He said he would come, so I said, "Wonderful! I'll send you a plane ticket tomorrow!" Of course, I phoned Carol right away and she was ecstatic. I phoned Craig every day for the next two weeks until the Chapel day.

We arrived early at the Chapel but chose to sit in the back of the sanctuary. We enjoyed Sara's sermon, and then the healings began. I was praying so hard for my brother, and hoping Sara would feel my vibes. I was impressed with the healings happening around the room. I thought it was the most fabulous, unbelievable gift anyone could have.

My heart began to pound faster as she came closer and closer to us. I nudged my brother and said, "Do you feel anything?" I told him I was burning up. He said he was warm but not hot.

I had neck problems, but I wasn't there for my neck. I was there for my brother. There was Sara, looking square at me, and telling me I was receiving a healing. I was shocked!

Through this I learned a great lesson. I believe God wants to heal us, but we must *allow* Him into our hearts to receive His beautiful blessings. He doesn't heal us in our sins, but heals us out of our earthly ways to His higher way of living. That was a day of change for me. I'm so humbly grateful for my healing and for the chance to grow spiritually. The Little Chapel is a house of miracles!

Why Choose to Hang On to Pain?

Carrie Mezes

*C*arrie is a travel agent and has lived in Arizona with her husband, John, for well over 20 years. They have raised three children and two grandchildren. She has always gone to church, but feels The Little Chapel has helped her to lift her thinking to another spiritual level. Carrie feels this has been the best time in her life because of her spiritual growth. She has learned so much through the services, and coming to Chapel means more than anything to her. Growing spiritually is what counts for all eternity.

"The Little Chapel is truly the little house of miracles. I receive them every time I attend a service. The first time I entered the Chapel I felt a cleansing of my spirit. At another service, I had a healing of arthritis in my hands. It felt so good to be able to move them without pain.

My lower back was always in a lot of pain, but I thought maybe God limited people to only one or two miracles. I had already received my quota, and hesitated to ask God for another one.

The next month Sara said in her sermon to not limit God, so I decided to pray for my back. The heat on my back became so intense, I knew God was giving me another healing and showing me I should never limit His wonderful gifts.

You learn to live with pain, but why choose to hang on to pain when God wants to free us from all of that misery? I thank God for opening my heart to accept the blessings. I truly have learned to believe and trust God in every way with my life.

Everything about the Chapel service is special. The beautiful music is always so uplifting, and Sara's sermons touch your soul in a way that you cannot be the same person when you leave. The Chapel is so filled with love, and everyone is there to help and pray for each other. I've never experienced anything like this in any other church.

Sara has shared many messages from the Holy Spirit to my husband, John. It has given us peace of mind with our business. I thank God for Kathy Bowen for introducing us to this Little Chapel, and for Sara who continues to bless all of us. My beliefs are so much stronger now, and I want to tell others and help them to find God in a real way.

The Most Important Part of a Miracle is to Accept It

Thomas Michaels by Joanne Michaels

Talking to Joanne Michaels is a treat. She is so filled with love for her husband, Tom, and her family, and so happy about Tom's fantastic healing. You can tell from the story about her husband what a terrific person she is.

"First I would like you to know that *everyone* loves Tom Michaels. He is very soft-spoken, polite, cuddly, and has something in his soul that tends to make other people want to take care of him.

He is a North Dakota-born transplant to Arizona, here since the late 1970's, and a Registered Doctor of Pharmacy who has owned drugstores in Idaho, Iowa and Scottsdale, Arizona. He currently works three jobs, but that's the norm for Tom. Working is his favorite thing to do, besides watching television.

Tom is very devoted to his family. He has 7 grown daughters and 5 grandchildren. We all feel blessed having him as part of our lives.

In November of 2000, a spot in his upper left lung was discovered to be non-small-cell cancer. Luckily, his 2 specialists were able to do a lobectomy immediately, as it was contained and hadn't spread. He didn't even need chemotherapy or radiation, and we were told that a healthy 2 year anniversary date of this surgery was a good prognosis for a 100% cure.

The same month of his surgery, Tom asked me to marry him, and of course I couldn't refuse. He was only on short-term disability from the end of December until the first of March—a speedy recovery that held high hopes and expectations for us both. Tom's positive attitude and dream of watching his grandchildren grow up is what kept him going.

Since that surgery, Tom let me take care of him and was a compliant patient, gleefully taking 15 or so types of cancer-preventing herbs and supplements to ward off a recurrence. Just 5 months away from his 2 year mark, I noticed him having some labored breathing. Something from within told me to call and have his October doctor appointment pushed up. That appointment really changed our lives.

His pulmonologist found the same type of cancer in a pleural effusion around his lungs where the upper left lobe was removed. This time it was not operable, as it involved the chest wall. We held each other and cried, then made our first appointment to meet with an oncologist. Tom and I had researched information on alternative treatments over the past year or so, in case the lung cancer would come back. It was July of 2002 when we met Dr. Sun and started IV vitamin C therapy. Poor Tom continued working the whole time (only two jobs!), stayed on chemotherapy, and kept up with Dr. Sun's therapies. I was the chauffeur for my husband, from job to chemo, to work to Dr. Sun, etc. One day, Dr. Sun told us about The Little Chapel.

The Little Chapel is closed during the summer but she told us to think about attending a service in a couple of months. We discussed the chances of faith healing on our drive home. It kind of scared us because we were not familiar with it, so we decided not to think about it until closer to September when The Little Chapel services resumed.

Throughout all his treatment, Tom only missed two days of work, but the fatigue from chemo was finally starting to take its toll. It caused other horrible side effects like awful sores in his mouth, making it hard for Tom to eat. We decided to try The Little Chapel, mainly—to be honest with you—because we were curious, and although we are Christians, we are terrible about going to church. Dr. Sun told us a little about it, so we put in our reservation for September 15, 2002.

By the time we arrived that Sunday, there were only two chairs left in the corner, way in the back of the Chapel. I was immediately filled with love and felt sort of anxious. Tom told me the same thing later, but he was very sick and weak from chemo that Sunday. I actually thought I might have to get him out of there and straight home to bed.

Miraculously, Tom seemed to get better after the service started. We were so impressed and felt so full of God's love when Sara O'Meara started her sermon. She is amazing and very serious when she is preaching, yet there is a glint in her eye one can detect from even in the back row; a sense of the soul and a sense of humor as well.

Her service was nothing like we imagined. It was not TV evangelism or a laying-of-hands. You can feel the love and hope coming from inside of everyone in that Little Chapel. Then, toward the end of her service, I began to feel confirmation in my heart that God and Jesus were coming through Sara to guide all troubled believers toward the right path in life. When she asked the ones in the room with cancer to raise their hands, I looked into Tom's eyes and smiled through tears as he raised his hand.

I couldn't believe that Sara was going to speak to Tom his very first day! Dr. Sun told us sometimes it takes a long time, so not to get discouraged at that first service but to keep the faith. She spoke and had Tom laughing—they were laughing together! Sara said, "You really never believed you had cancer in the first place, did you?" Tom said no. Then Sara said something that changed our lives.

She said, "First you have to *expect* a miracle." She and Tom talked a bit longer, and then in her soft pink chiffon, she floated away. I was so excited. I think I drove Tom crazy all the way home in the car because I couldn't stop talking about The Little Chapel. I expected Tom to share my enthusiasm, and was disappointed when he started to sleep on the ride home. "Oh, well. It's from the chemo," I told myself.

Over the next couple of weeks, Tom was so sick from chemo that I finally talked him into getting his chemotherapy evaluated. He took two weeks off from it, and then they lowered the dose and frequency. He regretfully started again.

Sometime between the September and October chapel services, Dr. Sun suggested I call Sara O'Meara and ask her if she could pray with Tom privately. She thought it would be good since Sara was guided to Tom right away on his first visit. When I called the number Dr. Sun gave me, I was nervous, yet I knew it was the right thing to do. It turned out that Sara was on her way to California for a while, but her secretary promised to give Sara the message and our phone number. We were so happy when she called me back that same day on her way to the airport. Tom was at work, and she assured me that she remembered talking to him at the recent Little Chapel service. She said she would be praying for his healing, and to tell him, "God bless!"

A week later, Sara called again, this time from California. She wanted to pray together with Tom on the telephone. When I explained he would be home at 3:30 that afternoon, she said she would be calling back. I couldn't believe our good fortune. I actually called Tom at work, and believe me—Tom was sitting by our phone at 3:15 waiting for her call. When Sara called, I went upstairs and left them alone, as I felt this was about to be a very personal time for my husband. I was right. I came down only when I heard Tom blowing his nose from tears of a poignant nature.

During this whole time Tom had been getting chemo, his other specialist, a pulmonologist, was having Tom come in every 3 weeks to check the status of fluid in his pleural space. He had aspirated most of it out when he initially found it, and sent it to be analyzed, leaving a small amount behind purposely, to be used as a marker for monitoring his condition. Another expensive scan, a PET scan, was also in the process of being approved for Tom to eventually get after chemo was finished. They use it to detect any new or recurrent types of cancers that are not calcified, therefore, don't show up on the normal scans. Tom's was one of this nature, which is why the doctor used his fluid as a tumor marker. These scans are very expensive, and have only recently been approved/paid for by insurance companies to detect certain disease progress, such as Tom's type of cancer.

We had been anxiously waiting for the next service at the Little Chapel, on Sunday, October 15, 2002. This time, during the part of the service where Sara connects with people who need healing from God, she asked for people with lung disease to raise their hands. I urged Tom to do so, because besides the cancer he had there was also an underlying lung disease, namely COPD. As Tom was waiting his turn to talk with Sara, I could feel an intense aura type of light with each step she made to finally speak with him. He was the 4th and last of the people who raised their hands. I know the feeling I had was real, an intense kind of urgency that Sara was being drawn to him quicker and quicker. She took her time with the other three visitors, then, just two short rows away from Tom and I, almost flew to Tom with a great smile on her face.

"You're Tom Michaels, aren't you? You came here expecting to be healed, didn't you?' "Yes, I did," said Tom. Well, you have been. All you need to do now is accept the fact that you've been healed. Remember, she said, "First you must expect a miracle, but the most important thing of all is to accept it!" Then she asked Tom if there was some way he could confirm his healing, such as a doctor appointment. It just so happened we had an appointment with his pulmonary doctor in two days to have the remaining fluid removed from his pleural space. Every 3 weeks he had been checking with radiographs to monitor any fluid increase or decrease. Since there had been no change at all for 9 weeks, the doctor wanted to remove that fluid.

On Tuesday, October 17th, Tom went to see the doctor. The severe effects from chemotherapy had masked some of the physical and spiritual signs. First he went to the lab for a chest X-ray, and then took it with him to show the doctor. The doctor was shocked when he looked at the X-ray, for all of the fluid he was going to drain out was completely gone!

The next day, he went in for a PET scan. On Friday, October 20th, the physician's assistant called the PET scan office and they confirmed over the phone to both of us that there was no sign of current or recurrent cancer anywhere in Tom's body!

We are so grateful for Tom's miracle from our Lord Jesus, and thank Him each precious minute of every day. He gives Sara the credit for teaching him to expect a miracle and-the most important part-to accept it. We share this wonderful miracle with everyone who will listen. We want to thank Sara for connecting us to God when she did, and for God allowing Tom more time with his earthly family.

Solving My Greatest Puzzle

Barbara Morgan

*G*od loves it when we don't give up in receiving a heavenly touch from the Holy Spirit for a healing. Jerry Lindberg first brought Barbara to The Little Chapel. She faithfully attended the services for a year before she received a miracle. Every month she kept praying that God would heal her of multiple sclerosis.

She was born and raised in Michigan and is now enjoying the Arizona sun. She is the mother of four fine young men. Her greatest hobby is putting together puzzles. It was quite a puzzle for her to watch the different healings happen all around her at the different services and for her not to receive one. She kept praying and believed it was possible.

She knew when you had all the pieces of a puzzle you could complete the picture. Barbara felt she needed to search for the missing ingredient to complete her healing. She worked on growing spiritually. She learned to forgive, let go of the past, and release all the negative barriers we carry around and love more.

Love is that gentle but powerful healing energy. Everyday she is getting stronger spiritually and physically, and is so thankful to God.

" I am so grateful that I had the courage to hang on to the spiritual truth and words given in the services at The Little Chapel. Each month the sermon had a wonderful message, and Sara would always say, "God can heal anything. There are no incurable diseases when we look to the Great Physician."

My M.S. was diagnosed in 1986. By the time I learned about The Little Chapel, I was walking with crutches. I was so excited the day Sara looked at me and said the light of the Holy Spirit was all around me and to stand up and claim my healing. She asked for me to walk up and down the aisle of the church and forget the crutches, for I no longer had M.S. All I could do was cry as I walked. The heat was so strong through my entire body I knew God was healing me. I felt close to God, and my faith increased immediately.

My one son is a doctor of internal medicine and I couldn't wait to show him what God had done. His belief system is very black and white. When I marched into his office the next day, it was hard for him to grasp what had happened to me and he couldn't explain it. He called in another doctor to verify my healing. Both of them had to admit something out of the ordinary happened. I'm still working on my son to attend a service in The Little Chapel.

I didn't make a promise to God for anything because I was afraid I might fail in keeping it. He didn't pass me by after all—I'm healed! I do thank God everyday for making me stronger and stronger and for solving my greatest puzzle. "

As the Pain Left My Body Complete Joy Filled My Heart and Soul

Ella Newkirk

*E*lla has quite an interesting story to tell. When her healing occurred, she felt as if she knew a great secret that should not be a secret. So, she is delighted to share her joyful experience.

Ella was telling a friend about how she went to hear Sara speak, and what happened to her. Her friend said, "That is really a miracle." Ella was asked to give her testimony at a Little Chapel Service. Her friend, knowing her fear of public speaking, asked, "What did they say when you said, 'No'?" Ella replied, "Well, I didn't say 'No.' I feel it should not be kept a secret. Everyone should know about The Little Chapel and the wonderful miracles that are happening there all the time."

She didn't say, "No" to giving her testimony at The Little Chapel or to writing her story for this book.

On April 4, 2000, I took on the project of painting my bathroom, and I had a really difficult time getting started. First, I couldn't find a paintbrush, then the paint needed more color added and mixed, then I couldn't find a newspaper, or the stepladder. Now, most people probably would have listened to that little voice inside of them saying, "This isn't a good day to be doing this," but not me. The more challenged I was, the more determined I was to begin this project.

When I finally had everything together, I started painting. I was making pretty good time, everything was falling into place, and there I was, standing on top of the stepladder when suddenly I felt my insulin kick in. In the rush to start this project, I had remembered to do everything except eat after taking my morning shot. I decided I needed to stop what I was doing and eat something quickly. I had a paintbrush in one hand, and a paint container in the other, and so I was going to step down very carefully. Unfortunately, that is not what happened. I lost my balance, and fell back, striking my head; first against the wall and then against the tub. My back came down full force, and there I was in the tub, legs sticking straight up with pain shooting through my body. I felt like my abdomen and my legs were both on fire.

I knew this was serious. I started to lean over to grab the phone, just out of my reach, when I discovered that I could no longer feel or move my legs. I lay there, crying, trying to figure out what I could do. Suddenly it dawned upon me that I was fine from the waist up, so I pulled my legs out of the bathtub, and pulled myself forward on my hands. As I did this, I could feel a slight tingling in my legs, like the pins and needles you experience when your foot falls asleep. I got to the phone, and remembering something my brother Grant said—He's a paramedic—about people calling an ambulance when they could just as easily drive themselves to the hospital. I called my husband instead.

We went to Good Samaritan Hospital, and I was put in a wheelchair right away. Then we waited. Three and one-half hours later we were still waiting. At this point I asked Derek to go to the desk and see if they would be seeing me any time soon, or if we could please go home. Much to my surprise, they saw me right away, and a very nice nurse took me back to a little curtained area where she explained that the only examining table they had left was a birthing table. At 52 I thought I'd never see one of those again! Everyone had a good laugh.

Next, I was taken off to X-ray, and felt sorry for the technician because at this point I started crying uncontrollably with pain. He kept asking if he was hurting me, and I said, "No, it's all mine." I know he was grateful to get me back to my little room. My doctor was young and personable, friendly and very busy, but he still took the time to tell me all of the things that I had not broken in my body, and how lucky I was. The bad news, however, was that I had a lateral fracture of the fifth lumbar, and I had broken the tip off one of my lamina (those are the little fingers that go around your spinal column). I had a massive hematoma that was now pressing against my bladder and my spine. I can only describe the pain as worse than childbirth. I was informed that there was nothing they could do except to keep me very still. They gave me some strong pain pills and I was to see my regular doctor on Monday.

My regular doctor prescribed a strong narcotic that I would continue in larger and more frequent doses as the days progressed. The time of healing was estimated at 8 to 10 weeks, possibly longer, depending on my ability to heal. The pain was bad but I learned a great deal about my tolerance for drugs and my ability to accept pain.

My husband was wonderful. He did all of the cooking, cleaning and care giving. He dressed me and helped me in and out of the shower. I am ashamed to say that I was not gracious or thankful for the things he was doing. I was, however, angry that I should have to endure this painful humiliation. I told him on many occasions that this is something you do for old people, and I'm not old. "Why is this happening to me?" All I could do was think of myself. Pain seems to make us very self-centered. Perhaps it's because we become more aware of our physical selves. It was much more difficult for me to hold on to that spiritual side of myself.

Because of this, I forced myself to attend the May monthly meditation group, and on May 6th, the universal healing circle, run by Philip Burley. Our guest speaker that Saturday was Sara O'Meara. She was going to address our group about God's healing power. Now, I must say that I've always been somewhat skeptical of faith healers, even though I was a member of a prayer-healing group myself. I had, however, seen the ones on television, and they all looked rather staged to me. I would be polite and supportive because I had a deep respect for the work of Philip and Vivian Burley.

Sara introduced herself to the group and started to share her amazing story. She was an energetic and thought-provoking speaker. I listened intently, hanging on every word. She had not come to do any healings that day, only to share her experiences with us. To my amazement, as she was speaking, I saw the strangest thing begin to happen. Three or four inches from her body appeared a white light. It completely surrounded her. I thought to myself, "This woman's soul is too big for her body!" Then to my amazement, I was suddenly seeing her through this bright, white light with swirling pink opalescence. Next, I felt energy-almost electrical-enter at the top of my head. It went through my body, first hitting my neck and shoulders. I had experienced a bad whiplash previously and couldn't move my neck and shoulders but this was to be addressed after my back was healed. I saw a dark, rock-like energy move away from my body, and my head and shoulders area. Then it continued down my back and I felt a slight "ping" in the back of my neck. I watched numbly as the rock substance broke away from my body. The energy continued through my body, hitting my fifth lumbar. Again I felt this ping sensation and the same rock-like energy moving away from my body. There I was with no pain.

As all this was happening to me, Sara said that God had just told her that there was a person present in this group who had fallen from a ladder. This person had hit their head twice and broken their back. He was healing this person as she spoke. I was already crying with joy and relief. There was no pain and a feeling of complete joy had entered my body. At this point Sara asked if this person might identify themselves. I slowly raised my hand.

Sara said, "Get up, move around. How do you feel?" I said, "I feel wonderful," and I sat back down, because I was a little overwhelmed. It was several minutes before I understood the enormity of what had just happened to me. God had healed me. Me, plain old, ordinary, imperfect, regular person, me. God had loved me enough, with all of my imperfections. I had always thought that God healed only the most deserving people; people who had done great acts in His name. The few things I had done in my life had been done because they felt like the thing to do at the time; no other reason. I felt a little embarrassed because I knew I was unworthy of such a blessing, but how do you question the Lord's actions? The answer was simple: we don't. We accept with grace and know that we are all indeed part of His divine plan.

The following Monday I had an appointment with my doctor. I went to see her because my throat was a little rough, and I had plans to go to Hopi and the Grand Canyon the following weekend. When she saw me walking down the hall toward her office, carrying my granddaughter, she said, "Ella, what are you doing?" I said, "Have I got a story for you!"

We went into her office, sat down and I shared my story with her. Much to my surprise, she told me that her mother had a similar experience and that she knew that things like this really did happen. I told her that my husband thought I should have another X-ray, and she said, "Ella, I don't think you need another X-ray. You wouldn't even be able to bend over and pick up your granddaughter, let alone carry her down the hall, if your back was still broken." I told her that I had just stopped taking the pain medication and didn't get sick. She was a little surprised at that, but thought that it must have been a part of the healing. I felt wonderful.

On the following Sunday, I climbed up Second Mesa, a huge mountain, to watch the Mother's Day Home dances on the Hopi reservation and visit my friends up there. The next day I hiked the South Rim of the Grand Canyon with my friends and my husband. I carried a full, heavy backpack with no discomfort. My usual fear of heights was no longer present, and I was able to enjoy the sheer beauty of this truly sacred place, pain free. My heart was full of gratitude and joy. I made my fall to grace, and I am so thankful.

How Comforting it is to Know We Never Have to Face Any Challenge Alone

Sandra Owen

Sandy is such a wonderful woman. She has such a big heart and always wants to help out in any way she can. She is a past president of our Arizona Chapter for Childhelp.

Professionally, Sandy worked for the phone company and has now retired. One day at work she had a serious back injury. She immediately asked God to remove all fear and surround her with love. She trusted in God's love to be a shield of energy around her that would protect her from any permanent damage to her back.

Sara prayed for Sandy over the phone, and she felt the love and assurance that God was with her. God always answers a sincere prayer. The most valuable possession anyone can own is an open heart to God and His unconditional love.

" I had an accident at work and injured my back. The first thing I wanted to do was to phone Sara. I knew I had to have back surgery, but I wanted prayers to surround me and the doctors so everything would go perfectly.

The prayers gave me a sense of calmness through it all. The inner peace that I was given transformed my feelings of anxiety and concern to serenity and faith. It is such a blessing to know that help is always there for the asking, and we never have to face any challenge alone.

My back was healing while taking therapy three times a week, but I had some nerve pain that was bothering me. The December Chapel service was coming, and I couldn't wait to experience the extra love and healing power that is there at every service. I knew God would heal me. I knew it from deep inside my soul.

Yes, I received a healing. It felt like a tingling feeling down my back. I was engulfed in peace and love and felt safe, which helped me to relax my body as the nerve pain disappeared. My promise to God was to continually thank Him and never doubt his powerful healing energy. The Little Chapel may be small in size but the power of God's love is mighty there. "

Releasing My Fears with Faith

Marianne Rice

Marianne Rice is quite an extraordinary woman. She is blessed with outward beauty, but it is her inner beauty that captures your attention. She is smart, but always gives God the credit for making her dreams become a reality to help mankind. She truly knows to get her little ego out of the way and let God work through her for His glory to allow greater works to be done.

She loves The Little Chapel and brings friends whenever she attends. She has had quite a positive effect in so many lives.

In January of 1998 I suffered a sports injury that left me unable to walk within one year. Doctors involved in traditional medicine were unable to diagnose my condition. In November of 1998, through prayer, I begged God that if He wanted me to come home to Him, I was ready. Should He consider me worthy of healing, I would promise to devote my life to helping those like me who could not find the answers in traditional medicine.

Through a series of miraculous events beginning on Christmas Eve of 1998, I was lead from one integrative modality to the next, from Reiki to Chi Gong, to homeopathy and Chinese medicine. I also used acupuncture, chiropractic and energy medicine through healers. The unusual effects produced by these various healers amazed me. I began to slowly but surely recover through 1999. I also began to realize that my covenant with God was beginning to manifest and my life's destiny was unfolding.

I started to study physics and quantum physics, trying to find the binding universal concepts that God had created to unite the various integrative techniques I was using to achieve health and wellbeing. Through the next four years, I devoted myself to following God's lead, which had culminated in a company called *The Miracle Product Group.*

The *Miracle Product Group* team postulates that disease disorders alter the electromagnetic properties of molecules within cells, tissues and organs of the body. If a frequency can be introduced that cancels a discordant or pathological frequency then a state of natural balance can be achieved. It is this natural state of balance (homeostasis) that is representative of a healthy body and mind. The *Miracle Product Group* team asserts that energy healers translate a quantum field called the unified field to the sick individual they are working on, effectuating a healthy state of being through the alteration of the electromagnetic field from a discordant frequency to a harmonic frequency.

When I met Sara O'Meara in The Little Chapel a few years ago, I realized that I was meeting one of God's most important examples of a great leader. She represented to me a dynamic woman who had vision and dreamed to make Childhelp, one of the most prominent charities in the United States, a reality. She has an extraordinary amount of credits to her name for that work. In addition, her monthly chapel services provide consistent examples of the extreme value of energy healing techniques.

Sara represents for me the crossover personality of a tremendous visionary in humanitarian work and one of the most compassionate and refined healers I have ever observed. I can only thank God for giving me Sara as an example of what I should emulate. I now know that she has been used by The Lord to show me how He can effectively work through us and our work.

Sara has healed me in a most important way. She has shown me how to release myself to God's ultimate purpose for my divine destiny. Through observation of this extraordinary lady of grace, I have found the courage to release my fears to be replaced by faith.

I plan to complete my promise to God and to build His three companies: *The Miracle Product Group*, *The Miracle Product Foundation* and *Circle of Light International Healthcare Research* for His glory. Through healthcare applications based in science, millions will find their way back to understanding that God is an accessible reality through prayer. Sara is one of the key individuals I must thank for showing me that God's divine plan can be achieved.

My allegiance to Sara and Childhelp will never end. She has taught me to have a willing heart, to be fearless and to always have faith, because belief is what gets us there.

Imagine the vision.

Step into the dream.

Make it a reality through faith and observation of a superior lady of grace…our Sara O'Meara.

Goodbye "Artie" and Hello God

Terry Rockwell

erry lives alone in Minnesota and has two grown sons. She is an aunt to Carol Hebets. Carol always talks about Sara and The Little Chapel when someone is in need of a healing, and Terry was.

Terry had suffered with arthritis for a long time. She said arthritis had been a part of her life for so many years. She looked at it as her best friend and called it "Artie." She is such a fine Christian and looks every day to God to keep her strong and healthy.

" When Carol first told me about Sara, I had to think about it and pray about it. I wanted to be able to let go, say goodbye to "Artie," and be open to the healing process from God.

Carol and Jim invited me to stay with them in San Diego during their summer visit. Most of the way flying to California, I was praying and getting ready for my healing. After I got settled in my room, Carol and I started talking. She got Sara on the phone to pray for me. I started to get very warm, then hot, and then the water just poured off my body. By the time she finished praying, I felt I had just had a hot shower. The pain had left, and it was like I never had it before. I felt normal again.

Carol asked if I would like to take a walk with her. I said, "Of course, I've had a healing." We walked so much my shins got sore. I was having such a good time with Carol, I didn't think much more about my healing. I just started doing everything that I hadn't been able to do in years. What a thrill it was to not have pain and be able to walk again.

That evening, I started to think about what happened to me and what a glorious, pain-free day I had. I thanked God for answering Sara's prayers for me, and asked that the pain from my arthritis never return. I gave "Artie" to God.

Sara prayed for me a few days later and once again I felt the heat. I have so much peace and joy in my heart every time she prays for me. The doctor still says I have arthritis in my body, but I have no pain. He has agreed that if I do not have any pain, I do not need to have surgery. He doesn't understand what happened to me, even though I told him Sara prayed and God healed me.

I got a bladder infection a while back and the doctor wanted me to do some things that I didn't want to do, so I phoned Sara and received another healing.

I am a whole person again. I attend Bible study regularly and teach children's programs. I started my own business specializing in home wrapping and window installation on new construction. I was once immobile, and now because God healed me, I am free. I want everyone to know how good God is. I hope everyone who reads these stories will tell at least four friends, maybe even five! God will bless you if you do.

Completing My Mission is My Number One Priority

Dola Rogers

When God first spoke to Dola, known as "D," she was just a little girl. "D" grew up in the beautiful country of Tennessee and then moved to the city for a different lifestyle. She was exposed to many kinds of churches and beliefs but her heart was searching to find her own path to God.

Sara and "D" first met in 1952 in Tennessee. Over the years, she has remained a dear friend to Sara and many of us in Childhelp. She attends the Little Chapel service as often as she can.

She is intelligent, has a lot of energy, and knows new and exciting things are opening up for her. She has two grown boys, Tip and Craig, who live in Tennessee.

In 1952, I attended the University of Tennessee. I married someone from Knoxville and lived there for many years. I met Sara and had the pleasure of knowing her entire family. They were very nice to me and introduced me to so many people. Sara went away to college and then moved to California, but I kept up with her through her family and friends.

During the period just prior to Childhelp coming to Tennessee, I attended a Chapel service. As I entered The Little Chapel, I felt great peace come over me. I sat and listened to every word of Sara's sermon, and knew I had come home. I found the church my heart had always longed for.

When the healings began after Sara spoke, I felt this trembling, tingling feeling going through my body. Later, I realized I had a total spiritual reawakening which continued progressing after the service.

I returned to my home in New York, and felt the negative energy all around me. I worked in the stock market for 30 years, and dealt with a lot of negative energy. Now it hit me so hard I could hardly breathe. The energy in The Little Chapel was so positive and uplifting, and made me retreat from negative places.

This was the beginning of changing my life and direction. Living in New York, I couldn't attend Chapel every month, so I bought tapes and videos of the services. Now I have church in my own home every Sunday when listening to them. When I get agitated about things, I go to the drawers of tapes and videos and run my hand over them. When I stop and pick one out, it is always just what I need to hear. It is like a small miracle every time.

I've actually had healings listening to the services. One day, I had fallen and hurt my arm, so I decided I needed to listen to a tape of Sara's. She called out a healing for a left arm. I surprised myself when my hand went up and I said, "I'll take it, I'll take it." Sara didn't hear me, but God did, and my arm was healed.

Each healing has taught me a lesson. My right hip needed a healing and I suffered with bad arthritis for years. At one of The Little Chapel services, Sara placed her hand on my hip and it was so hot I thought I would have her handprint on me for the rest of my life. I had never felt such heat before. I received a beautiful and complete healing.

In January 1999, I tried to move an immovable bed and really hurt my back. I had two ruptured disks resulting in a lot of pain. Sara began praying for me over the phone. In May, I flew out for the wedding of Dionne Fedderson, Yvonne's daughter. I had to wear a back brace, which was extremely uncomfortable. The night of the wedding came, and we arrived early at the church. When Sara entered on stage where she was going to perform the marriage ceremony, my back began to feel funny. I thought the brace had killed all my nerves and I was going to die. A swirling kept going up my back all during the wedding ceremony and continued in the car to dinner.

After being seated for the reception dinner, I finally realized what had happened. I had received a healing on my back. Immediately I went to the ladies room, removed the back brace and threw it in the garbage can. I danced every dance and had no pain.

When I returned home to see my doctor, he insisted on taking another X-ray even though I kept saying I was healed. The ruptured disks were gone. My back was completely healed and I have never had a back pain since that day.

My next healing I call my "ground zero" healing. I was to meet some friends for breakfast at "Window on the World" at 9:00 AM on 9/11/01. I decided not to go at the last moment, which saved my life. My friends were all killed.

After 9/11, a small police force that manned the *World Trade Center* asked me to volunteer. My work was not down in the pit, but several blocks back behind gates and patrol centers in trailers. It never occurred to me that when I was brushing this white dust off my clothes, I was breathing it in.

In April 2002, I was rushed to the hospital with a temperature of 106°F. I had pneumonia and developed a bizarre lung infection. I was told I had lost the complete capacity for breathing in the lower right lobes of my lung. I would have to learn how to breathe, have a lot of therapy, and a lung specialist to monitor me. Part of my lung was dead.

When I phoned Sara she started praying immediately, and the healing process began. It took me a long time to get my body healthy again. The last X-rays of my right lung looked fine. I told the doctor that God had healed me. He said something was wrong with the X-ray and first diagnosis because he did not know how to explain the miracle.

Two years ago, I was rushed to the hospital with a double heart blockage, and I needed to have surgery right away. They phoned my brother and my children. I was in the emergency room for 6 hours before they assembled the cardiac team. They wouldn't give me a phone to call Sara, but I kept praying silently. I was given an anesthetic as they wheeled me into the operating room. I could hear the doctor say that I was clean as a bell and he was not going to operate. I could not open my mouth to talk, which drove me crazy. I wanted to shout, "God healed me again!" They apologized to me, but to this day, they have no clue why I had every single sign of double blockage and then I was perfectly okay.

I'm grateful to be given more time here. I want to complete my mission. I've promised God that for the rest of my life, I will listen and obey. Wherever He leads me, I will follow. Every day, I pray for the highest good for me, for all those I love, and for all those who need love.

He is the Master of Miracles

Reverend Philip Rye

Reverend Philip Rye and his faithful, sweet wife, Gloria, love to attend The Little Chapel services and watch God work through Sara. Miracle after miracle, they feel it is a true joy to watch.

Reverend Rye was born in Santa Barbara, California on his mother's birthday. He and Gloria live in Phoenix now, and they are both ordained ministers.

Elaine Jarvis always attends The Little Chapel services. She is a member of Reverend Rye's church and goes there on alternating Sundays. It was Elaine who first told the Rye's about The Little Chapel.

Reverend Rye now brings his congregation with him once a month to hear Sara speak. Many of them have received healings, and they all feel they have been greatly blessed by the power of the Holy Spirit in The Little Chapel.

They enjoy sitting in The Little Chapel and feeling the powerful love, energy and peace that surpasses all understanding.

My story begins in the middle of April 2003. Everything was going well in our ministry and we were happy with our lives. Three things happened that brought us much pain, but they were the very things we needed to bring us closer to Him so we could experience His great healing power and blessings.

My wife, Gloria, and I took a couple out for lunch at a western restaurant. We wanted to have a photo of the four of us, so I picked up my chair to move it around the table and it caught on something on the floor. I fell on the window frame and cracked my head. A big lump formed on the back of my head but I really wasn't hurt badly. Being a minister you have to be hard headed, you know. I bled a little, so the restaurant gave us a free meal. They were concerned I might sue them, I guess. We accepted it as a blessing and thanked them for being so kind about it.

The second thing that happened to me was one morning I picked up a very large, heavy bag of clothes, and like Santa Claus, I swung it over my left shoulder. I felt something pull on my shoulder as I said, "uh oh."

A couple of weeks later, the third thing happened to me. A relative was leaving for Spain, and they asked me to drive them to the airport. Of course, they had large suitcases that were quite heavy. I picked up the luggage to place it in the trunk of my car. As I did, I felt severe pain in my back and left shoulder.

When I got home, I took some pain pills but they did not help. Joint Riders Rub with hot packs helped a little. The doctor said, "Just take it easy and it will go away." After two trips to the chiropractor, the diagnosis was that I had a pulled muscle or separated a rib. Our ministry has to keep going, so I suffered the pain.

On May 27th, Gloria and I were to conduct a memorial service for some deceased members of the First Families of Arizona, a pioneer organization here in Phoenix. I serve as their chaplain. The pain was so severe that morning in my chest that I was doubled over.

Paramedics were called and I was taken to the emergency room in St. Luke's hospital. It seemed I was having a heart attack.

This was the day after Memorial Day, so there was only one doctor on duty to take care of all the sick people coming to that hospital. I couldn't go anywhere as I was hooked up to a drip system and a heart-monitoring device while lying on a gurney, which was not very comfortable. Being a minister, I began to pray for the sick folks coming in to the emergency room.

About eight hours later, I was taken to a room for a CAT scan, and then taken to another room to spend the night. I shared space with another clergyman, so we prayed for one another, our loved ones, friends, and the world. It was a prayerful evening.

Gloria was so upset worrying about me, she developed shingles. The next day I had a stress test on the treadmill and I barely passed it. They sent me home later that day with positive results about my heart. I did not have any heart trouble but I still had severe chest and back pain.

On June 1st, we went to the service in The Little Chapel. My chest and back pain was horrible. The only way I could help the pain abate was to lean back on the bench hard against it to keep it from hurting. The soft, gentle voice of the Holy Spirit said, "Trust in me."

Sara came out and began her message, and my pain began to subside. I was sitting next to Atlee Tucker and our wives were sitting behind us. When the healings started happening throughout The Chapel, Sara turned to Atlee and me and said, "The Holy Spirit is all over you both. Accept your healings now." Praise God, my pain went away. Atlee got a wonderful healing of his knee.

My pain came back a little when we got home, but I knew some healings are progressive. The Holy Spirit assured me my comfort would come. Several weeks later, I was completely healed of all pain in my chest, back and shoulder. Praise God, and thank you Sara. I love to bring my congregation to The Little Chapel once a month and see the wonders of God in action through Sara.

On December 18, 2008, I was blessed again with a wonderful healing. The Christmas service is always popular and on December 18 2008 the Little Chapel couldn't hold everyone so it was moved to the *Franciscan Renewal Center*—a much larger church.

My right arm from the elbow to the shoulder had been in constant pain for quite some time. I don't believe in taking pain pills, so on the way to the service I was in a lot of pain. The word FROG came to my mind while driving that evening which was a sign to me to "Fully Rely On God".

Gloria and I sat in the fourth row in the middle of the sanctuary. Being a minister, I love to watch everyone during the service, and see how God touches them. I have such long legs I prefer to sit in the aisle seat.

Yvonne gave her opening talk and asked everyone to quiet their minds and open their hearts to the presence of God. The love energy is always so strong during the services and Yvonne encourages us to make the most of every precious moment. God never forces us to receive his blessings, but His love is free for the asking.

The mood in the room began to shift as we focused our attention on why we were there in The Little Chapel. As we opened our hearts to His love you could feel the power of the Holy Spirit.

Sara's grandchildren were next on the program, and I continued to relax and thank God for taking away my pain. Sara began her sermon, and I got caught up in the scriptures being read in a spiritual moment (not a senior moment!)

When the healings began at the end of the service I listened carefully as she began calling out different body parts and diseases being healed. She always reminds us that God does the healing, and she does not have to touch us. However, that night as she walked down the aisle past me she laid her hand on my shoulder, and I felt a very warm feeling right down my arm all the way down to my hand. The pain was gone completely.

I thank God for my healing. I can do anything and everything with my right arm again. Praise God! If we truly rely on God, He will never let you do down. He is the master of miracles.

God Has Been So Good to Me, I Wish I Could Do More for Him

Maria Sau

Maria lives in Arizona where she attends The Little Chapel services as often as possible. She has two daughters and one son. God has touched them all and they are so grateful for The Little Chapel.

Maria appreciates everything you do for her, and always has a smile on her face, no matter what she is going through personally. She doesn't complain about the challenges she has been given. She does what she has to do, and is constantly thanking God for His love and blessings. We could all learn a lot from her sweet spirit.

"I am a single mom with three children to raise. My son, Juan, is an angel sent to teach me many things. He has always been on medication to help his mental challenges, and is very hard to control and handle. My two teenage daughters tried to help me with him, but it was impossible. Sadly, he had to be placed in a foster home. He was very unhappy there and became even more aggressive and unmanageable. They gave him higher doses of prescription drugs, which broke my heart.

Juan loves to go to The Little Chapel with me. He begged God to help him, so he could come home and live with me. I kept telling him, "no", because he was just too hard to handle. A lot of struggles happened for him in foster care, and Juan ended up being sent back to live with me. I was so concerned, but it has been easy this time. I surround him with love every day, and I believe *that* is the best medicine. He is now on the minimum dose of drugs—a baby dose. He and I thank God each and every day.

All my life, I had practiced Yoga, but the pain in my right knee got so bad I had to quit. By the time I heard about the Little Chapel in October 2001, I was wearing a brace. Every night was miserable. I slept on my side with my knees bent, but the severe pain would always awaken me.

I was excited to learn about the Little Chapel, or what is lovingly called "The House of Miracles." You can feel the power of God when you enter, and I couldn't wait for the healings to start after Sara spoke. I couldn't believe all the miracles that were happening all around me. Sara said knees were being healed. I held my breath and thought, "Would God really heal me?" I was so nervous I didn't feel anything like great heat or cold.

I went home and thought I had been touched, but I wasn't really sure. Monday morning I realized I had slept through the night with no pain. I got up and walked without the brace and felt no pain. I thought, "I really was healed at the Little Chapel! Miracles truly *do* happen there!" I started to phone my family and neighbors and decided to wait a day or two to make certain. Well, I was certain after that.

Months later my knee started cracking. I heard the Father say, "Reclaim it." I did. I know the cracking in my knee came back because I was listening to my mind, not my spirit. It was so awesome how God heard my prayers again. I was able to keep my healing.

Through Sara, God has also healed me of high cholesterol and so many other things. One of my daughters received a beautiful healing of cancer through prayers at The Little Chapel. So did my other daughter who was a victim of sexual abuse, and after attending The Little Chapel, our relationship is improving. I know putting all our names on the prayer request cards every Sunday has helped. Sara prays over our requests daily, and I know what a difference that has made for my family. We always need all the prayers and help we can get.

I wish I could do more for God because He has done so much for my family and me. I thank Him for Sara, and pray for The Little Chapel all the time. It truly has been "The Little House of Miracles" for me. "

He Answers All Prayers Perfectly

Analisa & Joann Sayklay

JoAnn was born and raised in El Paso, Texas. She attended the University of Texas in El Paso. She was married and traveled around quite a bit before settling in Arizona. She and her daughter live in Cave Creek, Arizona presently.

Her daughter, Analisa, was born in Santa Monica, California. She attends Saint Theresa Catholic School in Phoenix. She is active in Girl Scouts®, her church, and is on the school volleyball team.

Both JoAnn and Analisa love the arts and attend plays whenever they can.

Marilyn Brownstein introduced them to The Little Chapel about two years ago. They feel Sara has been so kind and loving to them and they love her. The Little Chapel has truly been a place of comfort and inspiration. They have been blessed with several healings.

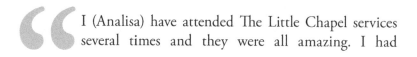

I (Analisa) have attended The Little Chapel services several times and they were all amazing. I had something wrong with my stomach. I was nauseous all the time and kept throwing up. I was really, *really* sick and every time I would try to eat something I would lose it. I was so freaked out.

My dad had me for the weekend; so, my mom went to The Little Chapel to pray for me. When Sara asked who was praying for their daughter, my mom not only raised her hand but also stood up. Sara walked over to her and said what your daughter is going through will bring her closer to God. Ever since that day I haven't thrown up or been nauseous. That experience did make me closer to God.

The second time I was healed I had sprained my ankle warming up for a volleyball game. I had gone to physical therapy, but it was still really stiff. It hurt a lot. Sara was healing people and walking around the chapel and she said, "Who is having leg problems." I thought that was me and I raised my hand. When she came up to me, she asked what was wrong with my leg. I told her I sprained it. Then she told me to test it by walking on it down the aisle of the church. It hasn't hurt since. I was so happy that I received another healing.

The third time God blessed me with an emotional healing. Things were going badly for me and I was getting upset a lot. I was arguing all the time with my friends and becoming kind of bitter. My grades were going down and I felt awful about myself.

My mom brought me to The Little Chapel and I prayed hard that God would help me. He answered my prayers, and I felt His touch upon me immediately! I am like a new person after that service. I'm feeling good and my grades are better. God answers all prayers perfectly.

My (Joann) healing took place just this last Christmas service. My neck had been hurting me for several days. I was managing it by taking a lot of ibuprofen. During the service, I started feeling pain traveling down my neck into my shoulder and through my arm. I love the Christmas service. It is one of my favorite chapel services of the year. All through the service, I just kept thinking when I get home I want to take some more ibuprofen.

After Sara spoke she started walking around and calling out healings. I was praying that she would mention a healing of a neck, but she didn't. Sara always tells us just because she doesn't call out something specific about an illness or problem doesn't mean God is not healing us. In fact she says we can receive a healing on the way to The Little Chapel, during the sermon, on the way home, or days later.

I decided to "act" and even though she didn't call out a neck healing I would believe God knew and would heal me. I started moving my neck left to right and each time I did, it moved a little bit more and more and more and by the end of the service I felt absolutely no pain.

Analisa and I feel so blessed to know about The Little Chapel and thank God for always answering our prayers. We both have learned about faith, love and perseverance through attending The Little Chapel and receiving our own personal healings. God never lets us down!

The Love I Give Returns to Bless Me Many Times Over

Rhonda Sehorn

Rhonda was born in Mount Ayr, Iowa and raised in Blue Springs, Missouri. She attended Missouri Western State University. She moved to Phoenix, Arizona in 2008 to help her mother take care of her father. He has a heart transplant and is on dialysis.

Karl Gosch is married to Taryn who is the daughter of Sara. His mother Karen was in Arizona visiting Taryn and Karl last year and phoned Rhonda and asked her to join her for lunch one afternoon. While they were out enjoying the day, Karen told her about Sara and The Little Chapel. Rhonda was anxious to attend a service after hearing many stories from Karen.

She was hungry to learn more about the miracles that happen in this small chapel and felt it must be a very sacred place. Rhonda loves to come to the services and experience God in action. It is so exciting for her to watch people get healed, and see the look on their faces when God touches them. Sara always says it is "God's call" who gets healed, when they get healed, or if they get healed.

Everyone who attends a service receives a blessing of some kind: A spiritual blessing about God's truth and how we should live our lives.

I had attended several services before I received my special healing. Every service is a treat and I feel so good during and after those hours in The Little Chapel. The power of love is strong and I'm always overwhelmed with the presence of God. It is an amazing feeling.

In September 2010 I had the unforgettable experience of sitting next to a woman who received a healing. Sara started her healing work. She asked who was suffering from neck pain. The women next to me raised her hand. Sara came over and started inquiring about her pain. The women said she felt heat on the right side of her neck. The heat was so intense that I felt it on the left side of my own neck. She was definitely healed.

My neck was hurt on the right side, but the heat was only on the left side. Sara asked if there was anyone else with neck pain, but I didn't raise my hand. I know I should have but I felt there were so many other people that needed healings more than I did. Many were there with cancer and life-threatening illnesses and I thought after all no one ever died from neck pain. So, I made the choice to go home with a sore neck. I must admit when I felt the heat coming from the women next to me there was a little voice inside of me that was saying, "Please, give some of that to me. I wouldn't mind being healed as well."

A month later my neck pain was getting worse. I was in tears most of the time because it hurt so badly. I had gone to doctors, chiropractors, I had laser therapy, muscle relaxers, pain pills, but nothing was working.

On October 17, 2010, I got up early to get ready in plenty of time for The Little Chapel service. I was suffering from excruciating pain down the right side of my neck. It was so bad that I could not turn my head to the right at all. I almost cancelled my plans to attend the service because it was very difficult for me to drive in that condition. I felt I just have to push and go to pray for my father who was a heart transplant recipient many years ago and is now on dialysis. He needs a lot of prayers. I was also asked to pray for other family and friends who were experiencing health problems and troubles in their lives. I knew God always heard the prayers that were said in The Little Chapel.

It was a beautiful day in Arizona and when I arrived the church was quite full so I sat in the second row from the back. Even though my neck was hurting it felt good to be in the chapel with so many prayerful and loving people. The atmosphere was heavenly, and I was praying hard for everyone.

It was sometime during Sara's sermon that I received my healing. I didn't feel heat or anything. I just tried to turn my head to the right and it didn't hurt. I kept turning my head and smiling at the lady sitting behind me. I did it at least twenty times and I know the woman had to be thinking, "What is wrong with her? Why does this woman keep turning around and staring at me and smiling?"

My smile has never left my face since my outstanding healing. I feel so blessed and thankful to God for his wonderful grace and healing love. Thank you, Sara, for allowing God to bless and heal others through you.

P.S. I received another healing after I gave my testimony in The Little Chapel. I had torn tendons in my leg and my leg is perfect now.

Blessed with a Physical Healing & Working on Spiritual Growth

Mary Severtson

*I*n 1960, Mary and her family moved from New Jersey to
Arizona. She loves the weather, with the exception of two
and a half months, and thinks the people in Arizona are
the best, anywhere. Mary and her husband are in business together
and have one son who is twenty-five years old and happily married.
She can't wait to have grandchildren.

When Mary has a free moment she enjoys crafting and sewing.
Every day she is working on overcoming any challenges that come
her way and looking for a positive outcome. She trusts the gentle
strength of God.

" In 2002, I had major back surgery and reconstruction.
At that time, I wasn't sure if I was going to be able
to walk again or have any feeling in my legs. My doctors were
phenomenal and I call them "my angels."

The degree of physical, mental and spiritual downfall was
overwhelming after the surgery. When you are in great pain, it is

easy to fall into the pit of self-pity and forget all about your spiritual beliefs. You put God on the back burner and indulge in feeling sorry for yourself. You dwell on the pain and give it great power instead of thinking about God and how wonderful His healing touch can be on your body. Painkillers helped ease my severe physical pain and enabled me to shuffle my feet to move.

One special Sunday morning, I forced myself to go to The Little Chapel. As I entered through the doors, a great calm feeling came over my body. Sitting in The Little Chapel, I began to think about my life and how I always had to control things. As I listened to the service, I realized I needed to relinquish some of my responsibilities to others. I began to let go and relax. My back and legs began to feel warm and tingle a bit. Because of my history, I just assumed that I had been sitting too long and needed to get up and move around. Suddenly, I heard Sara say, "Someone is having trouble walking." My arm shot up like someone pulled it. She turned to me and asked if I could walk up to the front where she was standing. I walked to her with no problem. She had me walk back and forth several times and I did so with ease.

Many outstanding healings occurred that beautiful Sunday morning as the Holy Spirit was so powerful around the room. Sara was the conduit for my physical healing and also helped me to see what I had to do to change in my life to make it better. Before that Sunday, I didn't feel worthy to receive a healing. I had to love and accept myself as a child of God before I could allow the Holy Spirit to heal my physical body.

I still have a few aches and pains, but I thank God for them because they remind me to be grateful for my miraculous healing. I will never be a gymnast again, but I have God in my life and that is greater, by far. I'm thankful for my physical healing and working everyday on my spiritual growth.

When the Student is Ready, the Teacher Will Appear

Susan Shakespeare

*C*arol Hebets is mentioned throughout this book because she is always bringing individuals to The Little Chapel. This story is about her lovely sister, Susan, who lives in California with her two children—Kelsey and Spencer.

Susan is so grateful for her life-changing experience and feels totally blessed. She always thought her sister, Carol, was an angel, and now she knows how correct her feelings were.

> My doctor found a tumor in my thyroid. When it was first discovered, it was very tiny. The doctor said, "If you see any growth in the next 6 months, I want you to go and see a specialist." It did grow. So, I went to a specialist. He did the usual testing and a biopsy. I had an ultrasound as well but everything was coming back inconclusive, which was not okay with me. I wanted to know if this was cancer or nothing to worry about. Having had cancer previously, it was frightening for me. When physicians know your history they want to do surgery right away.

I talked to my doctor and we agreed to monitor it and do another biopsy in six months. I went back in 6 months and had another biopsy. It came back inconclusive but it did have some suspicious cells. Again, with my history, the physicians were strongly recommending surgery. I just didn't want to have another surgery.

I hadn't told Carol and Jim, because I didn't want them to worry. I finally phoned Carol and told her and she invited me to go to the next Chapel service with them. The service was in two weeks. Carol had already told me about Sara's gift so I said I would love to join them.

It was October 2001 when I first came through the doors of the Little Chapel. I was filled with doubts and fear, and all the negativity that goes with that. Those negative feelings didn't last long in the Chapel because I was so overwhelmed with the love and light all around the room. I felt so warm and safe there.

All through the service, Carol kept telling me, "Just be in surrender and open your heart and trust." So many miracles began to happen and then Sara called out a healing of upper leg/hip. Carol reached over and said to raise my hand and take the healing because I had injured my upper leg the week before while crawling under a corral fence. It was very painful and made it difficult for me to be as active as I'd like to be, but it wasn't life threatening.

I reluctantly raised my hand and Sara came over to me and stood right in front of me and said, "You're praying very hard for something here." I was crying so hard, I had to talk through the shaking of my head. She said, "God's love and light are all over you." I felt heat all through my body and I know it was the Holy Spirit.

Sara asked, "Is there anything that you would want more in your life right now than to be healed?" She went on to say this was a learning experience for me. "It's about your priorities." I didn't understand at that time, but I do now. I was not putting God first.

She asked if my leg/hip felt better and asked me to stand up and test it. I was shocked when I stood up and realized all the pain was gone. I squealed, "Yes, it's completely gone. It doesn't hurt at all." She told me to thank God and moved on. I was left with no pain in my leg, but huge disappointment in my heart because my prayer was for the nodule on my neck not my leg. After the service, I wanted to thank Sara for the message and tell her about my illness. I started to talk and she said, "May I pray with you?"

Sara put her hand on my neck where the tumor was and proceeded to pray. What happened was so miraculous. Through my whole body I felt an exchange of energy and felt warmth everywhere. At the same time, I was sobbing and releasing so much through my physical body. It was unbelievable. It was as if I was lifted up and out of my body, and something incredible was happening to me. I was absolutely healed there at the service and I'm so grateful. After she prayed I felt my throat and couldn't feel any nodule, or anything. Yet, I still had a thread of "doubt." Could it be completely gone or would it come back? I shared my doubts with Sara and she asked whether I believed my leg had been healed earlier. I said, "Yes absolutely it had." She then responded with "Well, if God can do that so instantaneously, why can't He take care of this as well?" She reminded me to keep affirming that I had been healed.

A little while later, I started feeling the nodule, and I said to Carol, "Oh my gosh maybe it's not gone." Doubt crept in and I remembered the man who gave his testimony. He had been healed of rheumatoid arthritis and said that a year later, he began experiencing that old familiar pain and took it as an opportunity to say thank you to God for reminding him of the miracle healing he had received. Soon, he was no longer in pain. I know his was a message I will always remember and I am grateful for his testimony that morning.

I wanted to get confirmation and had one more doctor appointment with another specialist that I had seen before. At my first visit he insisted that I needed surgery. After my healing in the

Chapel, he took another biopsy and it came out that it was just multiple cysts that are always statistically benign. He said, "I just don't believe this. I do not recommend surgery for you now." This was the added confirmation I needed to hear. Doubt left, and joy and peace filled my heart.

The day I received my healing, after the service, four women asked my name and said they would pray for me. Everyone who attends The Little Chapel is so wonderful to pray for each other. I have never seen or experienced anything like it.

"When the student is ready, the teacher will appear." *[Buddhist Proverb]* I believe that so much now. Jim and Carol are beautiful blessings in my life. I thank God for healing me through Sara, for all those who are praying for me and for others who are in need.

I am clearer within myself after the healing. I'm working very hard to get my priorities straight, and spend my time and energy on worthwhile things. I am always telling others about the Little Chapel. All of you in Arizona are fortunate to have this Chapel and the benefit of Sara's blessed ministry. It is a gift from God, be thankful.

The Little Chapel is Big When it Comes to Miracles

Reverend Margo Shatto

Reverend Margo Shatto was born and raised in Phoenix, Arizona. She met and married the love of her life, Reverend Ryland Jones, in 1994 and they were fortunate to have 10 years together before he passed away in 2004.

Reverend Ryland was a wonderful gentleman and loved the Lord with all his heart. He was the one responsible for leading Margo to the Lord, teaching her how to pray and eventually opening her heart to receive a healing through one of Sara's Christmas services in The Little Chapel.

After Reverend Ryland died, Margo became a reverend and started a ministry on behalf of Ryland and herself. She has three doctorates, a Master's Degree in Religion and a PhD in Philosophy. She has mass every Sunday morning with a small group of friends.

She was first told about The Little Chapel from her neighbor whose child was receiving therapy at our Childhelp Children's Advocacy Center.

Margo loves The Little Chapel and receives great comfort when she attends the services.

" It was the second time Ryland and I attended The Little Chapel on a cold December evening in 2000, but inside the Little Chapel it was warm and cozy. The room was filled with God's love and the sound of Christmas music filled the air. Sara gave a beautiful sermon on the life of Jesus and then the healings began.

Ryland held my hand and prayed so hard for me to receive a healing. Sara announced there was an anointing of healings for those who had breathing problems. My mother passed away years ago, but at that moment I felt her loving arms pick me up as she whispered gently that I was receiving the healing I had prayed for.

My heart was overjoyed. I could hardly contain myself. I was healed miraculously of COPD, a pulmonary disease. I was taking Prednisone at the time, and I was using a breathing machine twice daily. After my fantastic healing, I quit taking all my medicines and did not have to use the breathing machine.

I will be forever grateful to my husband for opening my eyes to see and my heart to accept the love that God has for me and each one of us. Thank you, Sara, for allowing God to use you as a vessel for His healing work. "

The Miracle Hog

Michelle Singleton

*M*ichelle was a California girl until 1987 when she moved to Arizona. She is the proud mother of two grown boys in their twenties—Christopher and Jeremiah. She attends the Fountain of Life Church in Mesa, Arizona the weeks there is no chapel service.

Michelle is such a fun person to be around. She has a great sense of humor and spreads God's joy wherever she goes.

She has received so many miracles in The Little Chapel that her friends jokingly call her "The Miracle Hog." Her mental atmosphere of love and acceptance is a magnet for miracles.

Michelle has truly learned that God's love and grace is unlimited. Jesus taught us "Above all else, love one another." When we truly have love in our hearts we can't help but share that love and joy with others.

I had been out of work for five months and then in February 2009 our Lord laid on my heart an idea to start my own business, "Organize It and Clean It Up." The first two months were very slow and I was barely able to meet my basic needs. Through my work, however, God sent me into several homes where my customers were in great need of prayer. I prayed with them and for them and saw many lives change. My heart was full of gratitude to God for using me to help others but I needed to find a way to help myself financially. I was at a crossroad and facing a very serious decision.

I have a special friend who is an ordained minister and lives in Camp Verde. She invited me to visit her for a couple of days so we could spend some quality time praying about my future work. I took her up on her invitation and drove to Camp Verde praising God all the way. My friend is such a wonderful prayer warrior and always willing to help when you need her. I was looking forward to our time together. Prayer time is special and always makes you feel better and more at peace with your current challenges. With God, there is always a way.

During our time together my friend kept talking about The Little Chapel in Paradise Valley, and her wonderful experience at one of the services. It made me curious and put the desire in my heart to attend a service so I could see for myself why she was so excited. She said the next chapel service was Tuesday evening and we could drive down the hill together. As she was talking I felt deep in my heart a great urgency to go.

I was offered a full time job in Camp Verde while I was there, but somehow it didn't feel quite right to give up my own business completely. I felt strongly that if I would go to The Little Chapel my answer would become clear.

Tuesday was a happy day for me. My friend and I drove down from Camp Verde to Paradise Valley talking, laughing and praying all the way. We arrived early for the service and I was amazed how peaceful I felt the minute I walked through the Chapel door. We were handed a program as we entered and it told the story about Sara's healing of cancer at a Kathryn Kuhlman's service. I knew I was in the right place, and knew that God would speak to me that evening. I was right! I listened to every word of the sermon and felt it was written for me. Then the healings began.

My first healing was when Sara called out for shoulders to be healed. I have long suffered from aching shoulders—years in fact — from a fall I took down a flight of stairs in 2003. I had not only torn my rotator cuff and dislocated that shoulder but I had broken the collarbone as well. That night the pain subsided into nothingness.

The second healing I received that Sara called out was for knees. Oh, my word! My knees had been in excruciating pain for years. Being 100 pounds overweight, I knew if I would lose some weight it would help. When I would stand up my knees felt like there was bone-on-bone burning pain. That night in The Little Chapel the pain went away. I know my part was *believing* it would be gone forever and that He would restore my knees to full capacity. This is a progressive healing for me but that night I had no pain—and now it continues to be pain-free.

The third healing came when Sara said there are three people needing healing in their business. I raised my hand quickly. Sara said that my plans were not necessarily what the Lord's plans were. I needed to diversify and not put everything in one place. These weren't the exact words but I knew what she was saying. I thought that I was to go up to Camp Verde and spread my wings.

Spreading my wings included getting involved with Childhelp®. I am now a member of the Phoenix Chapter of Childhelp® and volunteered my time at an event in October 2009.

I have received from God so much and I want to show my deep appreciation by giving back to those in need. There is no better cause than helping the abused and neglected children who cannot help themselves.

After the long hot summer in Arizona, the first Little Chapel service was on September 27th. My friends, Marjorie and Saretta, attended with me. I was praying so hard for them because they both needed a healing.

All of a sudden I heard Sara say there was an anointing of spines happening and everyone who was having trouble with their spines should raise their hands. I couldn't believe it. You see about a month and a half ago, a group of friends and I decided to believe that we were young again and go to Sun Splash, a water amusement park.

After going down the slides several times I thought it would be fun to try the Bonsai. Well the name alone should have given me a clue. It was almost an 80 foot drop straight down. Now, mind you I hadn't been on those kinds of slides in almost 15 years. When I hit the bottom of the slide, I knew that the middle of my spine had been really hurt. In fact, I had the breath knocked out of me. It almost felt like one of my vertebrae was sticking out. But this didn't stop me. I went down six more slides. Again, I believed I was still young enough to do this. Ha!

It was the third day after the slides that my entire back went out at work and I couldn't breathe for the pain. I could not afford to go to the doctor so I did what I could to relieve some of the pain.

In the Chapel service Sara said God is going to heal spines today. I couldn't raise my hand quickly enough. Sara said, "There is someone that is having great heat in their spine area." I felt I was burning up, so I knew she was talking about me. She had me stand up and touch my toes I had no pain and to this day my pain is gone.

I don't mind being called "The Miracle Hog." In fact, many times people ask why my friends call me this, and it gives me an opportunity to tell them about how good God is. I invite them to come to The Little Chapel, but the choice is theirs to make. Choices make the difference in our lives. Choices can create a life of negativity and pain or a life of unlimited joy. I know what I want, do you?

Trusting in the Future

Chrissy Smith

*C*hrissy lives in Michigan with her two boys, Michael and Lucas. She attends the Renaissance Unity Church every Sunday and she makes certain her boys go to church also. She is raising her two sons in a very spiritual environment.

Chrissy came to Sara's church service with a broken heart and after hearing Sara, she left with a joyful one. It became clear to her that afternoon while Sara was speaking that we must let go of the past, live in the present, and trust in the future. Her heart was deeply touched with the wonder and power of God's healing love.

" I have been a material planner for seventeen years, and in my spare time I do yoga. I'm also a scoutmaster and keep busy doing activities with my boys.

My church is a very important part of my life. I was at a low point after my dear grandmother passed away and my marriage fell apart. I was miserable, unhappy and in limbo. My heart was aching with such deep sorrow. When the announcement was made about Sara giving a healing service in our church, I knew it was a must that I attend.

As Sara was speaking that afternoon, I was praying desperately for a release of the sorrow and heaviness in my heart. I felt the tender touch of the Holy Spirit. I felt heat and tingling in my foot and throughout my body. It was like a shot of energy, and then great peace came over me. I felt the release of all the hurt and sorrow I held onto for such a long time. Now, I have never felt better in my entire life.

I have started a daily journal of my feelings and experiences. I feel my healing was the beginning of a great spiritual growth period for me.

My sister is going through a difficult emotional time now and I promised God that I would help her. She has moved in with me and the boys and she is improving every day. I pray the ripples of my blessings never end for me and will continue to bless the lives of countless others.

He Held
My Heart in His Hand

Dolly Smith

olly heard Sara speak at the National Conference for the *Association of Christian Therapists* (ACT) in February 2004. She is a registered nurse and lives in San Juan Capistrano, California.

She is a part time stage and screen actress and loves to do needlework in her spare time. Dolly has five children and nine grandchildren who are scattered all around the country. Her heart is overflowing with love for each one of them.

I was suffering with heart problems for a few weeks so I was looking forward to the healing service Sara was giving at the ACT National Conference. The sermon was fabulous. I was praying throughout her service that I would receive a healing of my heart and a release of the fear that had such a hold on me.

I knew I had to let go of the fear so that God's love could reach and heal me. All of a sudden, I felt a warm sensation over my heart. God's love engulfed me and I felt all warm and cozy. It was like He held my heart in His hands. This lasted for a few minutes and then I felt a jolt.

I prayed for this healing, but when it happened I was shocked and stunned. I knew at that moment God had completely healed me. I was excited and grateful but could hardly believe God did this for me but it proved He absolutely did. I'm so grateful Sara came to San Diego for our conference. She touched a lot of lives that evening, including mine.

Every Beat of My Heart is for His Glory

Glada Mae Sprenger

*G*lada Mae Sprenger started her interview by saying, "This is difficult to explain, but miracles speak for themselves" She is a solid believer in God's miracles after her fabulous healing in the year 2000.

Glada Mae has a beautiful spirit, great faith and trust in the Lord. She is married and has 3 grown sons. Her son, Thaine, attends the Little Chapel services with his mother, and feels better every time he comes.

" In 1960, I was standing on a chair cleaning windows, fell backwards and landed in a sitting position. From that time on, I was in too much pain to sit. At times the pain was so bad, I had to kneel on a chair at the dinner table. I would always lie down when riding in the car.

In 1962, my husband purchased a van so I could go on vacations. I lay in the back on a foam mattress, but we hadn't traveled very far before I realized that the vibration and movement of the car caused more back pain. When we arrived home, I was in such great pain, I phoned the doctor immediately. He told me to come right in and he would examine me. The doctor found that my tailbone was loose and dangling and suggested I have surgery. My answer was a firm, "No!"

I then went to another doctor who fitted me with a corset. This helped some, and I wore it for several years. It was impossible to sit through a church service, so I stood up in the back most of the time. If I had to drive the car, I would rest my left arm on the armrest, lifting my body enough to take some of the weight off my back. I found walking fast would ease some of the pain for a short while.

My son, Thaine, had a dear friend who went to The Little Chapel. She told him about Sara and all the incredible miracles. Thaine offered to take me to a service hoping I would receive a healing. Sunday came and we were most anxious to go to The Little Chapel. As we walked through the door, I felt a warm, loving presence. I was thankful Sara's healing chair was offered to me in the back of The Chapel so my standing wouldn't be conspicuous. The healing chair was the one Sara was sitting in when she herself was healed through Kathryn Kuhlman's ministry. Sara's husband had purchased it from the Shrine Auditorium as a gift to Sara.

I was up and down throughout the service and was standing when Sara finished her sermon. As Sara began the healings she said God was touching someone's lower back and they were being completely healed. I shot my hand up immediately because I knew it was mine to take. Sara saw the light all around me. She looked straight at me and assured me that indeed God was healing my back. It was so powerful, I could hardly stand up. It felt like God was healing my bones, nerves and muscles. I felt warm throughout my body.

After the service, we decided to eat lunch (another hour of sitting). Then a 75 mile drive home (another hour and 15 minutes of sitting). As we drove into our driveway, I was pain free! Our neighbors arrived home at the same time. I jumped out of the van and hurried over to tell them the wonderful news. In an excited and loud voice, I told them what God had done for me during the healing service. They all rejoiced and thanked God for the beautiful blessing.

It has been over a decade now since God touched me in such an outstanding way. Most every day I claim my healing and say a prayer of thanks. I thank God for His loving, healing touch, for Sara and for the Little Chapel. The healing of my back made me stop and think deeply about the privileges we have as God's children.

I have a new respect for my back now. I am so happy and grateful that I can do the things that are important to me: sit through church, sit to visit with friends, and play games with my darling grandchildren. What a joy and what a blessing!

At another service, months after my first healing, God touched my heart. My heart seldom skips a beat now and is quite regular. I only need the pacemaker when I am sleeping. Attending the services gives me a supportive healing presence and I continually improve. I am relying on God more and more every day to keep my heart beating regularly. Every beat of my heart is for His glory.

Accepting God's Light and Love Changes Your Life Completely

Jerry Tassone

*J*erry and his lovely wife, Crysta, have been personal friends since all of our family moved from California to Arizona. The two of them worked with some of our family, and we did a lot of special things together. Now, they are living in Atlanta, Georgia but we keep in touch. Jerry continues to participate in Childhelp®, and for that we are deeply grateful. It is especially rewarding when someone gives from their heart and you can give back to them with yours.

"While Crysta and I lived in Arizona, we loved to attend The Little Chapel services. One Saturday, I jammed my foot into a stool. It was so painful I could hardly sleep all night. The next morning I asked Crysta to go to the service without me.

I couldn't walk and my foot was swollen with a large, brown, ugly bruise. I decided to read the Bible and spend some quiet time alone. There was a person I wanted to pray for and I thought this would be a good time to do it.

When Crysta returned home she asked how I was feeling. I told her it didn't feel any better, and she asked if I had prayed about it. I said I had other things to pray for and did not concentrate on a healing for me.

A couple of days passed and people were noticeably watching me walk and hobble and some suggested that I go see a doctor. I'm not one who runs to the doctor at the drop of a hat, so I resisted the suggestions.

Sara noticed I missed the Chapel service on Sunday, so she phoned me Tuesday evening to see how I was doing. My foot was still black and blue and swollen. I knew something was wrong, but I didn't know if it was a bone or cartilage. I just didn't want to take the time to see a doctor. Sara asked if I would give a little time to her for prayer. God can heal instantaneously but we must stop and ask. She prayed and I thanked her.

Wednesday morning I woke up and looked at my foot. There was no bruise and no swelling. On the day of the injury, if I touched the top of my foot, pain would shoot all the way up my body. I touched my foot that morning and there was no pain.

Crysta and I had been attending Sara's services for two years and it finally dawned on my consciousness what she was talking about. It's not enough just to see the light or want the light, you have to be open and accept the light. On that day I accepted God's light.

When you receive a physical healing, it makes you feel filled with gratitude in your heart. The spiritual blessing that you receive along with the healing changes your life. You can never be the same after this type of experience. I know I'm not.

God Specializes in Everything

Atlee A. Tucker

*A*tlee was born in Manila, Arkansas and moved to Arizona in 1940. He has been happily married to Grace for 53 years. They were blessed with three sons. The middle son died of cystic fibrosis at age 30. They have eight grandchildren and four great grandchildren. Atlee loves to play golf and work in the garden at home.

Atlee's mother taught him and his four siblings to always stay close to God, and Atlee has and always will. He feels coming to The Little Chapel has made his faith even stronger.

"Grace and I attend Pastor Rye's services every Sunday. Once a month, Pastor Rye brings us all to The Little Chapel. Each one of us has been blessed coming to hear Sara speak and watching God in action heal people through her.

The first time we attended a service, I knew when Sara started to speak that the Holy Spirit was with her. I got all excited because I needed a healing badly in my legs. It hurt me terribly to walk. My legs would get excruciatingly painful cramps in the calves.

As I prayed for God to heal me, I felt His power and knew my legs were healed. I am so grateful. It means a lot to be able to walk anywhere you want without pain. I tell everyone about my wonderful healing and about The Lord. I even told a lady in the grocery store while we were standing in line. Who knows, she might need a healing one day.

We all need healings of some kind and God is the greatest physician we can go to because He specializes in everything.

I Put My Cancer in a Tiny Box and Gave it to God

John R. Tucker

ohn was born in Jacksonville, Florida and is happily married to Nora. They moved to Arizona in February 2000. He is a wonderful Christian who hadn't yet become familiar with God's healing power. He was also unfamiliar with healing services. People don't always speak out to others about The Little Chapel and Sara's healing gift unless someone is ill.

Sara's husband, Colonel Bob Sigholtz, met John when Bob became a commissioner of the *Arizona Department of Veterans Services*, which operates the *Arizona State Veterans Home*. When Bob learned about John being terminally ill with cancer, he invited him to The Little Chapel. John was fascinated with what Bob told him about Sara's own healing and about her gift. He told Bob he would definitely attend the next service.

John's heart was asking God to help him, and Bob was there to tell him about The Little Chapel. Timing is everything, and God's timing is perfect. There are no coincidences.

Learning is an everyday event. Every obstacle can be a wonderful step upward toward a spiritual unfolding.

I am a healthcare administrator. From a very young age, I have enjoyed being around my elders. I began my career in healthcare as a volunteer at a busy county hospital emergency room.

From volunteer, I became a janitor, a nursing assistant, a social worker, an administrator, a regional director, and then an executive vice president—all in the healthcare arena. I was so passionate about my elders that I even pursued, and obtained a Masters in Gerontology. My life was going very well, and just when I thought I was my very happiest, life got even better.

I met, fell in love with, and married the girl of my dreams, Nora. I became the administrator of the Arizona State Veterans Home; the home of America's heroes. My life was full and I was so happy.

Then my life took an unexpected turn. What I had mistaken for a sports injury was diagnosed as lymphoma. It was a terminal diagnosis. I did receive radiation before work and chemotherapy after my workday. The Veterans Home was in the middle of a critical turnaround and I could not have people see a weak leader. After my treatments, and six months on crutches, my life returned to normal. I was in remission, but I was not cured. I was told and knew my disease would return and this time I might not be so fortunate.

When I became ill, I made a list of things that I wished I had done. I had been so blessed throughout my life the list was extremely short. When my health allowed, I began working on this list.

I am now teaching as adjunct faculty at the local community college, I have begun my PhD program, I began the book I had always meant to write, and I started to renew my faith. I believe this last step was rewarded by the Lord acquainting me with Colonel Sigholtz.

The Colonel found out about my cancer and invited me to one of Sara's services. I was delighted, and accepted his invitation. Unfortunately, that Saturday I became ill and was unable to crawl out of bed. That Sunday passed, but Sunday night I had a vivid dream.

In my dream, the Colonel stopped by, and asked if he could use my Bible. I was a bit embarrassed and said I "know it was around here somewhere." The Colonel was kind enough to help me look. When we finally found it, the Colonel opened it and began to read from Matthew 8, verses 5 through 13.

It was about a centurion asking Jesus to heal his servant who was lying paralyzed at home, suffering great pain. Jesus told the centurion He would go to his home and heal him. But the centurion said, "Lord, I am not worthy for You to come under my roof, just say the word and my servant will be healed. Jesus was so impressed with his faith. Jesus told the centurion to go home. "Let it be done to you as you have believed". The servant was healed that very hour.

The next morning, I saw Commissioner Sisco who had attended The Little Chapel service the day before. She was excited to share with me what had happened on Sunday. Sara announced during the healing portion of the service, four people were being healed of cancer. Only three came forward. Colonel Sigholtz held up his hand and said, "I am praying for John Tucker who was too ill to come today." Sara gave the message to Bob for me to find a small box, put my cancer inside, put the box away, and accept God's gift of healing. I was completely speechless.

That past Friday someone had sent me a tiny empty box. The box had been made from a Christmas card that I had given my friend the year before. I had thanked my friend for the thoughtfulness of her gift, but I remembered thinking at the time, "What am I going to do with this tiny, little box?" Now, without a moment's uncertainty, I knew exactly what I was going to do with that tiny, little box! The gift of the tiny box and then the incredible dream all came together when Commissioner Sisco told me the wonderful news about Sunday. I had goose bumps on top of goose bumps.

Sara asked me if I would like to give my testimony in The Little Chapel. It is a pleasure and an honor to tell others how wonderful God is. I feel the gentle and powerful love of God moving in and through me daily, and in each moment I know I am being renewed. I go in every six months for a check up, and I'm perfect now — thanks to God and Sara. My "remission" has become a *healing*. I thank Sara and the Colonel for their kindness, and I thank The Lord for His fantastic mercy!

I Believe in Miracles Because I Believe in God

Pamela Ulich

*P*amela is a bright, bubbly, outgoing woman you love to be around. She is a lawyer, past mayor of Malibu, CA and is married to David Ulich, who has been Childhelp's lawyer for over 25 years. They are blessed with two adorable children, Katarina and Konrad.

Pamela and David are so wonderful to support Childhelp® in every way, and when The Little Chapel was in California, they attended the services whenever they could. They have come a few times to Arizona for a service and we are always happy to see them. They are truly two bright and shining lights for God.

" After I had my first baby, Katarina, I could barely use my right hand. It hurt to type on the computer and to even simply sign my name. My right wrist was so useless I could not even open bottles.

It bothered me so much that I went to see Doctor Waxler in April 2000. He told me I had Carpal Tunnel Syndrome in my right wrist and there was no cure for it. I asked him how I got it. He said that it is caused by repetitive motion, such as nursing my new baby. He suggested that I wear a wrist guard but it did not help. I could barely move my wrist because of the pain.

The doctor didn't have an answer, but I knew something he didn't. I knew about the "Great Physician" who can cure anything. Deep in my heart, I knew all things were possible with God. David and I had attended many services at the Little Chapel, and we saw, with our own eyes, healing after healing. I couldn't wait for the next service.

Throughout the service, I kept thanking God that He was going to heal me. My wrist began to get warm then quite hot while Sara was speaking but it still hurt. The wrist was hot for the rest of the day and all night. I woke up perspiring and soaking wet for about a week straight. My wrist slowly got better, and was perfect by the end of the week. I felt so relieved, lucky and blessed to have been touched and healed by God.

I learned not to take small things for granted like being able to open a bottle of orange juice or a can of pasta sauce. I promised God to thank Him every day for all of the little things. It took something as small as my wrist to wake me up to realizing that little things mean a lot, and we should never stop being grateful for them.

My enthusiasm never dwindles for telling others about Sara and the Little Chapel. It gives me such pleasure to offer others hope and encouragement to look to God for a miracle. He is the great miracle worker. To quote Kathryn Kuhlman, "I believe in miracles because I believe in God."

God Always Knows Best

Gerald "Jerry" Van Slyke

*J*erry was born and raised in Lone Rock and Kenosha, Wisconsin. He and his wife, Pamela, moved to Arizona in June 1996. They have enjoyed nearly 40 years of marriage and have three children. Major Bradley Van Slyke, USMC, Alicia Anne Hasemeyer, Curtis Van Slyke, and an adoptive greyhound, Kiki, complete their family.

Jerry and Pamela were invited to attend a service at The Little Chapel by a member of our Childhelp® Arizona Chapter, Teri Leveton. They both are gifted spiritually and felt the power of God the minute they entered through the chapel doors. Jerry has written several books about angels and he knew the chapel was overflowing with God's healing angels. You can't be in this atmosphere without receiving blessings of some kind. Every one can take as much of God's love as they want if they are open to receive it. God always offers His great love and grace but He never forces it upon anyone.

“ Pamela and I love to attend The Little Chapel services and sit near the back so we can watch all the healings when they begin to happen. As we arrived at the evening service in October 2007, Yvonne greeted us and asked that we pray for the gentleman seated next to Pamela. When I looked over at him I realized it was John Reid, the Executive Director of Childhelp®. His back was in great pain and I knew how he was feeling.

Yvonne didn't know that I was at the service hoping to get a back healing. Several weeks prior to this evening, I had experienced severe pain in my lower back. It was so painful it took my breath away and the agony brought me to my knees. Being brought to your knees does help you to start thinking about praying to God for a healing.

The pain was severe and it went all across my lower back. There was numbness and tingling from my right hip to my big toe. When I finally saw my doctor she examined me the best she could. She took X-rays and gave me two prescriptions: one for pain relief, the other a muscle relaxant. I followed her instructions and took the medication. One made me feel numb, and the other put me in the twilight zone. "No more medication for me", I thought. I purchased a mat and began doing exercises and stretches for back pain. If it is natural, I'm for it. Natural treatment feels better for me. I received some relief but I couldn't walk without limping with constant pain. The doctor informed me I had degenerative arthritic condition of the lower spine. I was going to have to live with pain the rest of my life.

Pamela and I believe strongly in God's miracles and had witnessed many phenomenal healings while attending the Little Chapel Services. I was thankful to be at the Chapel service to ask for a healing. That night I hobbled in the Chapel with Pamela's assistance and we sat in our favorite seats in the back row. My right leg and hip began to throb. It was very hard for me to get comfortable. I tried to get my mind off my pain and listen to everything that was being said by Sara. When Sara began calling out the healing she said someone who came in the door at this chapel could hardly put one foot in front of the other. She mimicked the very slow painful walk. She said, "A man will be totally healed and he will walk perfectly normal."

Ralna English finished singing a beautiful song and then introduced her friend, Dee Cupchak, who had received a healing of cancer at a previous service. As Dee gave her testimony she said, "God lives within each one of us." I had heard Sara say this many times, but tonight it hit me so hard. It was like a light bulb turning on in my head. Yes, His love and light is within each one of us but we must be open to let His love flow through us. As I relaxed and gave my pain to God I felt the warmth of the Holy Spirit flowing through my body. It touched my back, my right hip and leg. I felt such peace knowing that God was healing my aching tired body. Yes, I was healed and walked out of The Little Chapel without a limp or any pain.

God's love and grace are the ingredients for all healing. Enough love can and does change things for the better. Nothing in the outer world is beyond the power of God's love to transform.

Every day Pamela and I open our hearts and minds to what God wants to teach us. We look forward to learning new ways of thinking and being that will enrich our lives and the lives of all those we love and meet along our journey in life. It is always good to pray our way to a divine solution for God always knows best.

God Has All the Answers

Peter Walser

eter and Janet have enjoyed many years of happiness together, and are the proud parents of Melissa, Peter and Michael. They live in Arizona and attend The Little Chapel as often as they can.

When Peter was asked to give his testimony for his first healing of his foot at one of the Sunday services, he said he didn't think his healing was profound, compared to the many other healings.

His healing is profound because God knew Peter was suffering, and with His loving touch God made Peter's body whole and pain free. Peter needed a second healing a couple of years later, and God blessed him then also. God is always ready to relieve us from our pain when we are ready and open to receive His blessing. His great love lifts us up and sets us free. Nothing is too small, too big or too impossible for God to change and make perfect.

> My lovely wife, Janet, had attended a Little Chapel service with a friend and enjoyed it so much she wanted me to go with her the next time.

It was October 2001 when I finally made it to The Little Chapel. I went to please my wife. I did not know Sara had anything to do with healing people. What a surprise I was in for!

For 30 years I experienced physical problems, especially in my lower back. I've been to medical doctors, chiropractors and done every manual manipulation and testing they could come up with. I ended up in worse pain than I was in the first place. I decided I just had to live with the pain because nothing seemed to work. I have always played sports in my life and, to work around my back problems, I had to do a lot of warm up before I stressed my back.

In January of 2001, one morning while putting my socks on, I discovered I had no feeling in my right foot. All of a sudden it was totally numb. I thought the numbness would go away, but it didn't. I went to see a podiatrist and he did some needle pricks in the office. Then it took me awhile to get an appointment with a nerve specialist. He hooked me up to a monitor and gave me all kinds of needle probing and electronic shocks to test my responses.

A few days later, he called me to say he thought I had one of two problems. I either had a pinched nerve or I had permanent nerve damage in my right foot. To this day, I still haven't been told what to do about it.

So I was sitting in The Little Chapel with my wife on a beautiful Sunday in October, enjoying the service and then the healings began. I was amazed at what began to happen. I looked at my wife and said, "You didn't tell me about this." She just smiled.

Sara stated that there were several people who had foot problems. Without thinking I raised my hand and identified myself as one of those people. Sara went to a couple of people before she came to me, but during that time I noticed a difference in my foot. It felt like it was tingling and it was also getting a little bit warm, generating some heat inside the shoe.

Sara finally got to me and stared right through me as she said, "God's light is all around you." She asked what my problem was, and I told her about the numbness in my foot. I never mentioned my back. She said, "Well, how are you doing now?" I said, "I really can't tell, but I'd like to take my shoe off and feel it." She told me to take off my shoe, and she would be back.

She left to talk to somebody else. I took my shoe off, and praise God, there was feeling there. It wasn't totally all right, there were still some areas, but the feeling started. I put my shoe back on. Sara approached me and said, "How is it now?" I said, "There definitely is feeling," and I explained about the tingling. It was similar to when a part of your body falls asleep, and when it starts to wake back up again. There was this prickling feeling. It was also generating heat inside the shoe. She said, "What do you think?" All I could do was say, "Praise the Lord!"

I went home and within two days the tingling and heat had subsided. Within a week my foot was normal and I just couldn't believe it. I don't know what was healed that day, but I know there was a healing. Remember I told you how I had to always do a lot of warm-ups before I stressed my back? Well, I've done no exercise in the past few days and I can bend over and touch my feet. Praise the Lord, and thank you Sara for bringing about this healing.

I received my first healing of my foot in November 2001. The following healing was received at a service in March 2003. In the early part of 2003, I finished playing basketball in the senior league in Tempe. Later that month I was playing a softball game in Surprise, Arizona and my heart started to beat uncontrollably. I knew there was something wrong. I began to gasp for breath so I walked off the field into the dugout.

The ambulance came quickly. On the way to the hospital my heart stopped twice. They were trying to get my heart to convert back to normal rhythm with medication. It was unsuccessful. They asked me if I had any chest pain and I said, "No."

I was in the emergency room of the hospital for 4 hours. The doctors finally came in to see me with two choices. We can send you home as you are, and hopefully your heart will straighten out. The valves are beating irregularly and could be fatal. Your other choice is to sign this form, and we will give you an electric shock to get your heart back beating in rhythm. I signed the papers immediately for the shock treatment, and my heart did convert back to normal. They gave me medication to take and recommended that I see a cardiologist as soon as possible.

The cardiologist checked me out, and arranged for me to take some tests the following Monday. He said I must take a stress test and something called nuclear imaging.

Janet and I went to The Little Chapel on the Sunday before the tests, and we enjoyed hearing Sara speak as we always do. When the healing began, Sara asked the people with heart problems to raise their hand. I was the second person Sara walked up to. I quickly told her my story and she just held up her hands and said, "I see God's light all over you. Don't worry, you are going to be just fine and let me know what happens."

The next day I had the session where you drink some nuclear liquid, and then you lie down and take a 32 film sequence of your chest as the fluid goes through you. Later that day, I took a ten minute stress test and then repeated the nuclear drink and more pictures. This equipment is quite reliable. I never had taken the stress test before, but I felt funny and knew something was wrong.

After I finished everything, I saw the doctor and he said for me to come back in ten days and he would have the results of the tests. I didn't feel up to par for about five days. Then one afternoon, I started to feel a warm sensation throughout my upper body. That was the beginning of my healing. I kept feeling a little better each day until I went back to see the doctor for my diagnosis.

I arrived about nine o'clock in the morning to see the doctor, and he confirmed that I had suffered a heart attack. I told him that I had never had any chest pains. He said you can have what is called silent heart attacks. The tests I had taken definitely showed that I

God Has All the Answers **347**

had significant heart damage. He went on to say that the left side of my heart was dead, and there was no blood flow whatsoever.

The doctor asked me to go in for an angiogram so he could determine whether I needed a bypass, a stint or a heart replacement. He told me I could take the test that day. I chose to wait until the next morning.

Bright and early the next day, I arrived at the *Della Hospital*. They prepped me and stuck me where they shouldn't, and I bled all over the place. Finally, I was mildly sedated and watching the monitors. They started the test and I kept my eyes on the heart pump and the blood flow through the various vessels. I'm no expert, but I couldn't see anything wrong.

After 20 to 30 minutes, the doctor called in another doctor. Finally, my doctor began to apologize and said he couldn't explain what had happened. They had never had a false positive before. They said this was the first time the equipment had failed. He went on to say my heart was just like new. Not a thing was wrong with my heart. He kept repeating that he couldn't explain what happened. I smiled and said, "I think I know what happened. The Lord God healed me."

The doctor just looked at me and said he would see me in the recovery room. Janet was with me when the Doctor came in to see me again. She was talking to him about what had happened to me, and he turned to her and said, "I can't explain what happened."

The doctor scheduled an appointment for me the following week. I told him again the equipment was not broken. God had given my heart a fantastic healing and I said so again. He didn't respond.

I feel great and I continue to play basketball, softball and run. I tell everyone my story and encourage them to attend a service in The Little Chapel. It changed my life, and I know it will change their lives too. Everyday, Janet and I praise The Lord and thank Sara for blessing me in such a miraculous way.

A Little Hockey Player will Never Be the Same

Justin Weber by Stacey Weber

S tacey Weber is a devout Christian and frequently attends The Little Chapel services with her husband, Kevin. She and her mother-in-law, Wanda, are very active in Childhelp®.

Stacey and Kevin have two fine sons, Justin and Zachary. The boys have heard their mother and father speak about the healings that occur at the Little Chapel but they never stopped to think too much about the subject. They had too many other things to think about, and anyway, sickness was for the elderly.

One morning, Justin had an excruciating earache. He asked Sara to pray to God to take away the pain, and He did. Children are so open to God's love and light when we as their parents encourage them to believe and accept God's beautiful blessings.

God took a problem and changed it into a miracle. Two little brothers will never be the same.

"On Thursday morning, January 15th, I dropped my two sons (Justin, 8, and Zachary, 7) off at school as I usually do. I was in a hurry because at 1 PM that day our family of four would be flying on an airplane to Salt Lake City, Utah. We were taking this trip because my older son, Justin, was going to play in a big ice hockey tournament. Being the busy Mom that I am, I left all packing to do until that morning while the boys were in school.

At about 9 AM, I received a call from the school nurse. Justin, my 8 year old, was there in her office with tremendous pain from his ear. "Oh my gosh," I thought, "anything but the ear when we are about to get on a plane!" After spending 30 to 45 minutes trying to get him into a doctor to get a professional opinion as to whether we could fly or not, Justin was quickly getting worse. Justin is very in tune with his body along with his spirit.

I brought him home and as he lay in his bed crying, "Why me, please God help me. Take this pain away" over and over, I thought "Yes, that's it! I'll call Sara." Justin knows Sara, however, he has never prayed with her. Justin does go to Sunday school each Sunday; he says the dinner blessing along with a daily devotion each evening, so I know he understands the power of God and the power of prayer.

When I phoned Sara, she was at a meeting, but thankfully she answered her cell phone and stepped out of the room so I could let her know what was happening. She asked to speak to Justin. He told her what was hurting. I left the room so as not to distract him, but was just outside his door. A few minutes later he came to me with the biggest smile I've ever seen and said, "Mommy, the pain is gone! Thank you God, and thank you Sara!"

I was so grateful to God and to Sara for allowing God to use her to heal my son. I asked Justin if he felt anything when he was being touched by God. He said he felt tickling in his ear.

We were able to make our flight, and Justin was no longer in any pain or discomfort. We feel so blessed to have Sara in our lives for she is such an amazing vehicle for God's healing work. Now, neither one of my boys are afraid of illness because they know we can just call Sara!

God Never Gives Up on Us, So Why Should We?

Suzanne Westfall

S uzanne is the fourth generation of her family to be born and raised in Phoenix, Arizona. She is the oldest girl in a family of 19 children. She had to help take care of a lot of children while she was still growing up herself. She'd have to wake up 8 or 9 children every morning, find their shoes, get them dressed, clean the whole house, all before she left for school. Then she would go to school, come home and repeat everything, plus help with the dinner.

This upbringing made her strong. Suzanne never let any obstacle stop her from succeeding. She was taught to keep going, and never give up. Her faith in God brought her through many tough times.

"   Growing up with eighteen siblings, you never have a free moment to get bored. I attended Catholic schools for 12 years, and then graduated from Arizona State University with a teaching degree. After working for the Watergate prosecutor for two years in Washington, DC, I returned home to work in a new position for two more years. I then got married, and moved to Washington State for a while.

I have a wonderful son from that marriage. My life has not been easy, and at times I persevered because of the love I have for my dear son. I am also a Christian and knew it wasn't right to give up. God did give me extra strength to endure the difficult times.

In the eighties, I worked for the US Army Corps of Engineers in Portland, Oregon at a large hydroelectric dam. There were 65 guys and I was the only woman, so I learned quickly how to communicate with men. They were fine Christian men and were not intimidated to talk about the Lord.

In 1990, I was asked to do the mail run. Some bags weighed up to 100 pounds because of the heavy steel parts in them. I thought the mail run would be easy but the bags were so weighty that I'd have to drag them to the van, and use my knees to lift them up. After six weeks of straining my back and legs, I could not even go to the grocery store and wait in line. I had to have help carrying my groceries.

I went to the doctor, and then took six weeks of therapy. This routine went on for 10 years. My back was in terrible shape and I was in pain constantly. In the year 2000, I decided to move back to Phoenix. I went to 12 specialists and endured lots of therapy. Finally, I heard about the Little Chapel.

I thought I'd never make it through the service, but I did, and then the healings started happening. Sara said an extra prayer for my aching back during the service and the healing began. I can roll over in my bed now, and my back won't go out. I'm over 50 years old, and feel like I'm 20. I'm pain free and so grateful.

The last time Sara prayed for me was for my ankle. I had fallen to the ground three separate times and my ankle was still weak and wobbly. I had gone to several foot doctors about it. Sara prayed for me one Sunday in Chapel and it felt so good. My ankle was perfect. When I went back to see one of the foot doctors, he wanted to check it out on a new machine he had just purchased. He was surprised to see my ankle was fine. He confirmed what I knew in The Little Chapel. God had given me another wonderful healing.

The Little Chapel has taught me so much. I want to help others to be free from pain, and more into the light. Thank you, Sara, for opening my eyes to see a little clearer and for helping me to accept God's beautiful healings.

In closing, I want to encourage everyone who is reading this and having a problem, to never give up. God always wants to help us, but we must ask. We are His children, and His love is always there for us. If we sincerely pray and ask God to send help, He will send earthly angels as His hands and feet to get the job done.

Tough Guys and Chihuahuas: Big or Small, God Loves Us All

Jeff Young

Jeff Young is a former Kent State football player, Sigma Nu brother, Army officer and avid motorcyclist with a Bachelor's Degree in Education and Master's Degree in Psychology. He currently resides in Wisconsin where he has worked in business logistics, transportation and operations for some of America's top companies. He is married to the beautiful and brilliant Dr. Yvette Young, PhD, who is a former Professor of French Literature and published poet. He has a daughter named Daphne who works as a professional writer in Phoenix at Childhelp® Headquarters. It was when he was visiting his daughter that Jeff came to The Little Chapel. Having never been there, he was not expecting anything more than an enlightening sermon and a pleasant churchgoing experience, but what he left with was a healing that brought him closer to God.

If someone had told me I'd ever be caught dead walking a Chihuahua, I wouldn't have believed them. I've been a football lineman, military officer, corporate executive and weekend biker. I ascribe to the manly arts of mastering the grill, charting unknown territory on my Gold Wing motorcycle and surveying my property from the seat of a riding lawn mower. Little froufrou lap dogs have never factored into my life until my daughter got a seven pounds soaking wet miniature dog called Buckaroo. At first I referred to him as "the rat" but as I got to know this Doberman trapped in a Chihuahua's body, I reluctantly developed affection for the creature I now refer to as my "grandson."

The day of The Little Chapel, I took Buckaroo around the block. Not only was the spectacle of me with a micro dog at the end of a leash absurd enough, but his head was ensconced in one of those Elizabethan collars from the vet. He had been having horrible allergies, itching his eyes and body until both bled. The cone had been on for weeks, and the little guy was miserable.

I wasn't feeling so hot myself. Back in the days of the Kent State riots, football was a rougher game. A lot of older players were drafted from a pool of servicemen back from Vietnam. If you want to face a fearless man on the field, look into the eyes of someone who has seen war. I had the nickname "Truck" because of a little toy truck glued to my helmet. During practice, I had to hit my opponent over and over again as hard as possible with my head until the truck would break. Men have been accused of being pretty thick-headed, but a fellow can only bash his skull in for so many years before back surgery and pain management become a way of life. So, here we are walking down the street: A limping man with pain shooting through his back, leg and arm and a morose Chihuahua wobbling along with a giant cone on his head.

It had been awhile since I had been to church. I suppose I had the same excuses as everyone else: work, work, *work*. Walking into The Little Chapel, I was overwhelmed by an indescribable feeling. I got choked up with emotion. The music, the beautiful serenity of the place and the presence of something greater than myself moved me. I sat in a side pew and enjoyed Sara O'Meara's inspiring service. As usual, I shifted around in my seat from the discomfort of old injuries. Sara shared a lesson of love, understanding and coming together in peace. She read a poem for men in uniform and I may have shed a tear thinking about those who risk their lives to protect our freedoms. Inspiring singer Robbie Britt sang stirring hymns with his deep baritone. I told my daughter "No, I'm fine. I just had something in my eye."

When Sara began the healing portion of the service, I was a little skeptical but my heart had been opened by her words and I felt closer to God than I had in years. I didn't raise my hand when she called out for members of the congregation who needed relief of the back, leg or arm. She said there were those who might not come forward but still could be blessed by God's healing grace.

There was no thunderbolt, no heat like some of those being healed described but midway through the service I stopped stirring in my seat. For the first time since I can remember, I was still. My back was free from pain, my leg was no longer restless and my arm was folded comfortably at my side. The aches and shooting pains that had been a regular day-to-day aspect of my life had subsided. I sat in peace.

I didn't speak on the car ride home. "Dad, are you okay?" my daughter asked. I couldn't express what had happened to me. When we returned to my daughter's house, I took Buckaroo outside. He walked around the pool miserably and came to sit on my lap. As I was petting him, I was struck with a confident assurance that if I removed his cone, he would be fine.

My daughter told me not to do it. She said each time she tried he would itch and scratch until he drew blood. Something had touched me at The Little Chapel and I was sure that this small dog would be cured of his ailments as I had been. I removed his cone and he shook all over with the recognizable canine joy of freedom. He pranced into the house and promptly fell asleep. No scratching, biting or bleeding. Within days, his sores were replaced with healed pink skin and he was happy again.

Something profound worked through my body and even more importantly in my heart. The Little Chapel helped me strengthen my relationship with God. When I am busy or preoccupied and I lean away from my awareness of the Lord in my life, I occasionally feel a pinprick of pain. When that happens, I excuse myself from whatever I am doing, say a prayer, realign myself with Him and all aches subside. I surrender. Sara O'Meara said that no request is unworthy and no problem is too small. If we can open our hearts to accept His gift, God wants to heal us all. Every man, woman, child and Chihuahua is deserving of His love.

God's Voice Speaks Through Us in Unique and Beautiful Ways

Wendy Young

Music has been Wendy Young's life. Throughout her childhood music was an integral part of her every waking moment. She loved to sing and dance. When she was 7 years old she began singing solos at church services, through high school she auditioned and was chosen to sing leading roles in school productions such as Josephine in the HMS Pinafore. Later in life, Wendy was invited to be the guest soloist at Lincoln Center in New York City and received a standing ovation for her performance. Wendy was told that she had an exceptionally clear voice with the capability of singing three octaves. People told her parents that they would see angels around Wendy whenever she sang. God's pure love radiated, and continues to radiate, through Wendy's voice.

God's Divine Guidance led me to work at Childhelp as a creative writer for the founders, Sara O'Meara and Yvonne Fedderson. Through working at Childhelp I was told about the Little Chapel services and started attending services in

October 2007. Following a spiritual path all of my life, I resonated to the love and healings which embraced everyone who attended the services. At every service I gave thanks for the goodness in my life and offered my prayers and energy to help and heal those needing a miracle. I witnessed many miracles at the services.

At the Christmas service I held God's Light for those seeking help and also asked God to heal whatever needed to be healed within my body and my life. I let go and let God's healing power, generated through Sara and all those present, to envelop my body. I felt a great heat and an overwhelming joy take over my being. I knew I was in the flow of God's healing and loving energy.

I didn't realize I had personally received a miracle until everyone in the Little Chapel was invited to sing *Silent Night*. As I love to sing, I very quietly started to sing because I was embarrassed that my voice cracked and sounded raspy due to a near fatal car accident which I thankfully survived. In that accident I broke my neck with injuries similar to Christopher Reeves and the doctors wondered how I lived. As a result of my extensive injuries the specialist had to slit my throat to insert a 2 ½ inch titanium rod to secure my neck. When my throat was slit, my vocal chords were severely damaged.

Throughout my healing from this accident and every day thereafter, I would try to sing but only cracked and raspy sounds could come forth. I was so disheartened. God had given me an incredible singing voice for me to sing His message of hope and in an instant it was taken away.

However, during the Christmas service at the Little Chapel a miracle happened for me. I began softly singing *Silent Night* and I could hear the clear notes coming from my voice. There was clarity and power in my voice and I was in perfect harmony with the music. Tears began streaming down my face as I realized that the Hand of God was upon me and His Healing Power had healed my voice. I could sing beautifully again. When I gave my testimony

I proved what God had done for me by singing a hymn solo with everyone in awe that voice was coming from me.

The light-filled energy that came forth through Sara and filled the little chapel during that Christmas service beautifully healed my voice and my being. Praise be to God for Sara and the tremendous healing miracles that take place in the Little Chapel. I joyfully sing praises to God every day for His loving gift to me through my clear and musical voice.

God Has a Wonderful Sense of Humor

Efrem Zimbalist, Jr.

*E*frem has a beautiful spirit and we are blessed in Childhelp to have him as a Celebrity Ambassador as well as a dear, *dear* friend. He never missed a Chapel service while we lived in California, and comes when he can to services in Arizona. He lives in Solvang, California. Every year, he reads the Christmas story at our holiday program at the Childhelp Merv Griffin Village in Beaumont, California for severely abused children.

Most of us know and admire Efrem as a great actor but he has also influenced thousands of lives through his work on CBN. He recorded the Bible on tape, which is a wonderful blessing for so many people.

He has gone many times with Sara to pray for the sick in hospitals and homes. He came over to be with Sara when she lost her son, Chuck, in a car accident. He is the best friend you could ever have.

You could never find a better example to follow than Efrem. He loves the Lord, loves people, has a tremendous sense of humor, and you just love being around him. He has such positive energy and a beautiful, giving heart.

I have received many wonderful healings through Sara and the Little Chapel, but this is a different kind of story I am going to share first. Then I'll share my latest healing for there have been several.

One of the things I have noticed in the great souls that the Lord has placed across my path during my life is that they all have a wonderful sense of humor. I just believe that's part of our life. We're filled with joy, we love to laugh, and I think the Lord loves it too. My personal belief is that His life was full of that. I think if you look at His life in that light, His sacrifice at the end, His death and crucifixion and resurrection, against that side of His life, means all the more. I'm absolutely convinced, and love to search the Scriptures and re-write them in my mind (not rewrite them, but restage them, if you will) and imagine how they might have looked.

Consider incidents like the woman at the well. There's a lot of humor in that, for me. If you look at the woman taken in adultery, and the Lord scratching in the dirt with a stick, that's pure Gary Cooper. He's not looking up, he's scratching away, and says, "I'll tell you what, the one without sin—let him cast the first stone." It's very funny—he was having a good time. When he looked up and said, "Well, where are your accusers?" It's mirthful. And there's Peter, walking on the water and looking down and realizing he was sinking. I don't just think the Lord was smiling, I think He was roaring with laughter, I really do. I think he was bowled over with laughter at that point, and I think his life was filled with laughter.

This incident I want to talk about is in that area of His life. Many years ago, my first wife had died, and I was living a very close life to Him with my two children in Connecticut. I was starting to come out of an envelope that I had put my life into for about two years, with the help of my father and second mother, and a dear friend of theirs who used to come up to our place in Connecticut every weekend from Philadelphia.

This friend of my family's began teaching me musical composition, harmony, theory, counterpoint, and so forth, and at one point she told me to write a choral work. I wrote a motet, which is a choral work based upon a religious topic, and I wrote this motet for eight voices, based upon the 150th Psalm. They arranged for a performance outside of Philadelphia, in Marion, Pennsylvania, by a great choral group in Philadelphia (probably the greatest in the city, and the city at that time was probably the most musical city in the United States). This was terribly exciting to me. It was the first composition I had ever performed, and I was looking forward to it eagerly. It was a Sunday and they were going to have this performance in a great house in Marion, out on the main line of Philadelphia, and a talented choral group was going to perform it.

I was going to drive my old Packard, a 1934 Packard, with four new tires on it, so I allowed an extra hour and a half to get there on time. I got up and put on my best suit, got all dolled up, slicked my hair down, and started off.

About 50 miles from home in Connecticut, the first tire went outside a town called Sherman. Luckily, I was right at a little gas station. I pulled in and they took the tire off. By the time they had fixed it, I still had an extra half hour. I got down by the Sawmill River Parkway when the second tire went, and I was again, almost miraculously, at a gas station. I was able to pull in, and they fixed it. I went to the phone and called my father, because the plan was that I was to go to their house in Philadelphia, and we would drive out together to Marion in their car.

So I called my parents and said, "You know, it's very likely that I'm not going to make this, so you go ahead, and you can tell me about it." It was killing me because I had so looked forward to this moment. My father said he would wait for me at the 30th Street railroad information station, and I told him not to wait too long in case anything more happened.

368 Miracle Healing: God's Call

So I got in my car and started off, with only 2 sidewall spares left. I'm traveling on the Sawmill River Parkway, moving as fast as I could in a deserted, open country place when the third tire goes. There is nothing around and it began to rain. I got out of the car, got my jack and started cranking the rear-end up. The jack breaks and the whole thing collapsed, with me under the car, covered with mud.

My suit is ruined. There's nothing I can do, so I start walking. I walk about a mile and finally come to a house see the car in the driveway and figure someone's home. I ring the doorbell but no answer. I pound on the door as hard as I can. Upstairs a window opens, and a woman says, "What do you want?" I answer that "my car is down the road about a mile, I've got a flat tire, and need to call a service station to come and fix it." She says, "There's nothing open today!" and closed the window. I start pounding again, and say, "Please, please help me!" Finally she opens the window again, and I tell her I don't want to come in the house, but to please call somebody. There must be somebody open, somebody who can come and fix the tire. She says she will try to find someone, and I should go back to my car, which I did.

I walked back to my car and about half an hour later a truck pulls up. The guy takes one of the spares off the side mount and nuts it on the wheel, and I was on my way. By now I was very late, there was almost no point in going so I decided I'll go home and clean up, and my parents will come and tell me what the concert was like.

I'm down on the Henry Hudson Parkway, which runs along the Hudson River down the west side of New York City. I'm going along and there's not too much traffic because it's Sunday, but the traffic is speeding at about 50 mph. I round the corner on the Parkway, and the 4th tire goes! Unbelievable—absolutely unbelievable. I'm so angry at this point, I'm furious with rage. The outrage of all this happening on my special day with all the precautions I took, and all the work I did on the piece, the one chance I have to hear it, and idiotic things are happening to me. I stop, get out of the car, and I'm so furious I want to literally kill somebody. I felt like I wanted to get a hold of somebody's neck and kill them.

Alongside the road, there were about four lanes, and no shoulder, and I couldn't get out of the lane I was in. I pulled over as far as possible but couldn't get out of the lane. There was a fence with wood and cable running alongside the road, and I got out of the car.

I sat on the fence with the river behind me and thought, "I don't care what happens anymore. If I get triple pneumonia, I don't care." I'm not going to ask for help, I just don't care. If a policeman comes along, okay; if a wrecking truck comes along, okay; but I'm not going to have my hand out asking for any more help. I don't care any more.

I'm sitting there in fury, absolutely consumed with rage, and I look up and coming around the corner in my lane is this old, *old*, high black sedan going about 5 mph. It pulls behind my car and stops. I look in and see this old man (who was probably younger than I am now). He turned off the engine and, leaned forward and put his head on the steering wheel. I just sat there looking at him and finally said, "What are you doing here?" He looked up and he had the most beautiful face you have ever seen. It was absolutely angelic. He had beautiful skin with no wrinkles and piercing blue eyes. The other thing was he had this ridiculous accent. It was a vaudevillian accent of comical proportions. It was a music hall sort of accent. You couldn't help but laugh at the way he talked, it was so ridiculous.

In answer to my question he said, "I was a little tired—thought I'd take a rest." I thought, "Sure, great place to take a rest. Why not?" Finally, he said, "What are you doing here?" "I'm here because I have a flat tire. I'm not here because I want to be here, I'm here because I have to be here. I'm not taking a rest!"

Long pause—"Why don't you fix it?" Because I can't fix it. The jack's broken, I can't get the wheels up. Do you think I'd be here if I could fix it? Stupid question!

Another long pause, and he finally says, "You take this road down here about a mile and a half, you get off the exit, take a left, go up the hill, there's a service station there, he'll fix it for you." I said, "Thank you so much. Just great, what am I going to run on, the rim for two miles?"

Now there's a long pause and finally he says, "I got a jack in the trunk." I get off the fence very carefully and walk by his window. He hands me the keys to his car. I open the trunk and he's got a bumper jack in there, so I take it out but am still furious at him, at everything. I don't speak to him at all, and walk around back to my car, hook up his bumper jack to the front, and turn the handle. The car comes off the ground and I get the wheels up, and I'm able to take my last tire off the side of the car. I take the wheel around, take the lugs off, take the wheel off, put this new one on, replace the lugs, take the wrench and tighten everything down, throw the wrench in the back seat, and take his keys and jack, walk around and put his jack in the trunk of his car. I walk back, toss him the keys, and go back to my car.

All I have left to do is replace the hubcap, which is lying on the pavement. I aligned it correctly and give it a good whack to seat it, and something happened in that action. I don't know if it was the sound of the smack, or the physical impact of it, but it suddenly woke me up, and I began to see daylight. I thought, "Good Lord, here's this lovely man who's done everything he could to help me. I've treated him like my worst enemy. I've screamed at him, I've cursed at him, I've made fun of him and he's saved my life here. I've got to thank him." I turned around and he was not there. The car was not there.

Now, I give you my word that not more than 20 seconds had elapsed since I gave him his keys and put the hubcap on. I ran out and looked down the road. I could see for two miles, and there were no cars. Well, I was shaken with this. I was really shaken. I didn't know what it meant. I got in my car and very carefully stayed in the right lane and made it to the next exit. I got off, took a left turn, went up the hill and there was a station. The guy treated me the way everybody did if you were in an old car in those days. He said, "Get that thing out of here. I can't be bothered with that." I said, "You fix the tires" and I left. I got a cab, went to the railroad station, and got on the train, went to Grand Central, took the shuttle over to Penn Station and got on the train for Philadelphia. I'm now about 3 ½ hours late.

I tried to go in the dining car for some food but they threw me out. I was such a mess, covered from head to toe in mud, everything ruined. I stood on the platform all the way to Philadelphia. When I finally got there, I got off the train and ran, full-tilt, through the 30th Street Station, grabbed a cab, and went to my parents' house. I don't know what I thought I'd do, probably get in the bathtub and wait until they got back.

The butler opened the door and said, "Mr. Efrem! Didn't you see your father at the station?" I said, "My father's not there. I told him to go on without me." He said, "No, no! He said he wouldn't leave without you. He's there waiting for you! He calls every five minutes to see if you've called here."

I got into a cab and flew back to the 30th Street Station, and there he was—my sweet, adorable, wonderful father. Well, we got in a local train that went out to Marion and got there in about 20 minutes. We took a taxi from the station and drove to this beautiful mansion where this group met every Sunday afternoon. The butler opened the door and let us in and brought us to this huge music room where the performance took place every Sunday. I saw the conductor with his hands in the air. As I stepped into the room his hands came down with the first notes of my piece, and I heard every note of that piece—every note.

Afterwards, I asked him what happened; how could he keep this group so long? He said, "Well, your mother told us the trouble you were having, so we went through our library and read a lot of works stalling for time, but finally we just couldn't stall any longer, so we figured we'd have to play your piece, and at that moment you walked in." But as I stood there listening, tears were streaming down my face, and I could imagine the Lord saying, "Well, Zimbalist, quite a day, wasn't it? You know, you were pretty mad there, weren't you? I was a little worried about my angel—I thought you might really hurt him. Next time why don't you try to work with me instead of against me? You know, you can put a lot of weight on my shoulders. It's light for me."

I tell you, I look back on that experience and can also imagine him saying to me, "You were pretty angry because you worked very hard on that piece. You were anxious to have people tell you how wonderful it was. But you know something, you didn't write that piece. I wrote it. Every note was my piece, and as far as the lyrics go, I wrote them about 2,000 years ago. I'm the one who was hurt by this, not you. It's my piece."

Well, I learned from that, and would never, today, dream of doing anything, *anything* of the slightest importance, without asking Him to be my arms, legs, hands, face, voice, heart and thoughts. I can't do anything without him. I thought you'd enjoy sort of lifting a corner of the veil and getting a little peek of our Blessed Lord that I love so much. A little different angle, maybe, from the usual, but something that I think is very much Him. A funny, *funny* story, but it's His joke, not mine.

And now, I want to share with you another story. I always love my time at The Little Chapel services. To see God in action and so many shocked people when all the pain leaves their body is a beautiful example of God's unconditional love. To see Sara remove her human self and let God take over to work through her is a sight to behold. I sometimes brought my son, Efrem Zimbalist, III and my daughter Stephanie to Sara's services with me.

When I was taken to the hospital with an acute blockage near my home in Solvang, California, my daughter, Stephanie, called Sara and said I was too ill to be transported to a major hospital and the doctors felt I was extremely ill with little hope of survival. I was in intensive care. Stephanie made an urgent call for Sara's prayers.

They allowed Stephanie to take her cell phone in and hold it up to my ear to hear Sara's prayers. The next morning, Sara called the hospital to inquire how I was. They told her, "I'm sorry, Mr. Zimbalist is no longer here." Her conclusion was I didn't make it. She decided to call my cell phone hoping Stephanie would answer. Instead I answered. Sara said, "Efrem, *where* are you?" I replied, "I'm out in my corral feeding the horses." When she inquired what had happened I told her I was healed. All the pain left my body after she prayed and I felt great by early morning and told the nurses on duty that I was *outta* there as I was healed by God. That's God for you—He wasted no time. He knew I had to get home to feed the horses.

Prayers Can Change Things Even When it Looks Impossible

Don Fedderson by Yvonne Fedderson

This book began with a story about my best and dearest friend, and I've chosen to end this book with a phenomenal miracle about my great love and partner for twenty-six years, Don Fedderson.

My Don, known to the world as a famous and successful TV producer, was a kind gentleman and his shows were created for the entire family to watch and enjoy.

Don began his career in Kansas City, Missouri, writing for a prominent newspaper. He then moved to San Francisco where he managed a radio station. He won the Peabody Award for being the first to broadcast the beginning of the United Nations.

He managed KLAC radio station in Los Angeles, and it was his idea to put music to the call letters of KLAC. This had never been done before at a station. He also had the idea of disc jockeys announcing and playing popular music. He started Channel 13 TV station for KLAC. Don produced, for and at the Los Angeles Coliseum, the first college football game between UCLA and USC.

Don was intrigued with TV when it all began, and in the early fifties produced his first show, *The Millionaire*, through Don Fedderson Productions. He discovered many TV stars and went on to produce several popular family TV shows—such as *My Three Sons, Family Affair, To Rome With Love, the Betty White Show,* and the *Lawrence Welk Show,* to name a few. He was president of the *Pioneers of Broadcasting,* and his shows won many awards over the years.

Don was a man of high principles, served on the Board of his church, loved his family, and was very generous to charities—especially Childhelp®. He gave of his time, energy and money to produce many fund raising events for our charity. He never missed The Little Chapel services and definitely believed in God's miracles. He was blessed with good health and lived every day to the fullest.

When we were first married in 1969, he had 5 shows on TV. He worked very hard but his true joy was coming home to his family and loved ones.

In the middle 80's, Don had a virus attack his heart resulting in a quarter of his heart function afterwards.

In February of 1988, Sara and I had Childhelp® appointments in Los Angeles and couldn't go to our Palm Springs home with our husbands. Don and Bob, Sara's husband, played golf Saturday afternoon with our friends, Wicki and Lloyd McDonald. That evening, Bob was driving the two of them to meet Lloyd and Wicki for dinner when Don suffered a massive heart attack and stroke. Bob pulled into a gas station and yelled for someone to call 911. He dragged him out of the car to lay him flat on the ground and started to perform mouth-to-mouth resuscitation.

A woman getting gas, who happened to be a flight attendant, came over to help Bob. The paramedics rushed him to *Eisenhower Medical Hospital* and he was pronounced dead on arrival. The doctors had no hope for his recovery and wrote hopeless on his chart. Wicki phoned me from the hospital and said, "They had him breathing again and have him hooked up to all sorts of machines. I don't know whether you should pray for him to live or not." The doctor had told them he would be a vegetable if he lived.

Sara's son, Chuck, drove Sara and me to Palm Springs, and I was on the phone with the doctors the entire trip. The doctor at the hospital told me to get there as soon as I could. He said, "Don't have an accident, but hurry. We will try to keep him alive until you arrive, but I'm not certain we can."

When we arrived and saw Don in the intensive care unit, he was hooked up to a life support machine and monitors of all kinds. I asked the nurses to step aside and let us pray. I told them Sara had the gift of healing, and we believed in miracles regardless of how things looked.

Don was lying in bed in a coma, completely motionless. Sara put her hand on him to pray for a healing and as the life came back into his body, he began to jump and they had to tie him to the bed so he wouldn't hurt himself. The nurses were in shock and said, "Look at the monitors! Look at the monitors!"

One of the nurses was the daughter of the president of the Childhelp® Desert Chapter. She went home afterwards and told her mother about what happened to Don and what a miracle he received. I spent the night with Don along with his son Dana and Dana's wife Marlene. The next morning as they removed the breathing machine from his throat, he started to talk although the doctors said not to expect it. They said his left side would be paralyzed—it wasn't.

Later that day, Sara and Bob came back to the hospital to see Don. Bob was visiting with Don when the neurologist came into his room. The doctors wanted to test Don to see to what extent his brain had been damaged. He asked Don all kinds of questions, such as "Who was the United States President in 1902?" His answers were all correct, including the difficult math problems to the astonishment of the doctor. As the doctor left the room, he admitted to Sara and Bob that, "If you didn't believe in miracles before, you would have to believe after seeing what happened to Don Fedderson."

Don's cardiologist from Los Angeles was out of the country at the time this happened. When he returned, he read the doctor's report and became confused when he saw Don. He thought the doctors must have made a mistake but we know that God performed a phenomenal miracle.

Two months later, on April 16th, I gave Don a big 75th birthday party. Our daughter, Dionne, produced a film of his life and many friends and stars put together a fabulous show. Don walked up on stage and thanked everyone and announced he was going to play in the *Childhelp® Merlin Olsen Golf Tournament* the next week. He and Bob, along with two others, won the tournament! What a celebration!

Don wanted to see his last child, Dionne, graduate from ASU, and God granted his wish. God allowed him to be with us until December 1994. That was almost seven more years. He never missed a Little Chapel service. Don received many miracles and enjoyed telling everyone about them. He loved to say he was like Lazarus. Don was so grateful to God and to Sara for all of her loving prayers that he commissioned an artist in Italy to do the marble statue of Jesus that is in the Little Chapel today.

Prayers can change things even when it looks impossible. Nothing is impossible with God. It is always God's call though. Our part is to pray and let God decide what is best for a soul.

Yvonne Lime Fedderson and Sara Buckner O'Meara

A Friendship Made in Heaven

he actresses met on the set of *The Adventures of Ozzie and Harriet* and have been best friends ever since. For more than four decades, Yvonne Fedderson and Sara O'Meara have devoted their lives to helping children in need. As *Childhelp*® co-founders, they remain actively involved, Yvonne as president and Sara as CEO and chairman, in the development and oversight of a leading national nonprofit dedicated to helping victims of child abuse and neglect.

They have received countless awards for their lifelong mission, including nominations for the *Nobel Peace Prize* and *Presidential Medal of Freedom*, a citation for international collaboration to prevent child abused presented by the Queen of England, the U.S. Department of Justice Award presented by President Ronald Reagan and the Apostolic Blessing from His Holiness Pope John Paul II. Yvonne and Sara's story is told in their co-authored book *Silence Broken* and the film *For the Love of a Child* currently playing on Lifetime.

Yvonne Lime Fedderson is the mother of two children and has three grandchildren. She was born in Glendale, California and now makes her home in Paradise Valley, Arizona. She is a graduate of the Pasadena Playhouse and has had an extensive acting career in film, television and stage. She starred in such memorable movies as *Loving You* with Elvis Presley and is probably best remembered for her first role as "Snookie" in *The Rainmaker* with Katharine Hepburn and Burt Lancaster.

Since 1994, she has also served as president and CEO of her late husband's company, Don Fedderson Productions. Her responsibilities include managing the rights of the television programs he produced, including *Family Affair*, *My Three Sons*, and *The Betty White Show*. She has served on the company's board of directors for more than 30 years.

Don Fedderson was not only a pioneering producer who developed fun family shows that defined an era, he was deeply invested in the Childhelp mission and originated the slogan "For the love of a child" which has become synonymous with the organization.

Sara Buckner O'Meara was born Sara Buckner in Knoxville, Tennessee and now lives in Paradise Valley, Arizona. She was educated at Briarcliff Junior College, New York; Endicott College, Massachusetts; The Sorbonne, France; and Pasadena Playhouse, California. As an actress, she enjoyed a host of engaging parts, including regularly playing the girlfriend of David Nelson on *The Adventures of Ozzie and Harriett*, but her most important roles were that of wife, mother, philanthropist and conduit of God's healing grace.

She has a son, John Hopkins, daughter-in-law, Celeste, a stepdaughter, Taryn, and three grandchildren. Her son, Charles, died in a 1988 auto accident but his contribution to children is memorialized at the *Childhelp*® National Headquarters and his bright spirit remains a source of inspiration for all who knew him.

Mrs. O'Meara lost her beloved husband Colonel Robert (Bob) Sigholtz in 2005. Bob was a highly decorated Colonel who fought in three wars: World War II, the Korean War and Vietnam. He held a PhD in Education and History, was the Athletic Director of Georgetown University and ran RFK Stadium and The Armory in Washington, DC.

Together Sara and Yvonne founded *The Little Chapel* in Paradise Valley, Arizona to share spiritual insight, allow people from around the world to experience God's great healing gift through Sara and create a nondenominational fellowship based in God's one and only religion: Love. The thousands of healings that have been witnessed by friends and followers inspire these best friends to welcome all who seek miracles to the Little Chapel. Through Yvonne's gentle opening prayer, Sara's stirring sermons and the open hearts of the chapel congregation, God's powerful grace and healing hand can be felt in this uniquely holy place.

Sara Buckner O'Meara and Yvonne Lime Fedderson

Made in the USA
Monee, IL
08 March 2023